Counselling Children
with
Chronic Medical Conditions

Melinda Edwards and Hilton Davis

Communication and Counselling in Health Care Series
Series editor: Hilton Davis

Counselling Children
with
Chronic Medical
Conditions

Melinda Edwards

Principal Clinical Psychologist,
Lewisham and Guy's Mental Health NHS Trust,
Guy's Hospital, London, UK

and

Hilton Davis

Professor of Child Health Psychology,
United Medical and Dental Schools, Guy's Hospital,
London, UK

Medical advisor: Gillian Baird
Consultant Developmental Paediatrician,
Newcomen Centre, Guy's and St Thomas' Hospital Trust,
London, UK

 Published by The British Psychological Society

First published in 1997 by BPS Books (The British Psychological Society), St Andrews House, 48 Princess Road East, Leicester LE1 7DR, UK.

Distributed exclusively in North America by Paul H. Brookes Publishing Co., Inc., PO Box 10624, Baltimore, Maryland 21285, USA.

A catalogue record for this book is available from the British Library.

ISBN 1 85433 241 4

Typeset by The Midlands Book Typesetting Co., Loughborough, Leicestershire
Printed in Great Britain by Redwood Books, Trowbridge, Wilts.

OTHER TITLES IN THE SERIES:
Counselling Parents of Children with Chronic Illness or Disability by Hilton Davis
Counselling for Heart Disease by Paul Bennett
Counselling in Obstetrics and Gynaecology by Myra Hunter
Counselling People with Diabetes by Richard Shillitoe
Counselling in Terminal Care and Bereavement by Colin Murray Parkes, Marilyn Relf and Ann Couldrick
Counselling People with Disfigurement by Eileen Bradbury

Dedication

For my parents – your love for our family, and for life itself, is my greatest inspiration.
M.E.

To my mother for the respect she has shown me throughout my life.
H.D.

Acknowledgements

We would like to thank all the children and families who have shared their experiences and taught us so much. Our warmest thanks also to colleagues at Guy's Hospital and to Susan Pacitti at the BPS for their support. Finally, our deepest thanks to our own families – we could not have done this without you.

CONTENTS

List of Figures   x

Foreword   xi
Dr Gillian Baird

Preface to the series   xiii

1. INTRODUCTION   1
What is meant by counselling?   2
Chronic medical conditions   3
Helping children in the context of the family   4
When and for whom is help needed?   5
Plan of the book   8
Summary   9

2. ADAPTING TO ILLNESS   10
Family adaptation   12
Factors influencing adaptation in the child   14
The process of adaptation: a framework   22
Summary   27

3. THE CHILD'S EXPERIENCE   28
Constructions of illness and disability   28
Development of children's understanding   29
The role of personal experience   37
Developmental challenges and tasks   38
Characteristics of the condition   40
Constructions of self   44
Summary   48

4 THE SOCIAL WORLD OF THE CHILD   49
Constructions of family   49
Constructions of siblings   52
Constructions of professionals   53
Constructions of treatment   55
School   57
Friendships   59
Summary   61

5. THE AIMS AND PROCESS OF HELPING 62
Aims of helping 63
The helping relationship 67
The process of helping 71
Basic helper attitudes and characteristics 78
Summary 81

6. ENGAGING THE CHILD 82
Setting the scene 82
Basic skills 86
The first meeting with the child and family 90
Difficulties in engaging children 94
Difficulties in communication 95
Summary 97

7. EXPLORING THE CHILD'S EXPERIENCES
AND UNDERSTANDING 99
Getting to know the child 99
Verbal exploration skills 101
Non-verbal exploration strategies 105
More structured exploration strategies 111
Summary 117

8. GIVING INFORMATION 118
The need for information 118
General principles for giving information 120
Information giving as a process 121
Communicating about the diagnosis and treatment 130
Information giving and consent 134
Summary 135

9. SPECIFIC STRATEGIES FOR HELPING 137
Preparation for medical/surgical procedures 137
Helping the distressed or anxious child 145
Encouraging co-operation with treatment 148
Preparation for leaving hospital and returning to school 150
Preparation for transfer to adult services 151
Pain management 152
Summary 161

10. COMMUNICATING ABOUT DEATH AND DYING   162
Children's understanding of death and dying   163
Children's concepts of life after death   167
Children's reflections about their own death and dying   168
Emotional and behavioural reactions to life-threatening
conditions   173
Ways of managing the child's emotional and behavioural distress   176
Children's indirect communications about death   179
Talking about dying   180
Caring for siblings   183
Summary   188

11. FINAL REMARKS   190
Referral to other services   190
Children's rights   197
A charter for children in hospital   198

Appendix A: A Relaxation Exercise   200

Appendix B: Books for Children   201

Appendix C: Organizations and agencies – UK   205

Appendix D: Organizations and agencies – North America   211

References   213

Index   218

List of Figures

Figure 3.1	Eight-year-old child's diagram of food inside the body	31
Figure 3.2	A drawing of the body by a child with bladder dysfunction	32
Figure 3.3	Drawing of the body by a six-year-old child	33
Figure 3.4	Inside the body, drawn by an eight-year-old with kidney problems	34
Figure 3.5	Teenager looking in the mirror	45
Figure 4.1	Depiction of a mother trapped by her child's illness	51
Figure 7.1	Picture of a butterfly, drawn by sibling	106
Figure 7.2(a)	Picture drawn in the initial meeting with the child	107
Figure 7.2(b)	Picture drawn by the same child after explanations had been given to the child, family and school about his condition	107
Figure 7.3	Picture of child's perception of catheterization	108
Figure 7.4	Louise's visual analogue scale	116
Figure 9.1	Picture of a migraine attack	153
Figure 9.2	Pain scale drawn by a nine-year-old boy.	155

Foreword

Aloof, aloof, we stand aloof so stand
Thou too aloof bound with the flawless band
Of inner solitude; we bind not thee;
But who from the self-chain shall set thee free?
What heart shall touch thy heart? What hand thy hand?

(From the *Thread of Life* by Christina Rossetti)

All paediatricians, among many other professionals, will come into contact with families dealing with their children's chronic medical conditions, both at the acute stage and then subsequently. Understanding and adapting to the medical situation and the consequent impairment and disability calls for resources and coping strategies from the child and the family many times over the child's life. Healthcare professionals are trained to deal with the physical needs of the medical condition but the emotional needs are also crucially important. Healthcare professionals get much less training in this area. Studies of chronic conditions indicate the vital role of the quality of the relationship between the carer and the cared for – the doctor (or other) and the child in the family. The components of this relationship are common to *all* medical conditions. *Listening* as the core skill is a recurring theme throughout this book.

Personal construct theory is the basis of the philosophy behind this book and the approach of Melinda Edwards and Hilton Davis who use their extensive clinical experience to illustrate their message. This book should give many professionals from varying backgrounds the confidence to look at their own practice, using the authors' clear advice for the many different situations one encounters in a busy clinical life. (For further reading and resource material there are some valuable addresses at the back of the book both for families and professionals.)

The family is seen as central throughout this book while recognizing the rights of the child. It is not forgotten that siblings and grandparents have feelings too. From the child's perspective, the importance of cognitive development is emphasized in combination with the child's experiences, in and out of the hospital setting. Key developmental factors are described; for example, the conceptual understanding of death at varying ages, how and when to discuss difficult diagnoses with children and adolescents, remembering that children grow older while attending the same clinic and their psychological, if not medical, needs may change.

How families cope with a sick or disabled child depends upon many factors. Personal construct theory teaches the necessity to explore the individual's perspective and responses and the collective mutual interaction. All of us should strive to combine these counselling skills with the competences of our individual professional backgrounds. We will do so better after reading this book and above all LISTENING to our children and families.

Dr Gillian Baird
Consultant Developmental Paediatrician
Newcomen Centre
Guy's and St Thomas' Hospital Trust

Preface to the Series

People who suffer chronic disease or disability are confronted by problems that are as much psychological as physical, and involve all members of their family and the wider social network. Psychosocial adaptation is important in its own right, in terms of making necessary changes in lifestyle, altering aspirations or coping with an uncertain future. However, it may also influence the effectiveness of the diagnostic and treatment processes, and hence eventual outcomes.

As a consequence, healthcare, whether preventive or treatment-oriented, must encompass the psychosocial integrated with the physical, at all phases of the life cycle and at all stages of disease. The basis of this is skilled communication and counselling by all involved in providing services, professionally or voluntarily. Everyone, from the student to the experienced practitioner, can benefit from appropriate training in this area, where the social skills required are complex and uncertain.

Although there is a sizeable research literature related to counselling and communication in the area of healthcare, specialist texts for training purposes are scarce. The current series was, therefore, conceived as a practical resource for all who work in health services. Each book is concerned with a specific area of healthcare. The authors have been asked to provide detailed information, from the patient's perspective, about the problems (physical, psychological and social) faced by patients and their families. Each book examines the role of counselling and communication in the process of helping people to come to terms and deal with these problems, and presents usable frameworks as a guide to the helping process. Detailed and practical descriptions of the major qualities, abilities and skills that are required to provide the most effective help for patients are included.

The intention is to stimulate professional and voluntary helpers alike to explore their efforts at supportive communication. It is hoped that by so doing, they become sufficiently aware of patient difficulties and the processes of adaptation, and more able to facilitate positive adjustment. The aims of the series will have been met if patients and families feel someone has listened and if they feel respected in their struggle for health. A central theme is the effort to make people feel better about themselves and able to face the future, no matter how bleak, with dignity.

Hilton Davis
Series Editor

1

Introduction

'When I grow up I am going to be a pilot in the air force and fly all over the world.'

This may sound like a typical statement of a nine-year-old boy's ambition, but it is made poignant by the fact that in this case the boy has a progressive neuromuscular condition (Duchenne muscular dystrophy). When he said this, he was already using a wheelchair and rarely went anywhere other than school or hospital.

How do you respond to this? You might think, 'Surely this child must have been told he is not going to get better and will not be able to fly?' If he has not been told, whose responsibility should it be to do so? Should he be corrected and reminded of the futility of this hope? Should he be placated with a 'Yes, dear' and left to dream, or does this need to be explored further, giving the boy the opportunity to talk about his thoughts, fears and hopes for the future?

'You can never understand what it feels like to be me. I'm never going to be normal now, am I? Why me? Why did it have to happen to me?'

These are the comments of a very distressed adolescent, newly diagnosed as having diabetes. Where do you begin in addressing this young man's questions? How can you help him to cope with his frustration, and enable him to manage the necessary changes to his lifestyle? For this young man, hospitals and illness had not been a part of his life up until this point; they happened to other people, other lives, but now it was something intruding on him. How do you help him manage his distress and help the parent or carer in this relationship cope with the painful emotions raised?

These examples serve to highlight some of the emotions, conflicts and dilemmas experienced by children with chronic medical conditions and disabilities and by those caring for them. Our aim is to help people involved with these children – parents, health care professionals, child care staff, teachers, and voluntary workers – to develop greater insights into the child's experience of life with a chronic condition, including the challenges, triumphs and difficulties they face, and the strategies they use to cope with these. On the basis of this understanding, we will move on to describe practical ways to communicate more effectively with these children, using counselling skills. Our intention is to enable carers to identify and develop the skills and opportunities they already have, so that they might help children to adapt well and face the reality of their disease with the greatest possible quality of life.

An experience that parents and professionals may sometimes share is the overwhelming sense of personal inadequacy at not being able to take away the problems and make everything all right for the child. We, the authors, are not exempt from these feelings. We do not always know what to say, nor how best to help. We certainly have no precise recipes. We do hope, however, that the book will stimulate you to think creatively about the problems facing children with chronic conditions and their families, and give you the confidence to be with them, to listen to them, and to provide support.

What is Meant by Counselling?

Counselling is a somewhat ambiguous word used to cover many different actions and interventions. In this book the term is applied broadly to refer to the process of helping children by communicating effectively with them. This implies LISTENING to them, coming to a shared understanding of their problems, and facilitating their own development of strategies for overcoming or ameliorating their difficulties.

Counselling is more than problem-solving. It is not about giving advice ('If I were you . . .') nor about taking problems away and making everyone happy. It is about helping children to share their distress and feel less isolated in their difficulties. The basic aim is to empower children to develop their own problem-solving strategies, and, as a consequence, help them to feel more in control and to feel better about themselves. This requires the active participation of the child, whether verbally or through other means of communication. It involves providing an opportunity for children to communicate their problems, to explore them fully, and to make explicit the goals they wish to pursue. The aim, therefore, is as much to do with the development of understanding and self-esteem as with dealing with specific problems.

Although the skills of counselling are varied, they are essentially based upon communication. Such skills are required by all who try to help others, whatever their profession or position. In the context of paediatrics, this includes all medical and nursing staff, teachers, play specialists, physiotherapists, dieticians, occupational therapists, speech therapists, social workers, health visitors, and allied staff such as ward receptionists and domestics. All of these have opportunities through communicating appropriately to enhance the quality of their care, to help and support both children and their families, to make them feel better about themselves, and to improve the quality of their lives. The aim of this book is not to make all healthcare workers into skilled and professional counsellors, but to help them identify and improve existing skills and to integrate them into their daily working practice.

We will distinguish between health professionals who employ basic counselling skills in their work, and mental health professionals (including psychologists, psychiatrists and psychotherapists) who have specialized training. The basic counselling skills used by both groups are similar, although it is important to be able to recognize when these basic skills are appropriate and when more intensive help and therefore referral to a specialist is required. Mental health professionals have access to a wide range of therapeutic skills and techniques, an understanding of psychological and social issues and an understanding of the therapeutic process of change. They may work directly with the child, or act as a trainer, supervisor or consultant to those using counselling skills as part of their more technical role.

Chronic Medical Conditions

Although chronic conditions vary in severity and the extent to which they affect a child's life, what they have in common is the fact that they do not go away. Treatment advances may extend the life of children who would previously have died; they may also improve quality of life by controlling pain and other symptoms, but, by definition, chronic illness and disability cannot be cured.

Between 10–15 per cent of children under the age of sixteen years are affected by chronic, long-term physical problems (Weiland, Pless and Roghmann, 1992). The most prevalent chronic conditions are eczema (8–10 per cent of children), asthma (2–5 per cent), diabetes (1.8 per cent), congenital heart disease (0.2–0.7 per cent) and epilepsy (0.26–0.46 per cent). Although less common, there are nevertheless many other painful, debilitating and frightening diseases. Many of these conditions have an unpredictable course, some involving degenerative processes, others posing a real threat to the child's life at all stages. These conditions include sickle cell anaemia, rheumatoid arthritis, cystic fibrosis, HIV infection, cancer and leukaemia. Other life-threatening conditions such as kidney disease, metabolic disorders, and neuromuscular conditions are also very rare, which in itself poses an added source of stress to the already serious nature of the condition.

We are concerned in this book with all children who have any chronic disease, as well as those who are disabled or handicapped.

Using World Health Organisation (WHO) terminology, 'disability' is defined as *the behavioural consequence of the condition* (what the child is prevented from doing), and 'handicap' as *the social disadvantage of the disability*. Children who require the use of a wheelchair, for example, will be less handicapped by their disability if living in accommodation which has been specially adapted to their needs and which consequently gives them greater independence. Disabilities range across all the senses (for example, blindness and deafness), and include motor difficulties (such as cerebral palsy), communication problems (for example, autism) and intellectual problems. All these children and their families require help and support of the type we are considering here.

Helping Children in the Context of the Family

Although the focus of the book is on communicating with children, it is vital to acknowledge that children do not exist in isolation. They are an integral part of a family system. They both affect the functioning of the family system, and in turn are affected by the other members of the family in terms of the coping resources and support provided. The family is, in the vast majority of cases, the child's main source of support. The needs of the whole family and the mobilization of their own resources are therefore paramount.

The need to understand and address the adaptation of families, and especially the parents, is discussed in an earlier book in this series (Davis,1993). The points made by Davis of working with and through the parents will be assumed in the present text, where we will draw upon many of the same models. For example, we will assume that it is important to engage parents in a working relationship or partnership, which includes establishing common aims, negotiation, and mutual respect amongst its qualities. We will adopt the same framework for exploring and understanding peoples' experience as described by Davis. We will conceptualize processes or tasks of helping in the same way and assume that the same qualities and skills are just as important for working directly with children. However, although the models may be the same for helping both parents and children, the way these skills are put into practice must take into account the characteristics of children and, in particular, their developmental level. It is this that we will pursue in the present text, even though parents will remain central to any work carried out on their behalf with their children.

It is important to recognize the situations in which help may be provided for the child. It is often possible to support a child individually while seeing the whole family, or (more usually) a parent accompanying his or her child. However, there may be times when parents are unable to listen to their child's distress, possibly because they are feeling so overwhelmed themselves. This may lead them to block in rather subtle ways the child's attempts to communicate their distress. It is, therefore, important to be able to gain the permission and support of the parents to talk to their child. This alone may facilitate work with the child, since it indicates the parents' acknowledgement of his or her need to talk.

The purpose of any such intervention is certainly not to undermine the parents in any way. However, one notable exception to seeking permission is where the parents are suspected of abusing the child. In such cases, permission and co-operation may not be forthcoming, and legal steps to protect the child (possibly removing the child to a place of safety) may be necessary to enable him or her to talk openly and deal with the situation.

When and for Whom is Help Needed?

Chronic disease creates a variety of physical difficulties, but also has practical, social and emotional implications. The child's ways of adapting to the disease are at least in part related to the coping resources and support available from the family. These are in turn affected by the stresses upon the family including their economic situation; the area in which they live; the personal characteristics of the family members; the relationship between the parents; and the wider support the family derive from their relatives and friends. The child's response is also influenced by his or her developmental level and other personality characteristics, such as anxiety, independence and sociability. However, the characteristics of the disease itself may influence the situation, including the aetiology and severity of the disease, the nature of the symptoms, its predictability, stability, restrictions imposed by the condition, and the nature of its treatment.

Adaptation is a continual process, and it is important to identify which children require help and at what point. Since problems and distress may occur throughout the adaptation process, children may require psychosocial support at each and every stage. This is particularly so if an emphasis is put upon anticipation and prevention rather than crisis intervention. Such help is best provided, therefore, by developing a long-term relationship in which the child develops trust and feels secure to discuss worries or difficulties, without feeling they will be seen as trivial or silly. Such a relationship also enables children to feel you are interested in THEM, and not just their illness or serious problems. Such psychosocial care should occur as an integral part of medical care, should encompass the needs of the whole child, and can be potentially provided by all with whom the child has contact.

It may be helpful to consider children and families requiring help as falling into three broad categories. Firstly, there are those who would need help, whether or not they had a chronic medical condition. These may include children from families who appear chaotic, unsupportive and discordant, and who are facing a range of pre-existing stresses with the child's disease as an addition. For example, an eight-year-old child with Perthes (a potentially crippling disease of the hip for which she required surgical intervention) was evidently terrified whilst immobilized in plaster in hospital; she screamed as if in great pain at the slightest movement and was inconsolable whenever her mother left her. It transpired that she had had many previous experiences of being abandoned by her mother and taken into care. Her mother often threatened her with this as a punishment, if she caused her too much trouble. The mother was unable to cope with her own distress at seeing her little girl in pain, and often left the ward suddenly without warning, returning at very irregular times. One could foresee this child and family requiring psychosocial support regardless of the child's medical condition.

Other examples are families in which parents have pre-existing mental health problems, where there is marital conflict or unresolved traumas. For example, the diagnosis given to her young son of (mild) epilepsy was totally devastating for a mother who had suffered the loss of an older child three years previously. Her older child had died from meningitis, and had suffered a prolonged epileptic attack during this illness. She had never spoken about her older child or received any support over his death. However, the enormity of her distress and grief was triggered by receiving this diagnosis of epilepsy in her younger child, and completely overwhelmed her.

Secondly, there are children who are not able to manage a particular aspect of their medical problems or treatment, or who are overwhelmed and unable to cope at a specific time or stage of their condition. At this time, children appear unable to mobilize their normal coping strategies effectively. For example, one young girl became very agitated and distressed when told that she would have to wear a brace and learn a particular, time-consuming way of cleaning her teeth. Although her reaction seemed excessive, exploration of her distress revealed that she already felt severely restricted as a consequence of carrying out three dialysis exchanges a day, and the thought of having to spend more time on another area of self-care was the last straw for her. Another child managed all other aspects of treatment including surgery and invasive scans, but could not tolerate the regular blood tests which were a necessary part of the monitoring of her condition.

Finally, there is a large group of children and families who cope well, albeit showing appropriate levels of distress at their situation, but who may well be helped by supportive counselling. For example, a young boy, on leaving hospital after a head injury in which he lost his vision, was having to contend with the situation of moving house with his family to more suitable accommodation and with a consequent change of school. He was adapting well, not only to a tremendous loss, in terms of his vision, but also to these dramatic changes to his normal environment. The high level of stress experienced by him and his family was perfectly understandable, and although the situation itself could not be changed, his distress was amenable to supportive counselling, which helped to contain his fears of change and mobilize his highly adaptive resources.

In most examples, we are considering normal families who find themselves in abnormal situations because of their child's needs as well as other life stresses. Specific help may be required from a variety of professionals. However, support in the form of a listening ear and validation of them as people is almost always needed, with the implication that all children and families will benefit from a combined psychological and physical approach to their care.

Although it is important to prevent emotional difficulties and to reduce the necessity for more crisis-orientated measures, the most common experience of professionals is seeing a child who is either of concern to others or who is clearly exhibiting distressed behaviour. This may be shown as defiance, unco-operativeness and aggression, or as upset, anxious, withdrawn, sad or tearful behaviour. It is important to consider *who* feels the child has a problem, as the child might be, or appear, the least concerned of anyone. For example, children who refuse to stick to a specialized diet or take medication may appear unconcerned about the long-term effects of this on their health, particularly if the treatment does not make them feel better. It is usually adults who are fearful of the long-term consequences.

It is important to explore the problem carefully, and not to make assumptions about the cause of the difficulty, since these may relate to factors in the child, or elsewhere. It cannot be assumed that every difficulty is a consequence of the chronic condition; children with chronic illnesses are children first and foremost (a child with epilepsy rather than an epileptic child), and are subject to the same range of positive or negative life experiences as other people.

Children's inappropriate or worrying behaviour is a communication of distress and not a generalized characteristic of the child. Labelling the child as being naughty, silly or immature is a value judgment that serves little purpose. Focusing on the behaviour allows the possibility of the child altering his or her behaviour, and does not add a set of negative perceptions to the child's existing difficulties.

Finally, it is useful to remember that children are sometimes the vehicle by which parents seek help for themselves. Some parents may be struggling to manage their children's emotional and behavioural responses and may seek professional help for this, when in reality they are finding it difficult to adapt themselves and as a consequence are unable to support their children. Others may also find it difficult to separate their own needs from those of their children. This is illustrated by a mother who kept her child in isolation at home and away from school for several weeks after treatment had ended. She felt both she and her child needed a long rest after the ordeal of treatment, even though the child was well, bored at home and impatient to return to school. In all cases, therefore, it is necessary to consider and separate the needs of the child and those of other family members.

Plan of the Book

Given that a shared understanding of experiences and problems is a pre-requisite of effective helping, *Chapter 2* looks at the processes of adaptation to stressful circumstances. *Chapter 3* is devoted to an exploration of the world of illness through the eyes of the child. Using a developmental framework, we will look at children's understanding of themselves, their conditions, and their treatment. All children will have their own unique perceptions of themselves, and the ways in which their condition affects their lives. *Chapter 4* will extend this exploration of children's perceptions to include other significant people in the child's life including family members, friends and school.

Chapter 5 is concerned with the aims of helping and a convenient model for understanding the helping process with children is introduced. This is elaborated in *Chapter 6*, which looks in more detail at the process of forming and developing effective working relationships with children and their families. *Chapter 7* looks at ways of exploring children's experiences and *Chapter 8* focuses on strategies for facilitating change, by the provision of information, including communicating the diagnosis. *Chapter 9* looks at more specific skills and techniques for working with children who are chronically ill, and includes preparation for medical procedures, strategies to help with pain management and adherence to medical treatments, and support for managing transitions such as returning to school. *Chapter 10* is concerned with children with life-threatening or terminal conditions, and *Chapter 11* focuses on children's rights, and discusses the need for healthcare workers to look after themselves, by obtaining the necessary support and supervision to be effective in their work.

Summary

❏ Chronic medical conditions and disability affect between 10–15 per cent of children under the age of 16 years.

❏ Chronic disease presents major challenges to the child and family, with practical, social and emotional implications.

❏ Adaptation to living with a chronic condition is a continual process and psychosocial care is therefore appropriate at each and every stage of the condition.

❏ Counselling skills can potentially be used by all healthcare workers, to enable better communication and the development of a more satisfying and helping relationship with young people and their families.

❏ Counselling implies listening, coming to a shared understanding of problems, and facilitating the development of the child's own strategies for overcoming and ameliorating their difficulties.

2

Adapting to Illness

The following poem was written by an 11-year-old girl following her treatment for a brain tumour. Her poem, entitled 'The Big T', offers a glimpse of her world since diagnosis.

THE BIG T

Because of the Big T, I have terrible mood swings,
This is the new me, the way things are going to be.
But let's not despair, there are lots of things out there.

The Big T is responsible for my diabetes,
Not of the sugar but of the salt,
But even this, many new friends this has brought.
Blood tests three times a week at the path lab,
But Tony he's great, he takes me by cab.

Diets, who needs them? 860 calories I'm on,
Believe me that's no fun,
But plenty of salads in the garden in the sun,
Having no salt can be such a drag,
All my favourite foods I lack,
Then I turn my back, and on my plate
There's something varied and exciting,
All the restrictions and Mum's still providing.

The Big T is responsible for my sight,
Now very restricted, but I'm all right,
I now have a telescopic lens and a scanner,
You just have to be a good planner,
Ok, I can't see the TV
But can everyone boast they have a CCTV?

The Big T is responsible for my nightly needle and medication
But after I've done it Mum says I'm real brave,
This gives me a great feeling of elation,

The Big T is responsible for my muzzy head,
This is the feeling I really dread,
It leaves me tired and weary,
Oh let's face it, it's not all dreary.
I have a sleep and wake feeling fine,
That's basically the bottom line,

The Big T is responsible for all my hospital appointments,
I'm always so frightened there's going to be a disappointment.
But we make them as fun as we can, even If I have to have a scan.
I can no longer skate or ride a bike,
But there's so many other things I like.

The Big T is responsible for my size,
This really gets me down, then this makes me frown,
Then mum pops off to town, and finds me a lovely blouse or gown,
This I find so uplifting.
I can't blame the Big T for anything else,
It's not that gifted!

Or still so many positive subjects,
I bet Mr T you feel really wrecked,
I'm stronger not harder, our family so much closer,
Not to mention so much bigger,
I have so much equipment-
That's not a fate but a real treat,
I have a wider range of friends,
And many different hobbies,
I collect keyrings, where I get them from, that depends.
I write more letters and have many more connections.

When I was in hospital everyone was there,
When I came home, some just seem to stare
But then came the collections, I had a brand new printer,
Which opened many doors.
For learning to touch type I need to see all the flaws,

So you see Mr. T,
You didn't get the better of ME!

This courageous and talented young poet has offered us a rare insight into her world and the daily challenges and problems she now faces. The diagnosis of a tumour has brought dramatic changes to many aspects of her life and to the lives of all members of her family. Before the tumour occurred, this child and her family could not possibly have imagined that something so devastating could happen to them, shattering their world and so entirely changing their hopes and expectations for the future.

Family Adaptation

The whole family has to adapt to the disease, with every member having to accommodate the demands made by the condition into all aspects of their daily lives. All of them have to deal with the potentially overwhelming feelings that arise in this situation. The distress, anxiety and fear can be enormous, and they may feel utterly helpless. They may be faced with fears of the emergence of new problems, or a recurrence of old problems, new treatment demands or the possibility of treatment failing and the condition deteriorating. Ultimately, a number of families are faced with the fear of the child's death. Relationships between family members are affected and the roles and responsibilities taken by adults and children within the family may be altered. It is almost impossible to appreciate the multiple problems and changes at all levels – emotional, social and practical – that are faced by such children and their families.

Parents

For the parents, adapting may involve additional childcare responsibilities such as catering for special dietary needs, supervising medication, carrying out home-based treatments such as physiotherapy or exhausting night-time feeding or monitoring regimes. It may also involve attending numerous appointments with a variety of professionals from health, education and social services. All of these duties may involve a disproportionate amount of time being devoted to the care of one child, at the expense of time parents would usually spend with each other, with their other children, in employment, or pursuing relaxing or social activities for themselves. There may be no time or money to tend the garden, mend the car, decorate and repair the home or participate in community or school activities. Parents' own work and careers may be severely affected because of the time needed to care for their child. This may involve one or both parents giving up work, or conversely one parent needing to work as much overtime as possible to meet the financial needs of the family.

Siblings

Siblings are also profoundly affected. They may be required to help more with practical tasks around the house or to take on responsibilities for supervising or entertaining other children in the family, including the child who is ill. They may have to cope with alternate care arrangements when parents are at the hospital. This can involve staying with relatives or friends at short notice, and may continue for months on end. Parents may not be able to participate so fully in siblings' lives, and this, for example, may place restrictions on the other children socially in terms of being able to invite friends home or being included in other social events. Siblings may feel that their wishes and demands as always considered in relation to the needs of the child who is sick and they can easily feel less important, special or loved.

The extended family

Grandparents and other extended family members are also affected and this often goes unrecognized. They may be called upon to help with childcare and other practical arrangements, and they may be the greatest emotional support for parents and siblings and carry a tremendous burden of care and worry for the family. However, they may also compound the problems if they do not understand what is going on or do not adapt appropriately to the situation. In one family, for example, the wife's parents blamed the husband for the genetic condition that afflicted their grandson.

Social relationships

Relationships with others outside the family, and social opportunities generally, can frequently become restricted for the family as a whole. This may be because of the perceived or real stigma associated with the child's condition, or by parents trying to restrict the sick child's contact with others to protect them from common viruses that are normally harmless, but may be very dangerous for their child. Restrictions may also be due to time constraints or to the fact that friends are not willing, or not able, to accommodate the special needs of the child or family in their social activities. Parents may be so exhausted from the physical demands of caring for their child that they do not have sufficient energy to maintain friendships and social activities. Practically there may be difficulties in planning and carrying out activities as a family, even if there is enough time, energy and money left after all the other arrangements have been made.

Each disease presents specific problems and stresses, resulting from the characteristics of the disease (the nature, severity and stability of the condition for example) and the demands of the treatment. Common to all conditions, however, is the fact that the child's well-being, physical and psychological, is dependent upon the ability of the family to adapt adequately. For example, if a family has adapted well, they will be better able to recognize and set realistic expectations and goals, and to support the child in achieving his or her potential. Conversely, when families are not able to adapt, children may continually be frustrated by failing to meet (unrealistic) goals or may be denied achievement opportunities. Children or parents who are excessively distressed may also not comply with treatment regimes. This in turn has a number of consequences, such as how well the child feels, whether symptoms are controlled, how much time the child has to spend in hospital, and therefore how much further disruption occurs in their lives.

In order to help children effectively, it is important to have some understanding of the adaptation process. In the next section, therefore, we will focus upon the child specifically and consider what factors impinge upon the level of adaptation achieved.

Factors Influencing Adaptation in the Child

Adaptation is a complex and dynamic process, continually influenced by one's experience of events. Some of these factors may challenge the process (*risk* factors) and make adaptation more difficult, whereas other factors may serve to protect the person from difficulties (that is, *resistance* or *protective* factors) and enhance his or her ability to adjust successfully. Risk factors include the characteristics of the disease or disability (for example, the diagnosis and severity), the extent to which independence is compromised, and other psychosocial stressors. Resistance factors might include the characteristics of the child him or herself, such as temperament, problem-solving abilities and coping strategies, as well as the social context, such as the family environment and social support available.

Numerous studies have explored the effects of these various factors on the child and family, and good reviews of these can be found in Wallander *et al.* (1988), Beresford (1994) and Eiser (1993). However, the practical application of the findings is limited. There has been a tendency to focus quite narrowly on the implications of one particular factor, problem or disease, at a specific point in time, without taking account of the interactions between different factors and experiences over time. Studies have also tended to focus more on the difficulties and problems encountered by children and their families, rather than considering these in the context of the family's lives generally and the ways families try to manage these difficulties. The number of children in particular studies has often been very small, or has been rather heterogenous, mixing together children with different conditions, different ages or at diverse stages in their disease, making it difficult to draw conclusions or interpret the results. For the present purpose, we will briefly consider what factors have been associated with adaptation in the child in terms of characteristics of the disease or disability, psychosocial factors relating to the child and family, and the characteristics of the wider support system.

The nature of the disease

Clearly disease is a major stressor and will be a risk factor for the adaptation of the child. The Ontario Child Health Study (Cadman *et al.*, 1987) indicated twice the level of psychological disturbance in children who are chronically sick, than in healthy children. Children with accompanying physical disabilities were found to be up to three times more likely to show disturbance. Behavioural problems and difficulties in cognitive and academic functioning are commonly noted, but also emotional distress (particularly low self-esteem and depression) and social isolation.

In addition to studies which have looked at the effects of chronic conditions overall, specific characteristics of the disease or disability may influence the adaptation process and we will consider the following: *severity, central nervous system involvement, visibility, course, onset, rarity* and *treatment demands.*

Disease severity. Disease severity does not clearly predict the level of psychological distress or adaptation that the child will experience. This is, in part, due to the different measures of severity used. For example, severity can be described medically in terms of the number of treatments, hospitalizations, frequency of symptoms or the degree to which the condition is life-threatening. It can also be rated by the parent or child more subjectively in terms of how severely they perceive the problems or stresses associated with the condition. Severity can also be measured more practically and objectively in terms of interference with the activities of daily living. When this latter measure is used, severity has been associated with more difficulties, particularly in relation to social withdrawal and isolation (Cadman *et al.*, 1987). Conditions which involve sensory or motor impairment, or which are debilitating through pain or other factors therefore present the greatest challenge to adaptation. Life-threatening conditions are also associated with more psychological problems (Cadranell, 1994; Woolley *et al.*, 1991).

However, in their review of this issue, Drotar and Bush (1985) concluded that personal perceptions of disease severity were more predictive than objective physical criteria. Mothers' perceptions of the severity of their children's condition have certainly been shown to be a powerful predictor of their own, the family and the child's adjustment (De Maso *et al.*, 1991).

Central nervous system (CNS) involvement. The evidence strongly suggests that children with conditions involving the brain or central nervous system have a greater incidence of psychological, social and educational problems than children with non-brain-related disorders (Breslau, 1985). Conditions associated with cognitive impairment (learning difficulties) are linked with more behavioural problems, and may affect the child's ability to achieve independence in later life.

Visibility.   Conditions which are clearly evident to others (for example, using a white stick or being in a wheelchair) can be construed as *either* a risk or protective factor, depending on the child's experiences. Pless (1984) suggests that visibility can force children to accept themselves as ill or disabled. If others recognize the children's needs and treat them accordingly, then the child may accept the condition and adjust better. This will be true, however, only if the response gained from others is helpful and enables a positive and affirming self-acceptance by the child. If the response is insensitive, offensive or demeaning, the child will be further handicapped. Staring, name-calling, bullying or total avoidance are sadly all too common and can be very destructive to the child's self-image and adjustment. However, the child's own resources for dealing with these social interactions will undoubtably be an important mediating factor in dealing with the responses of others.

Pless suggests that the so-called invisible difficulties, such as renal failure, mild spina bifida, or diabetes, for example, will cause the most difficulty. Children may be confused about their identity and not know whether they belong to a 'normal' or 'disabled' group. They may find it difficult to identify or to feel accepted by either group.

Course.   Conditions which have an unpredictable or uncertain course (such as poorly-controlled asthma, epilepsy or renal failure), particularly those which are life-threatening, or which require frequent hospitalizations for treatment, are associated with poor adjustment in the child (Koocher, 1984). They severely disrupt the child's life, interfere with any plans made and reduce any sense of control the child has over what happens to him or her. Opportunities for social and school integration may become restricted because of frequent or sudden absences. Uncertainty regarding sudden changes in the child's well-being also poses particular difficulties in terms of how to balance the child's needs for participating in activities or developing independence with the risks involved if the child should suddenly become unwell.

Onset/aetiology.   There is little to suggest whether congenital or acquired conditions pose more of a challenge to adaptation. However, the age of the child at the onset of the condition will have implications for the developmental tasks which are most affected. Onset during adolescence, for example, is commonly believed to be particularly difficult. The young person's transition towards independence and their hopes and plans for their future are threatened by conditions which lead to increased dependence on family and carers. Having to deal with a disease in a developmental phase of great personal, social and emotional change, often results in problems about self-care, adherence to treatment and being able to make realistic plans for the future. Inherited conditions may be a risk factor because they have implications for how responsible and guilty family members might feel. Guilt is commonly felt by parents when a child is sick or disabled, but this can be intensified if parents consider that they have caused the condition by transmitting it genetically. As a result, parents may act inappropriately, allowing their children to dictate what they want or how they will behave. They may not set clear boundaries for behaviour and they may constantly give in to the child's demands. There may also be increased family conflict, if blame for transmitting the condition is attributed to one of the parents.

Rarity. Rare conditions pose their own unique stress. Lack of professional knowledge may result in delayed diagnosis or inappropriate treatment, and non-specialist agencies outside the hospital may have particular difficulties in understanding and communicating with the family. This may leave them feeling isolated, unsupported and not understood, especially if they require treatment at specialist regional (or even *supra* regional) centres. This situation increases the stresses on them enormously because of the cost, time and effort needed to travel to appointments. There may also be long absences from home for some of the family for inpatient treatment, and limitations in continuing support from services when at home. Lack of knowledge and understanding of the condition may also limit support and help available from family and friends. Organizations such as Contact-a-Family, which place families whose children have similar conditions (particularly those which are less common) into contact with each other are extremely valuable in reducing these feelings of isolation (see *Appendix C*).

Nature of the treatment. Conditions which require either frequent visits to hospital or intensive treatments to be carried out at home are risk factors as they can severely disrupt child and family life. Home-based treatments are not only time-consuming and physically demanding (for example, setting up dialysis machines, daily injections, physiotherapy or catheterization), but they may also have consequences for the child–parent relationship. In situations where a high level of physical care is required, parents may spend all their time with the child in doing physical chores and tasks rather than enjoying something pleasurable together. Children may not be given sufficient privacy and space to develop their own individual identity, leading to an overinvolved and intrusive relationship between parent and child.

The amount of responsibility children take on regarding self-care and management of their condition can be a risk or protective factor. Inappropriate expectations from adults about responsibility are associated with poorer compliance with treatment and poorer health status (Ingersoll *et al.*, 1986). If expectations are too high, this may place too many demands and too great a burden on the child, but if the child is given too little responsibility, this may undermine their abilities and may lead to resentment. Those who are able to take on appropriate responsibility and have control of some aspects of treatment are likely to have a greater sense of control, higher self-esteem and therefore better adjustment.

In summary, chronic disease is a considerable stressor to the child and other family members. The conclusions that can be drawn about the extent to which specific characteristics of a disease place a child at psychosocial risk are limited. However, most difficulty is associated with conditions which are more disruptive or limit daily living (painful, debilitating conditions and those requiring intensive treatments); those where there is CNS involvement and disability; and those where the course is uncertain or life-threatening. However, the individual variation in adaptation between children cannot be accounted for by the condition itself. Research suggests, for example, that the parents' perception of the severity or the challenge presented by the condition is more predictive than the condition itself, although other characteristics of the child, family and wider support system need to be considered when attempting to predict adjustment.

Characteristics of the child

Moos and Tsu (1977) have identified a number of tasks facing the child with a physical illness:

1. Dealing with pain and incapacitation.
2. Dealing with the hospital environment and developing relationships with the hospital staff.
3. Preserving emotional balance by managing feelings of anxiety, resentment, and isolation.
4. Preserving a positive self-image.
5. Preserving relationships with family and friends.
6. Preparing for an uncertain future.

A number of characteristics that children bring to the situation are likely to be important determinants of the extent to which they can meet these challenges. Confidence, positive self-esteem and self-reliance are strong protective factors, as are their cognitive abilities, both in terms of the understanding of the condition and the range of coping strategies available to them. Age is important both in terms of the experiences and possible coping resources available to them, but also in terms of how the child may be affected. For example, younger children seem more affected in terms of scholastic achievement, whereas older children are most affected in the area of social adjustment.

Coping skills. Coping skills vary from one child to another and are influenced by developmental stage as well as personality variables. Coping may involve denial or minimizing the seriousness of the condition, seeking relevant information, rehearsing possible outcomes and strategies for dealing with these, seeking emotional support from family, friends and medical staff, mastering specific illness-related self-care tasks, positive thinking, setting concrete goals and finding purpose and meaning in life-events. However, it is more difficult to determine from studies which coping strategies are most helpful for which children.

Children's coping will be influenced by the actual stressors facing them; for some children this may be pain, and for others the fear of medical procedures or the amount of disruption to their school life. It will also be dependent on what support is available to help them identify and put coping strategies into place. For example, a study by Gaffney and Dunne (1987) indicated that many children (particularly those who were younger) rarely initiated their own coping strategies in dealing with pain.

Peterson (1989) studied characteristics in children's coping when facing medical procedures. She categorized two coping styles: an active, information-seeking approach, and an avoidant, information-denying style. She concluded that children adopting an active approach were less anxious, more co-operative and were able to demonstrate higher pain tolerance than the second group.

Characteristics of the parents

The child exists as part of the family system and is dependent on the parents and family for support, and for developing significant relationships, a sense of self-identity and self-esteem. Parental coping and adaptation are therefore very significant in predicting the adjustment of the child. Parental coping strategies such as a positive approach to life (optimism), sense of humour, and an ability to focus on the positive aspects of the child are important protective factors. Excessive parental restriction, anxiety, overprotectiveness or emotional distancing are all associated with poorer adjustment in children (Johnson, 1985).

Parental stress and mental health problems are significant risk factors for the child's adaptation. High levels of depression, anxiety and social isolation have been found in mothers of sick children (Davis,

1993), and these mothers report more physical and health complaints compared to mothers of healthy children (Wallander *et al.*, 1989). As mothers tend to take responsibility for most of the daily care of the child, their levels of stress and adaptation will influence the child significantly. For example, the more stressed and distressed the mother, the less security she will provide for the child. She will have difficulties in facing and containing the child's own distress, and will generally be less able to support the child in developing appropriate and effective strategies for dealing with the illness.

There is a significant relationship between parental coping and the child's response to events such as medical procedures (Melamed, 1992). Children model their behaviour on people who are significant to them, and they are sensitive to the reassuring safe signals or the anxiety-heightening cues which they pick up from them. Parents who are anxious, depressed or overwhelmed will be less able to identify or meet their child's emotional needs. The child may feel abandoned and insecure, and this may manifest itself in emotional or behavioural problems. Alternatively, children may feel the need to take responsibility for their parents and try to protect them from their distress. As a result, they may attempt to take on the emotional and practical demands of their condition by themselves without support, and this may create a heavy burden, which is not shared by anyone.

Family relationships

Cohesiveness and harmonious relationships within the family, open communication and the opportunity to express emotions are strong protective factors for children. Such characteristics obviously reflect a healthy psychosocial environment, and good adaptation of all members of the family, and are likely to influence the positive adaptation of the child. In contrast, conflict, particularly between the parents, is one of the best predictors of psychosocial problems in children whether suffering from medical conditions or not (Bloch, Block and Morrison, 1981).

Chronic disease, as with any other stressor, places a strain on the relationship between the parents as well as on all other relationships within the whole family system. There is evidence of increased marital disharmony in families of children with chronic illness, although research does not support the commonly-held view that marital break-up and divorce are more likely (Sabbeth and Levanthal, 1984; Johnson, 1985). Nevertheless, this means that children with chronic medical conditions are more likely to be affected by family discord, which may be an additional stress factor on top of others related to the disease. By way of caution, however, it is important to note that some families report their relationships to be improved by the child's condition, which brings them closer together and enables them to be more considerate of each other (Johnson, 1980).

Other relationships within the family can also be important. In particular, good sibling relationships can protect children against mental health problems. Brothers and sisters can help and support each other by providing models of how to cope, comfort, ways of exploring difficulties, and ways of helping them to keep a reasonable perspective on events. However, this pre-supposes that the siblings are reasonably adapted to the situation themselves. Some studies have indicated high vulnerability for siblings of children with chronic conditions (Eiser, 1990). For example, they have been found to be more socially isolated, more likely to underachieve academically, and to present increased somatic complaints and health preoccupations. On the other hand, such findings are not universal, and Horowitz and Kazak (1990) have found evidence of improved adaptation, with higher social competence, and increased sensitivity and empathy in pre-school siblings of children with chronic conditions.

Concurrent stresses on the child and family

All families experience a variety of stressful events throughout life, and the more of these there are, the more difficult it will be for them to adapt, to support each other and to cope with the disease-related demands or stresses. Such stresses can include: school-related or social pressures for the child, such as taking examinations; relationship difficulties with peers; and a variety of pressures on the family such as moving house, redundancy, financial concerns, or any other life events. Concurrent stresses may serve to exacerbate symptoms, by exhausting normal coping responses, or may influence coping indirectly by reducing motivation or resources to comply with treatment, which in turn may compromise the well-being, and adaptation of the child.

Social support

Social support is an important coping resource in mediating stress for the child and family. The better the support that is available, the more likely families are to cope with adverse events and adapt effectively. However, it is a complex resource to measure and has a number of functions or components including emotional support, information, practical help or encouraging feelings of normality, and may be provided by one or many more people. Research clearly indicates that perceived support is more important than the size or density of social networks (Kazak, Reber and Carter, 1988). Available resources affect appraisal of stressful events and determine which strategies are accessible for the individual to use. Availability of support may vary according to the child's condition and the feelings this raises in others (Burden and Thomas, 1986). For example, a family with a child who has cancer may receive tremendous generosity, warmth and support from neighbours and friends, whereas families with children with profound physical or learning difficulties may find themselves shunned or ignored by others.

Service support

Professional support is obviously an important aspect of all support for families and hence should have beneficial effects upon the adaptation of all family members, including the child. The importance of professionals in terms of the security provided by their status and expertise is not to be underestimated as a factor in the adaptation of the child and family. However, this is mediated by the professionals' ability to establish relationships with them and to communicate effectively.

Formal support agencies have the potential for relieving the burden on informal support networks. In addition to specialist medical support, such agencies may support people emotionally and hence serve an important protective function, if they are geared to assess and meet the specific needs of the child and family. However, formal agencies are often criticized for their poor communication or inflexibility (Davis and Fallowfield, 1991). As a result, this may severely compromise the families' confidence and trust in their help, and restrict their ability to meet the child's and families' needs at any level. Such difficulties are at best frustrating, but, at worst, may exacerbate the stress already present in families, and make it more difficult for them to adapt.

The Process of Adaptation: A Framework

Analysis of all of these factors gives useful and interesting information, but questions remain about how they actually impinge upon the individual child. In order to be able to provide effective help on an individual basis, we need to know the child (and members of their family) to understand the process by which he or she adapts and the difficulties encountered in the process. Although complex, it is these processes that will determine why children can face the same situations and yet act and adapt so differently. It is important, therefore, for the helper to learn about the individual child's experiences, what meaning he or she attributes to particular events or challenges, and how he or she evaluates what is helpful in dealing with specific situations.

Personal Construct Theory

A useful framework for understanding the way people make sense of events and experience is Personal Construct Theory, developed by George Kelly (1991). He proposed that individuals develop their own unique model or theory of the world on the basis of their past experiences. This model is then used to try and make sense of all subsequent events with the aim of anticipating the world and adapting appropriately. Everyone develops such a model, from the baby who anticipates being fed or held, if he or she cries, to the boy who refuses to accept white medicine as his previous experience was that pink medicine was palatable and white medicine made him sick. These examples are no different in essence from the doctor who identifies symptoms and puts them together to make a diagnosis as a means of deciding upon treatment; he is using a model or theory, just like them.

The child's model. The child's model determines how the child sees, perceives, or construes events. It is therefore not events in themselves which determine how the child reacts, but the individual interpretations (or constructions) of the events. For example, to one child, a blood test may be seen as a momentary discomfort and little else. To another it can have enormous significance of possibly taking him or her into hospital and away from family and friends. For another child it may seem terrifying to lose what looks like a whole finger of blood, with considerable fears about whether they will have enough blood left! It is the uniqueness of the child's personal model that explains the variation in meaning and hence the individual response to the event.

Using his or her own unique model, the child tries to make sense of a particular problem and formulates ways to anticipate what will happen. These constructions are hypotheses, or best guesses, which are then tested out against what actually happens. For example, children who are helped to understand that a blood test will be less painful and take less time if they keep still, may only believe it if they put the strategy into practice and find it successful.

Some constructions held by the child may be incorrect or unhelpful and may need to be revised. For example, one young girl with diabetes kept cheating on her diet. Her mother and doctor were concerned about her blood sugar levels and did not understand why they were so high, until the mother found sweet wrappers in her daughter's bag. The doctor explored this with the young girl, without accusation and learned a great deal. Firstly, the girl knew that her behaviour was wrong. She revealed that she anticipated enjoying the sweets and also that she felt no adverse effects physically after consuming the sweets. As a result she concluded that no harm had been done! Although the conclusion was wrong, she was, nevertheless, testing the hypothesis by cheating.

Furthermore, she also admitted to asserting a measure of independence from her mother, since she construed her mother to be generally very controlling. Her behaviour in eating the sweets was also then a test of the construction that she could be independent and not controlled by her mother all the time.

Whenever constructions are tested, they may prove to be invalid and require a change to the underlying model and the way particular events are perceived. For example, the doctor in the previous example was able to show the girl that although she might not feel ill, the sweets were still damaging for her. He was also able to help her to find other, less dangerous, ways of being independent; for example, he encouraged her to take the lead in discussing the management of her condition with the diabetologist, rather than letting her mother. As a result, the child was able to alter her construction of eating forbidden sweets, and began to test new ways of asserting her independence.

The process of adaptation

The process of adaptation is, therefore, one of:

a) using the existing model to anticipate events;
b) testing these anticipations by what actually happens as a result of what we do; and
c) changing these anticipations, if they are found to be invalid, so that we are more realistic in future predictions.

Although the process may be conscious, it is just as likely to be unconscious and may certainly not be logical or easily understood. Intellectually, children are not the same as adults, and therefore the ways in which they make sense may be entirely different. To understand their construction specifically, we must listen very carefully to what they say and explore the meaning of events without making assumptions. It was only by doing this that the doctor understood the girl with diabetes. It may only be by listening to the child's protestations (as opposed to dismissing them) about not wanting to take the white medicine that the adult can construe his or her behaviour as anything more than a childish fad or as the child just being difficult!

Such a model helps make sense of adaptation to illness. For children who have acquired a chronic condition, they will have developed a construct system within health. All aspects of life will be involved in this including their constructions of themselves, parents, family, friends, the home, school or social activities in the community. Suddenly the child is ill and this whole model has to change.

One young man described a recurrent dream while he was recovering from surgery following the diagnosis of cancer. He described feeling totally alone in the ward as the walls of the hospital were pulled down around him. He pictured himself in the middle of this chaos, helpless, bewildered and terrified. As this illustrates, many children (and parents) feel their world and all its meaning has been shaken to its very foundations on being given the diagnosis of a chronic or life-threatening condition. Children may feel their construct system is invalid as their world ceases to make sense using it. For example, built carefully into the construct system of many people is that they are safe, that nothing awful can happen to them or anyone they care about. We hear about catastrophes that happen to other people, but somehow believe this could not happen to us or those we love. When it does happen, therefore, it is not surprising that extreme fearfulness and insecurity might result, with the worst possibilities being imagined in any situation, including the outcome or prognosis of the condition.

Following the diagnosis, all aspects of their constructions, including self-perceptions, are likely to change. A new area to understand is the illness, the symptoms, the treatment and the consequences of all of these for their lifestyle. The child may have to take in vast amounts of new information about his or her own body, develop new self-care skills and also learn what he or she is able to do, or now prevented from doing. For example, a child diagnosed with epilepsy may not be allowed to go swimming or ride a bike as independently as before.

Such changes, perhaps to a lesser extent, have to occur with any alteration or development in the child's condition, and these may be positive or negative. For example, a child may have to adjust to being able to consume previously forbidden food and drink after a kidney transplant. Such changes may appear small to adults, but can seem an enormous upheaval to a child. There are also new people to meet and frightening places to go, such as clinics and hospitals. Parents may not be what they were once perceived to be; for example, they may become much more anxious or more controlling. They may be seen as less powerful, less able to provide a totally safe environment, and not able to control everything (for example, the illness) as they did before.

A major diagnosis implies fundamental changes to all aspects of life and the child may lose, at least temporarily, the ability to anticipate and make sense of the world. Such a state is the source of enormous anxiety. The child may be unable to answer the question, 'What is going to happen to me?' at any level. As a result, a process of change is instituted immediately and automatically. This is the process of adaptation, which occurs constantly, is never finished and has to be understood in relation to the individual child. For example, we might take the child who was quoted at the beginning of the book as expecting to become a pilot, and ask whether and to what extent he is well or poorly adapted. An answer is impossible without much more information. However, what can be said is that he has come to this point no doubt via a complex set of changes, and that this belief may be something to which he needs to cling in order for him to retain self-esteem or hope for his future.

The process of helping is one of exploring children's perceptions or constructions of the world; helping them clarify, and, if necessary, change, their assumptions or beliefs, when they are not helpful. This can be done by listening and discussing, supporting the child in testing out constructions to find those which are useful and those which are not, and which need to be revised. This may be accomplished by presenting them with new information, which challenges their previous beliefs, or by the child carrying out a particular action or behaviour and evaluating the response, as in the example of the child testing out his new strategy for coping with needles.

Enabling this process is what this book is about, and the processes of exploration and change will be covered subsequently in some depth. However, before moving on to this, it will be helpful to set the scene in the next couple of chapters by exploring children's constructions of their condition and treatment and the other significant aspects of their lives, such as family, friends and school.

Summary

❑ Children with chronic disabling conditions (and all their family members) face many challenges and difficulties in all aspects of their lives, including at the physical, emotional, social and practical level.

❑ Research studies indicate raised levels of psychological and social problems in such children, their siblings and parents, and for the family unit as a whole, as compared with non-affected families.

❑ The factors which predict the level of adaptation include characteristics of the disease (disease severity, CNS involvement, visibility, course, aetiology, prevalence, and nature of treatment), characteristics of the child (including the child's development stage, personality and coping style), family characteristics, including family relationships, support and cohesiveness, other concurrent stresses on the family, and the level and availability of social and service support.

❑ Such factors do not yet allow us to predict the adaptation of an individual child and there is considerable variation between children in the degree of adaptation achieved.

❑ The process of adaptation is understood in terms of assuming that each child has a model of the world in his or her head and that this model enables anticipation of and adaptation to all events.

❑ Each child (and model) is unique, and it is only by listening carefully to the ways children make sense of the impact and meaning of their condition that any useful understanding of the tasks and available resources for adaptation can be achieved.

❑ The onset of illness may invalidate the model that the child has constructed to that point, and the process of adaptation is one of changing the model so as to enable appropriate and effective anticipations to occur.

❑ Adaptation is a process which happens over time, involves exploration and testing of all the implications of the disease and may be aided by all professionals in contact with the child and family.

3

The Child's Experience

Using the framework discussed in *Chapter 2*, we will explore the child's experiences further, including clinical examples to illustrate the changes and problems faced in adapting to a chronic condition or disability. The aim is to illustrate the diversity and range of experience. We will first consider the child's perceptions of their condition and treatment, and look at how this affects their view of themselves. We will continue this theme in *Chapter 4*, looking at children's constructions of their families, friends and school. It is important that adults working with children understand how children might view these areas so that they can communicate effectively with them, and help them develop both a useful understanding of, and ways of coping with, their experiences.

Constructions of Illness and Disability

As discussed in *Chapter 2*, a chronic condition has a profound impact on the child's model of the world. For some children, with early or congenital conditions, there is not a specific point at which the diagnosis is given. Instead, they gradually acquire and assimilate knowledge of their condition. For these children there may be a rather protected period within the family, where they are not aware that there is anything special or different about them. One young girl recalled that until she started school, she believed that every girl had to use tubes (catheters) to urinate. It was only when she realized that no other child's mother came into the school to help them that she began to be aware that she was different.

At whichever point children develop an awareness of their condition, they will initially have very little *specific* knowledge about it. They will, however, make their own sense of it, from their knowledge of how bodies work, what illness in general means to them, and their beliefs about illness causality and treatment. This knowledge will then be modified by further information as it is acquired, enabling the gradual rebuilding of the child's construct system.

Children may actively search for information, with some being very receptive and sensitive to any cues or information available to them (Kendrick *et al.*, 1986). Other children may initially find it too difficult to accept such unwelcome information, and will opt out of knowing anything more. Some may find it too hard to believe that a problem cannot be made better, particularly if their parents (or doctors) have always been able to make everything alright for them before.

Whatever the initial reaction, children will continue to acquire and update their knowledge as time goes on. This information may come from accurate sources, such as healthcare professionals or books, but also from inaccurate sources, such as television drama programmes or gossip at school. This means that inaccuracies and distortions can always occur, and need to be considered when trying to help them. What is particularly important to know, however, is that every child will be unique, and their construction will vary according to a number of factors. These include:

- their understanding of the illness;
- their intellectual capacities and developmental level;
- the characteristics of the condition; and
- the ways in which their condition compromises or challenges both developmental and daily living tasks.

Development of Children's Understanding

Attempts have been made to categorize the development of children's understanding of their bodies and illness as being a systematic and predictable sequence of stages, mirroring their acquisition of causal reasoning, as described by Piaget (Burbach and Peterson, 1986). On the basis of this, it is suggested that children of a particular age (and stage of thinking) will have acquired a corresponding level of understanding of illness.

Very young children have a limited number of constructs from which to make sense of the world. Most of their knowledge is acquired through direct experience, is very concrete, and bound very much within the here and now. They are likely to have little ability to generalize to related situations or to appreciate the multiple aspects of one situation. Their thinking may seem illogical and dominated by magical or superstitious thoughts.

With increasing age, thinking becomes more sophisticated, and logical thought processes become more evident. Initially these tend to be quite concrete and literal, in that children are only able to think and reason about real objects or events and to carry out basic problem-solving in the here and now. During adolescence, children acquire an increasingly mature and adult comprehension. They are able to reason logically and to think in abstract terms. They also begin to be able to explore problems systematically.

Using a Piagetian framework, it is assumed that understanding of illness causality progresses from vague, magical and illogical thinking, through to the identification of concrete, external causes of disease and ultimately leads to more abstract physiological and psychological theories. However, the process of acquiring and developing understanding is very complex. Piaget has been criticized as not sufficiently acknowledging the important role played by experience, social and cultural factors in the development of cognitive skills. It would be misleading to assume that children have a particular level of knowledge about their bodies or illness based on their age or even on their general cognitive abilities. However, as children progress in their ability to process information and make sense of their world, different characteristics in their thinking and understanding of illness and treatment may become apparent. We will go on to describe the major characteristics of the child's thinking in relation to these general trends and the implications of this for informing and supporting children. At the same time we will try to illustrate which factors influence the processes in determining how children come to have their own unique knowledge and understanding about how the body works, how illness is caused and why treatment is like it is.

Understanding of the body

At the most basic level of understanding, children will be fascinated by what they can actually see on their body and may delight in naming their eyes, nose, mouth and any external marks or scars! Children will need to have developed a concept of 'inside' to be able to think about what is going on inside their body. They may have an immature understanding that the body is made up of skin which holds all the blood and bones inside the body, and consequently become terribly upset by any puncture holes (from needles) or grazes to their skin, since this might let all their blood out. This is illustrated by a four-year old's fearful comment when seeing a few drops of blood on his arm following an injection, *'My blood keeps falling out!'* Plasters (band-aids) can be particularly reassuring for young children who have this belief! An explanation of the healing skin which starts to grow straight away and covers the graze or hole may also be valuable in this context to relieve this kind of anxiety or fear.

A simple knowledge of internal body parts tends to include organs about which the child has acquired information through direct experience, such as stomach ache. The heart, lungs and brain are often known, although children may be uncertain about their function. When asked, they might tell you that the heart is for loving people (and will frequently draw it in the shape of a love-heart), or for beating, or for keeping the body alive. One boy of four said the lungs were 'for going in and out', and that the brain was 'for being brainy'.

As children acquire more information, they are able to identify more organs and give more comprehensive definitions of their function. There will, however, be considerable variation in what children of any age may be able to tell you about what is inside their body. Some children may simply report what they have just eaten, as depicted in *Figure 3.1* by an eight-year-old child!

Children with a medical condition or disability may have specific knowledge about one particular organ or part of the body, perhaps related to their illness or condition. However, this knowledge may be dramatically in advance of their understanding of the body more generally, as shown in these figures (*3.1–3.4*) drawn by children with kidney, bladder and neuromuscular conditions.

Understanding of causality of illness and treatment

Again there is evidence in children of a developmental process in the understanding of illness and its treatment. We will illustrate some of the major themes here.

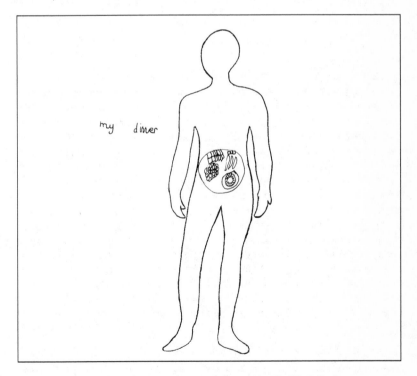

my dinner

Figure 3.1 Eight-year-old child's diagram of food inside the body.

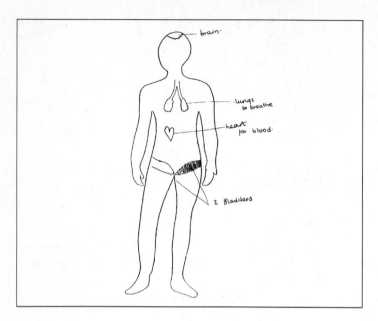

Figure 3.2 A drawing of the body by a child with bladder dysfunction.

'Mummy kiss it better!'   Infants and very young children may not be able to understand the meaning or cause of pain or other unpleasant sensations. The most important support for these children is a familiar and constant caregiver (usually the parent) who is able to act as interpreter for the child and is able to give security and reassurance, usually by physical comfort or a soothing voice. To enable this the caregiver must be well supported, adequately prepared for what will happen to their child, and as calm as possible so as not to transmit their own anxieties or distress to the infant.

Young children will try and make sense of what is happening to them and explanations tailored to their level of understanding should always be provided when trying to support them through treatment or tests. Although explanations or preparation may not be understood by very young children, they will still be helped to feel more comfortable and less frightened by someone who is calm, gentle, patient and friendly (see *Chapter 9* for strategies to prepare children for procedures).

'I've got a tummy-ache in my head.'   In pre-school children, comprehension of events is usually in advance of their verbal skills. This can make it difficult to assess what they have understood and it is

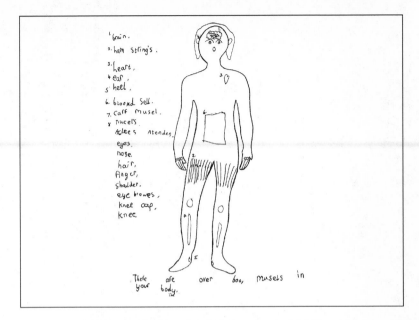

Figure 3.3 Drawing of the body by a six-year-old child.

easy to underestimate what a child has noticed or understood at this age. Practically, this indicates the importance of using verbal and non-verbal means of communicating, and listening carefully to children. One should use vocabulary which is meaningful or within their grasp, and speak in short uncomplicated sentences which the child can follow. It may help to talk to the child about what you are doing, even if it is not clear that he or she is able to understand; your presence, calmness, and tone of voice will still be comforting and reassuring.

'My lungs are broken.' Young children may be quite concrete or literal in their thinking. Illness may be construed as something broken as in this statement from a five-year-old boy with pneumonia. He was confident that the horrible tasting pink medicine was 'mending his lungs'. Children may also be baffled as to why they are receiving medicine through a drip in their arm when it is their head or their leg which is 'ill'. On a practical level, careful thought needs to be given to the information provided, as it may be taken literally. For example, one four-year-old refused to go out in the wind after she was jokingly told that she needed to wear a hat on a windy day or the wind would blow away her curls. She was very fond of her curls and did not want to take any chances!

Many health professionals aim to give explanations for tests or

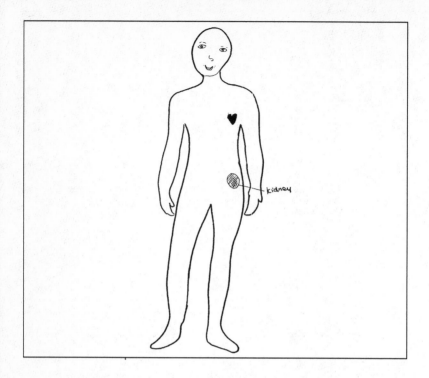

Figure 3.4 Inside the body, drawn by an eight-year-old with kidney problems.

procedures in the least threatening way possible, and they try to draw on the child's own experience. However, following the explanation being given that an X-ray was like having a photograph taken, a five-year-old boy was seen to put on his best beaming smile for the camera during the X-ray of his foot, much to the amusement of the technicians! Analogies which may be suitable and reassuring for an older child, such as likening the revolving motion and appearance of an MRI scan to a front-loading washing machine, may be taken quite literally and become very frightening to a child who has not grasped the 'as if' component. One can imagine the child's fears of being in a washing machine, or of being submerged in water and spun round very fast. One child, when told that he was to have a shunt in his head, with the explanation that it was like a tap to drain off excess fluid, pictured this quite literally as a tap in a sink coming out of his head. He described an image of turning it off and on as necessary.

'I have magic cream on my hand so the needles don't hurt.'

Magical thinking is prevalent in pre-school and primary children, and many may not be able to reliably distinguish between reality, dreams or make-believe. Their understanding is dominated by magical thinking in a world where Father Christmas, Snow White and the Easter Bunny are very real and loved, and monsters and ghosts are feared. Not surprisingly, therefore, magic is sometimes invoked to help young children cope with medical procedures; for example, they may be told about having a magic sleep when having an operation. However, it is important to make sure that 'magic sleep' is not also a euphemism, as it is in some families, for death. Alternative terms might be 'special sleep' or 'healing sleep'.

Children may also be told about magic cream, such as EMLA, which anaesthetizes the skin and helps to stop the needle hurting so much. They may also believe that they can get better by magic, if they do what they are told and take their medicine. However, this may be very frustrating, if they do not get better immediately like magic. As a result they may not understand long stays in hospital, continued treatments, and especially treatments which initially make them feel worse.

An understanding of children's magical thinking is also relevant when considering how they make sense of what happens to other people. For example, it is not uncommon for a sibling to have strong feelings of jealousy and resentment about the attention given to the sick child, and to wish they would go away. If the sick child then goes away into hospital for a long time or even dies, the sibling could be left with very frightening and guilty feelings about causing this to happen.

'Mummy, I'll be good, I promise. No more needles, please.'

The belief that illness is related to punishment is common in children, although it can occur at all ages when people in distress search for answers for why they have become ill. Such beliefs are not helped by adults who tease or threaten children by saying, for example, they will have an injection if they are naughty, or will have all their teeth out if they disobey the dentist. It is also perpetuated by our language in which words like 'bad' are commonly used to describe being ill. It is not surprising, therefore, that children might ask themselves what they must have done to deserve this illness and might believe they are being punished or that they are jinxed and that awful things will continue to happen to them.

One 11-year-old girl with cancer tearfully admitted that she had always tried to be good, and was desperately searching her mind for what she had done wrong to deserve such a serious illness.

The parents of a 12-year-old boy undergoing tests for Freidrich's Ataxia (a degenerative neurological condition) reported that he had become very helpful and his behaviour had improved significantly since the medical investigations had begun. They construed this as though he were bargaining and saying to himself, 'If I am good, then the tests will show nothing serious'.

Children will often resort to a magic or punishment idea when they do not have a more appropriate model, either from their experience, or from what they are told. This clearly highlights the importance of giving all children (and adults) an explanation which is meaningful for them, so that they do not misconstrue the situation, feel frightened and guilty, or that they are being punished. Contributing to this is the fact that a child may have been punished prior to the diagnosis of their condition for naughtiness, poor concentration or other problems which are likely to have been misinterpreted and not related to the medical problem diagnosed subsequently. Also, some religions perpetuate the belief of adversity as punishment or atonement.

Germs and contagion theory.
Children who are able to apply basic problem-solving strategies in their thinking may construe illness in terms of contagion, believing they are caused by contact with germs. This may be grossly over-applied, with some young children having the belief that *any* form of illness is spread by contact with others, including cancer, epilepsy or even broken bones. This has important implications since children may become frightened in hospital, for example, when put next to another seriously ill child, from whom they think they may catch something. For the same reason, peers may react badly and avoid a child who is returning to school after the diagnosis of a particular condition. Appropriate education and information rather than just reassurance is often necessary.

As children gain more experience, they will understand that illness (or disability) can be caused by a number of different factors, not just by germs which get into the body. They may begin to grasp the notion that illness can be located within the body, yet still assume it has an external cause. For example, a young girl who sustained damage to her optic nerve could not understand why the doctors simply did not give her a pair of glasses to make her see again.

Psychophysiological explanations.
A mature psychophysiological understanding is that illness can be caused by an interaction between environmental factors, germs, individual susceptibility (that is, low resistance) and psychological factors. Children and young adults will also come to recognize that specific organs may malfunction, as in renal disease or diabetes. However, again there is a wide diversity in understanding, and even many adults are poorly informed about their bodies and have limited knowledge about disease causality – one only has to consider the continued ignorance about HIV and AIDS in spite

of extensive publicity. It is also important to be aware of the child's understanding of death whenever talking about illness. Again, this is not an all or nothing concept, but changes with development and is influenced by the child's thinking, emotional state and experience, including cultural or religious teaching and beliefs about death. However, we will look at the implication of this in *Chapter 10* where we will look at issues of loss and bereavement in children.

The Role of Personal Experience

A developmental framework for making sense of children's growing awareness and understanding of their bodies and illness is useful, but not a substitute for listening to them. One must explore with every child their unique understanding, since what they think is dependent on their own individual experience.

Children are reliant on their own routines and rules which familiar adults apply for making sense of their world. Any situation which is unfamiliar and unknown is potentially distressing. Children's perceptions of these situations will be coloured not only by previous experience, but also by how they are feeling; for example, how anxious or upset they are.

Most of us would agree that the world of hospitals and treatment is perplexing and strange, and normal, everyday routines and rules are virtually absent. It is, therefore, difficult, particularly for younger children, to make any sense of events which they may perceive as incomprehensible and distressing. They may not understand why they are taking medicine to make them feel better, when it tastes awful and makes them feel worse. They will probably be very puzzled by a number of routines, such as using a bedpan (potty) when they have mastered the use of the toilet at home. They may have to stay in bed when they are not tired or not be allowed to eat when they are hungry!

Changes at home may be similarly confusing and unsettling in terms of different routines or expectations of behaviour. Children may find they are able or not able to do certain things as before, and that adults respond to them differently. Children who are very anxious may show signs of regressing both in their behaviour and their understanding of events. Children who are anxious may also selectively attend to the most disturbing or frightening aspects of a situation, as in the following example.

Sarah, who suffered with a form of dystonia (a degenerative muscular condition) came into hospital for the first time for respite care. She was horrified to learn that she needed to have a naso-gastric tube, as feeding had become so difficult. Her feelings, however, were not to do with the tube on its own, but because she thought she would lose her hair. When this was explored with her, she explained that she had seen two other children on the ward with tubes, and both of them had lost all their hair, one from surgery following a head injury and another through chemotherapy. She assumed, therefore, that she would lose her hair also, even though there were many other children she had met with tubes who had not lost their hair.

Children will make the best sense they can of what they see and experience around them in hospital. It is very important for adults to be sensitive to what the child may be concerned about, as in the following example.

One seven-year-old was very concerned about his brother having a blood exchange. He became very agitated after asking his mother quite calmly what would happen if all the blood came out of the body, to which his mother replied that you would die of course. In exploring this, it became clear that he had construed the nurse as removing large quantities of blood via a syringe, but had not realized that the clear liquid in the plasma drip was the main constituent of blood to replace what was being removed. He thought it was water and could not be blood, because it was not red. He was very angry, both with the nurses for harming his brother and with his mother for just letting this happen. His mother, quite obviously preoccupied by the child who was ill, just answered her young son's question literally without making sense of the context and her child's concerns inherent in the question.

Developmental Challenges and Tasks

In terms of understanding the child's experience of his or her condition, it is also important to consider the developmental tasks which are challenged at any point in time. There are different concerns for children at different ages, and diseases may compromise these. For example, neonates who have heart disease may be so unwell that they do not progress in motor skills or other areas of development. For infants and pre-school children, separation from parents and disruption of normal routines will be particularly difficult. The process of asserting their individuality and exploring their environment physically and socially may be curtailed because of the condition. Children whose immune systems are compromised following organ transplantation or chemotherapy may be isolated because of the risk of infection from others. Other children may be immobilized for long periods of time when undergoing corrective surgery. However, even without these constraints, parents may find it difficult to allow their pre-school children the same experiences as others, because of concern and feelings of protectiveness. For example, they may not let them go to nursery in case they are bullied, teased or accidentally hurt by other children.

In school-aged children, acceptance from peers and academic achievements become important issues and again these may be compromised. Children may resent missing time from school and not seeing their friends. They may experience considerable pressure to keep up with work and feel inferior to their peers who achieve more. Just being different may be enormously distressing for children beginning to identify with people outside the family.

Children of any age may have difficulties in considering their future and this can have particular implications when trying to encourage adherence to treatment regimes, especially when the effects are long-term in nature and not immediate. For example, a young child with PKU (a metabolic condition requiring a special diet) constantly tried to eat forbidden chocolate. Although his doctor and parents had explained the consequences (possible deficits in intellectual abilities), he seemed unable to grasp the seriousness of his non-compliance; he wanted the chocolate now, and did not want to contemplate anything negative happening in the future.

In adolescence, there may be a greater understanding of the long-term aspects of the condition, with the realization that they will have it for the rest of their lives. They have to face the limitations this may place on career choices, and ambitions, such as having a family or even living independently. Such knowledge can bring fear and resentment. The knowledge that they will have to take sole responsibility for the problem (rather than parents or doctors) may produce a deep sadness and despair, a sense of mourning for the loss of the perfect future.

Although adolescents still require support from the family, young people will be trying to assert their independence, having a greater reliance on, and allegiance to, their peer group. Responsibility for self-care shifts from adults to the adolescent, often with an uneasy period of adjustment on both sides. The dilemma of being expected to accept responsibility for something you do not want and yet needing to assert independence when others are protective and uneasy about letting go is complex. Non-compliance with treatment will often be tied up with these conflicts.

Particular challenges to adolescents will be conditions which restrict their independence or privacy. Young men and women who require supervision when in the bathroom in case of an epileptic seizure, or who cannot cross the road or travel independently, may experience tremendous frustration as a result of the restrictions on their personal and social activities.

One teenage girl, with spina bifida, always required the support and assistance of another person when walking. She bitterly described her frustration with her mother who would not let her go out with friends. Her mother felt that hanging around on the streets, apart from being a waste of time, was also unsuitable for someone who depended on others to be mobile. She did not feel her daughter's friends would be able to take the responsibility of looking after her seriously enough and was only prepared to allow her child to go to activities she considered suitable.

Adolescents are acutely aware of how others perceive them and how they feel society sees them. They may have a strong sense of injustice and anger at being isolated and made to feel different at a time when identification with their peer group and emergence as individuals in society are important.

Characteristics of the Condition

Children's experience of their condition will certainly be affected by the specific aspects of the condition or illness itself. In *Chapter 2* we considered how illness characteristics might predict adaptation. Here we will look at the particular difficulties children have with the many aspects of the disease that create problems for them and affect their adaptation. However, pain and preparation for treatment procedures are faced by so many children and are so frequently problematic, that they will be tackled separately in *Chapter 9*. Similarly, the issues faced by children with degenerative and life-threatening conditions will be considered separately in *Chapter 10*.

Unpredictability and uncertainty are important issues in many conditions. They are particularly apparent in conditions which may relapse (for example, cancer), or change suddenly in severity, negatively as in epilepsy or asthma, or positively following surgery or organ transplantation. It can be very difficult for children to make plans or to commit themselves to activities even one week in advance. As a result, they often find themselves excluded from these events or have difficulty in maintaining friendships at school. Other children may not want to start projects with them or have them in their teams, because they are perceived to be unreliable.

Julie, an adolescent with brittle diabetes, had to drop out of a number of school committees and to resign as publicity officer of her local drama group as she was often unavailable at very short notice to carry our her commitments. In addition, she often needed to cancel social activities with friends. It was with great sadness that she acknowledged that her friends rarely called for her now to go out and that she had stopped volunteering for anything so that she did not let others down. As a consequence, she rarely went anywhere and depended quite heavily on people at the hospital as her social contacts.

Much of the experience of illness is about waiting, for tests, test results, or treatments. The uncertainty of outcome in each of these is very difficult to contain, and this is true for most people, as uncertainly is very much the basis of anxiety. Many conditions involve tests (for example, scans, blood tests) at regular intervals throughout the child's life. For many children, there is unease and anxiety surrounding each test, perhaps a sleepless night beforehand, or perhaps several days of tension leading up to the test or the test result. Some people are totally incapacitated by the uncertainties around their condition and are unable to make plans or carry them out. When children are awaiting particular results about their condition, or are waiting to be called for an organ transplant, they may feel that their whole life is on hold, and everything is secondary to it. This is illustrated by a poem written by a teenager who was on call, waiting for a kidney transplant.

On Call

The phone rings,
My heart stops,
Starts beating again,
Faster than normal.

Wait for a moment,
Is that the Call?
Steps on the stairs,
Will they lead to my room?
Silence calls out,
NO ONE comes in.
I am disappointed and relieved
at the same time.

This poem also reflects the ambivalence that may be experienced about having treatment which might change the condition. This includes all the worry about the treatment itself (surgery is frightening) but also the uncertainty and delay in knowing whether it will be successful. Some children are fatalistic and prepared to take a chance. Other children are terrified of the possibility of success and change, as there are no guarantees, and the possibility of losing the gains can feel too distressing.

One young woman, following her kidney transplant, admitted to feeling very depressed. During the previous six years on dialysis, she had always imagined that her whole life would be wonderful after having a kidney; she thought she would have the health and energy to do everything she had always dreamed of doing. However, in the event she felt uneasy and was unwilling to try out this new life-style in case something went wrong and it was all taken away from her. The fear of losing this new-found life almost paralyzed her; it prevented her from testing out the new situation and realizing her dreams.

In addition to dealing with uncertainty and anxiety, it can be very difficult for children to know how or when they are feeling better. This may be due to doctors and others telling children they are getting better, when they still feel unwell and not at all sure that they are really improving. Children may also find it difficult to interpret their own normal body sensations accurately, particularly if they are very anxious about a recurrence of the condition and are hypersensitive and hypervigilant about their bodies. They may also lose confidence in their ability to know if they are well or not, especially if previous illness episodes begun suddenly without obvious physical symptoms. However, in addition to children's own dilemmas about their health, others around them may give inconsistent messages. They may themselves be very worried or protective, or alternatively expect the child to be better and want to treat him or her as normal. It appears very difficult to negotiate the grey area between these extremes in a way that is comfortable and consistent. One parent described this as travelling on a journey without a map and compass, having to find your own way without clear guidelines.

Another issue is that some conditions are stigmatized, whether in reality or as perceived by the child. For example, in certain cultures, epilepsy carries such a terrible stigma that families are ostracized. This may also be true in relation to intellectual disability. In a similar way, HIV and AIDS carries a stigma in Western cultures so that children are unable to tell peers or friends at school for fear of being excluded, or even terrorized at home if their neighbours find out.

In addition to social beliefs, children themselves construe certain causes or aspects of their condition as more or less acceptable. For example, one young man always told others that the problems with his legs resulted from a car accident, which he perceived as being a reasonable and acceptable explanation. The real explanation was that he had a congenital neuropathy (a neurological weakness from birth) which to him carried connotations of being born damaged, which he construed as less acceptable, both to himself and others. Similarly, a girl with spina bifida, who required sticks to get around, was very open with friends about her physical problems and was articulate and outspoken about the needs of people with restricted mobility. However, she went to great lengths to hide the fact that she also needed to self-catheterize, as she felt that her visible disability was acceptable to others but her special toileting needs would 'freak them out'.

Obviously the visibility of the condition or disability will influence how other people respond to the child. A problem for some children, however, is that they may find people responding to a stereotype of what they see, rather than to who they are as individuals. As a result, people may ascribe characteristics to them (for example, all children with Down's syndrome are happy and cheerful; children with cancer are brave), and talk accordingly, being very surprised when the child's own personality shines through. The classic scene is where questions are not addressed to a child/adult in a wheelchair, but to the person pushing it. Needless to say, dealing with responses purely based on appearances can prove very frustrating, particularly for children who have restricted growth. They are often treated as if they were much younger, and may even be refused entry to events (for example, films or clubs) as they look under the age limit. Some find it helpful to carry their birth certificate with them, but the initial embarrassment of being refused entry when with a group of friends is still painful for them.

Many young people with evident physical signs of illness, disability or disfigurement describe a hypersensitivity and hypervigilance when they are with other people. Unfortunately, the reality is that visible differences do often prompt attention. However, in being constantly alert to how others may perceive them, there is a strong tendency for children to assume that the attention will always be negative. They will tend to assume the other person thinks they look odd, ugly or fat, rather than that their hairstyle is attractive or that they simply want to ask the time. As a result, many children are upset and embarrassed and feel unable to handle any questions about their condition, whether concerned, intrusive or blatantly unkind. The organization Changing Faces has produced some very helpful leaflets and videos for young people to address these difficulties (see *Appendix C*). In *Chapter 9* we will look further at how to help children deal with such situations.

Some visible characteristics are associated with particular conditions, such as hair loss in cancer. Although this may be transient, if it remains after the condition has been treated, it can be difficult for the child to move on from being unwell. For example, a number of children whose hair does not grow back after therapy are treated by unfamiliar people as if they are still ill. Some feel they are carrying an indelible placard with them wherever they go, indicating that they are one of the 'cancer children'.

Children who have invisible difficulties are posed with different problems. Although they have a disability, they look and act normally in most respects and may be considered normal by others. They may then be faced with a choice about whether or not to tell other people about their condition. The consequences of not telling might be acceptance of them as normal, with the same opportunities and rights as everyone else, but feeling very different to others, holding on to what they might consider to be a dark and shameful secret and fearing being found out. Telling, on the other hand, involves the anxiety that others may be intolerant of their behaviour or needs associated with the condition. This might include, for example, needing rests, extra meal breaks, or visits to the toilet. It may also lead to being treated differently with possible repercussions for social or employment opportunities. The decision as to telling others can be a major dilemma for children who are struggling to establish their identity, since they will have difficulty in knowing to which group they belong and feel comfortable, disabled or normal.

Constructions of Self

Children's views of themselves may be radically changed as a consequence of the realization that they have a particular condition or disability. Central to these changes are those to do with their self-image, which is based on how they feel about themselves, what they can do, and how others see and respond to them. This is illustrated by the following picture (see *Figure 3.5*) and accompanying poem, composed by a teenager who lost her sight and hair as a result of her brain tumour and treatment.

Life after My Operation

After my operation,
I feel so low and ugly
Compared to before,
I used to be so bright and bubbly.
'You're so pretty, You'll knock 'um dead'
People used to say to me,
But now when I look in the mirror,
That's not what I see.

The condition may render it impossible for children to carry out activities which are central to their self-construction. For example, one 12-year-old boy was something of a local celebrity within his school and local community for his talents at judo. All his time was taken up with judo practice and tournaments. Following a serious accident, however, he was left disabled and intermittently in severe pain, making even walking difficult for him. As a result he had to change his view of himself dramatically; he lost both his status and passionate interest at one go. He had to develop alternative interests, which were not physically demanding; he had to cope with people reacting differently to him, and he had to develop a new circle of friends outside the judo club.

Figure 3.5 Teenager looking in the mirror.

For some children, being informed about their condition may enable a positive change in the way they perceive themselves. For example, some children experience considerable relief from the knowledge that they are not mad, that there *is* actually something wrong with them, particularly if they have been suffering symptoms which have previously been dismissed or trivialized. Many children have been told by parents, teachers or even their GP that they are making a fuss or attention seeking, and need to 'get on with things' rather than complain, until the reason for their pain, tiredness or other difficulty is diagnosed. Other children may derive positive benefit from being able to understand why they find particular activities difficult, as opposed to the construction that they are clumsy, stupid or wicked as in the following example.

Ana was 12 years old and had an atypical form of spina bifida which placed considerable stress on her lungs, making her breathing laboured, particularly at night. Her family did not realize she had a physical condition until she was nearly seven, when she required surgery and a corrective spinal brace.

Ana remembered with considerable sadness her mother's fury

*towards her for sleeping so poorly during the night and the disappoint-
ment her mother so clearly expressed that she was so ungainly and life-
less during the day. She grew up believing herself to be lazy, stupid and
useless. It was only after appropriate treatment and discussion about her
condition that she was able to free herself from her mother's misplaced
negative perceptions of her, resulting from misconstruing the situation
where her condition was not recognized.*

Some children feel very special because they can boast of having
experienced something others have not (in a similar vein to the 'my
brother is bigger than your brother' debate!). For example, the young
child with the 'broken lungs' was heard to brag to his siblings that he
should now be the first to play on the computer because of his condition.

For other children, there are negative connotations to being different and a constant need to prove themselves as good, if not better than,
healthy children. This may depend as much on the child's perception
of how others respond to disability or chronic illness, as on the reality
of the stigma or assumptions which are often made.

*Sarah was dismayed by her teacher's comments when she started a new
secondary school. She said she was pleased that Sarah had arrived, as
another pupil, Hannah, would now have a good friend. Hannah and
Sarah were the only pupils using wheelchairs in the school. Sarah then
went out of her way to be friends with every girl in the school other
than Hannah, as she did not want to be identified as disabled and different from the others. Throughout her schooling she felt under
tremendous pressure to achieve more than her peers academically. She
wanted to participate and be as good in all their activities (whether
smoking, truanting or exams) in order to be accepted by her peers.*

The influence of their own constructions of what constitutes disability
and how others relate to them is illustrated by a group of teenagers
requiring haemodialysis (as their kidneys were non-functioning). They
were adamant that they were not disabled. They considered themselves
normal, as it was just their kidneys that did not work. It was a source
of shock that others might regard them as disabled as they did not look
different to anyone else. According to them, the disabled were those in
wheelchairs or special schools. However, the anomaly of not perceiv-
ing themselves as disabled and yet receiving disability and mobility
allowances seemed to be ignored.

The reactions of others may have both positive and negative implications for how children construe themselves. Getting special attention
or being able to avoid tedious tasks such as homework may have positive implications, but being overprotected, prevented from joining in
with peers, or singled out may be negative, isolating or rejecting. As
stated earlier, there may be a hypersensitivity towards the reaction of

others, with a tendency to misconstrue all reactions as a result of their condition. The illness or condition becomes the most important construction, determining how everything else is perceived. This is illustrated in the case of a boy who kept insisting that all the other children disliked him because of his condition. His mother's attempt to correct the misconstruction involved her categorically telling him that their reaction was much more to do with him not sharing his toys or taking his fair turn in games!

However, the reactions of other people are particularly important in terms of forming a sense of oneself. It is hard, for example, to feel confident, successful and handsome/beautiful when confronted with embarrassment, concern, curiosity, disapproving stares or even being overlooked by others.

One teenager, recently diagnosed with multiple sclerosis, needed to spend some time in a wheelchair. She was infuriated by how family friends changed towards her when she was in the chair. Instead of talking to her, they began asking her parents how she was, as if she were not there or not able to talk. She described how she would furiously wheel her chair away in disgust, until the friends realized she was upset at their behaviour towards her.

Children may need opportunities to explore who they are, how their condition affects them, and how they are perceived by others. This can be achieved by listening carefully to them or by exploring their perceptions through drawings and play. Examples of how to do this are given in *Chapter 7*. Children certainly need to be able to see themselves as more than someone with a disability. This may involve thinking with the child about all aspects of their lives and relationships with others.

Summary

❑ Children's perceptions of themselves, their condition and illness were explored, because these determine their adjustment and are the starting point for providing help.

❑ Children's constructions of their bodies and conditions will develop and become more complex as the child gains more experience and knowledge of the world.

❑ One cannot make assumptions about understanding based on developmental abilities alone. Distortions and inaccuracies can occur at any age, and anxiety may interfere with children's acquisition of information and perception of events.

❑ Common themes identified in children's thinking which may lead to misperceptions include: concrete or literal thinking, magical thinking, viewing illness (and treatment) as punishment, and over-application of contagion as a means of becoming unwell.

❑ Children's experiences are varied, illustrating the importance of individual meaning and the necessity of listening carefully to them in order to make sense of what they feel is happening to them.

❑ Illness or disability presents different challenges according to the developmental tasks facing the child; for example, social acceptance and academic abilities in school age children and separation and independence in adolescence.

❑ Characteristics of the condition will also be an important factor influencing children's experience, affecting both the response of others and children's view of themselves.

4

The Social World of the Child

In this chapter we will continue to look at the child's experience, extending the exploration to consider constructions and problems in relation to the social world, including family, professionals, school and friends.

Constructions of Family

The way in which family members respond and interact with each other and with the child who has a chronic condition will have profound effects on the child's confidence, self-esteem and social relationships. If the child is made to feel an important member of the family unit and have something of value to contribute to other family members, he or she will be able to feel loved, valued and accepted as a person. It is important for children to know that their condition does not change this, even though many other events or activities may be different as a result.

When children are very young, most will probably believe that a cuddle, rub or kiss from their mother or father will make everything better! Following the diagnosis of a serious condition, the child may see their parents very differently, and there may be a change in their behaviour at least temporarily. Many children become very angry and difficult with their parents, partly because this feels a safe outlet for their distress, at a time when everything else seems less certain and safe. Sometimes children feel furious at their parents for somehow letting this awful thing happen to them. This can be particularly true for children undergoing painful or invasive procedures, who see their parents just letting it happen, or even worse, holding them still for the procedure to happen.

'You promised you wouldn't let them hurt me. I hate you!'

The situation can be especially difficult and distressing if the diagnosed condition is inherited from the parents. In anger and frustration, some children will blame their parents for their difficulties, and many parents will feel responsible and guilty for causing them, however illogical this may be. Parents may have difficulties in setting limits and disciplining their children appropriately. They may feel that the child deserves all the happiness they can get, and that being firm, scolding their child, or punishing him or her detracts from this directly.

Francis, the seven-year-old daughter of a woman with epilepsy was also discovered to have seizures. She refused to take any of her medicine and threw it at her mother screaming that it was all her mother's fault that she had 'caught' epilepsy. Her mother felt powerless to get her daughter to do anything she did not want to do, including taking her tablets.

Parents who suffer with a similar condition can also find it difficult to understand their child's experience. This may be either because they are unable to separate their own experience from the child's, or because it is just too painful to listen to their child talk about the feelings and distress they also experience. One teenager, Danny, recalled how, as a young child, he had been frightened of his father's anger every time he dropped something or fell over. He had assumed that as his father was in a wheelchair and could not carry out many practical tasks, he got very cross when other people were clumsy, or did not help him properly. It was only as a teenager when he discovered that he and his father had the same neuromuscular condition, that he understood his father's behaviour. He realized that his father had not been able to face the reality that his son would become disabled, and tried to deny it. This led to him being very punitive when Danny showed any signs of the condition, preferring to construe the behaviour as laziness or stupidity, and therefore not part of the hereditary condition and not his 'fault'.

Although children may feel very close and protected by their family, there will inevitably be periods of conflict, which may be exacerbated by the fact that children are dependent on their family. It can be difficult to communicate frustrations and negative feelings safely and openly to the person on whom you are dependent for care.

A teenage girl with spastic quadriplegia was extremely frustrated with the limitations caused by her condition. She depended on her mother for all her physical care, and the only way she could get out of the house with friends was if her mother or school auxiliary came with her and attended to her needs. She unleashed many of her frustrations by being verbally abusive towards her mother, or refusing to comply with her mother's requests. Her mother's response to this was to put her to her bed and refuse to do anything for her until she apologized and was more polite.

Any separation from the family and identification with a peer group can be very difficult in adolescence when there is such dependency in all daily activities. It can also be difficult to initiate conversations about more intimate problems or issues such as emotional or sexual experiences when you are 'infantalized', being perceived as being highly dependent. One teenage girl resorted to leaving the problem pages of a magazine in very conspicuous places, so as to indicate some of the problems she was also experiencing. One teenage boy became increasingly frustrated and resentful of his mother's plan for him to pursue a 'safe' career in the bank because of his epilepsy. He wanted to go to college and study nursing, but found it too difficult to challenge his mother and instead was resigned to following the career path she set.

Many children feel very guilty about the stress they think they cause their family. If their parents have financial concerns, they may believe this to be their fault, particularly if one parent has to leave work to care for them. They may also be acutely aware of the level of stress caused by worry over them, and might have considerable concern that all arguments between their parents are because of them, or that their parents may become ill as a result. Sadly, children's perceptions of family stress can be very astute, and so it is of the utmost importance that children realize they are not responsible. They need to learn that it is not their fault, but that it is just something that has happened to them and their family. Many parents are very good at feeding back positive feelings to children about how they contribute in a good way to family life, and emphasizing that as a family they will get through the difficulties together. However, this can be problematic when parents are feeling overwhelmed, restricted and hopeless themselves. *Figure 4.1* is a picture drawn by the mother of a chronically ill child, depicting how she saw her life, restricted, isolated and trapped. It would be hard to imagine these negative feelings not being communicated at some level to her child.

Figure 4.1 Depiction of a mother trapped by her child's illness.

Sometimes children will hold back distressing or worrying information from their parents as they are worried about their parent's response, or are concerned about burdening them further with more problems.

This is well illustrated by one girl's comment, '*My mum gets upset when I start to cry which makes me feel awful. I hate making her upset*'.

At times, both the parents and the child are 'holding back' in order to protect each other. In a study of dying children, Bluebond Langner (1978) observed a high frequency of mutual pretence between parent and child that death was not imminent as a means of both parent and child protecting each other.

Sometimes children feel deprived of their privacy as their parents are always talking about them to others. As one child expressed it, '*I don't know half the people that know all about me*', and continued, '*This is my story, and I never get a chance to tell it; my mother always talks for me.*'

Constructions of Siblings

Relationships between siblings within any family vary enormously. They may be extremely close and loving or alternatively hateful. What is even more complex, however, is that they might be both fiercely protective and loving, yet aggressive, resentful and hateful at the same time.

When one child in the family has special needs or requires special attention, it can create an imbalance and alter the dynamics between family members. As a result, some siblings become much closer. In some cases, children with a disability depend on their siblings both physically and socially. This may be particularly so when it is difficult to get out of the house to meet friends, or when the child attends a special school, which is a long way from home, making social contacts outside school difficult.

However, there may come a time when healthy siblings become preoccupied with their own social life, to the exclusion of their sick brother or sister, and this can be very difficult. Children might become resentful of their 'selfish' sibling, or begin to believe that they are too much trouble for anyone to spend time with. They might also feel that they are seen as an embarrassment to their sibling and friends. This can make them feel less confident in approaching others outside the family to go anywhere or do anything with.

Children with chronic conditions may feel resentful of their healthy siblings, who are able to go out independently and do what they like. Seeing one's brother or sister lead a full life is a vivid and constant reminder of everything they are not able to do. It can also be difficult when a younger sibling is more independent or academically able than the child with the illness. This may produce considerable frustration, and even a sense of humiliation. '*It makes me feel stupid. He does it easily, which just rubs it in for me that I can't.*'

One teenage girl noted how useless she felt as her mother rarely asked her to help around the house or pop to the shops, unlike her younger sister who was always helping. She also hated the fact that her younger sister was allowed a door key and could have the freedom to come and go as she pleased. In contrast, her parents always wanted to know where she was and would not even contemplate allowing her to be in the house on her own, let alone have a door key, which they believed she would promptly lose.

In these situations, parents can find themselves in the difficult position of trying to encourage and praise one child for their achievements without ignoring the other child or making her or him feel worthless. All children can be helped to succeed in something and feel good about it. It is a challenge to find something that a child who is severely restricted or disabled can do; something that feels special to them, regardless of what others achieve. With creative thinking, children can be helped to compete with themselves (and strive to do better) rather than compete with others.

Children with chronic conditions may also experience considerable anger and resentment from their siblings for the disruptions and inconvenience they cause them. *'I can't wait for HIM to go back into hospital, at least there will be some peace and quiet around here and we can be happy again.'* Although siblings' distress may be understood, it can be very hurtful and some children are bullied, or feel alienated from their family as a result. They may also feel guilty that their brother or sister is so unhappy. A number of children have wondered whether it would be better for everyone in the family if they were not around. The importance of positively involving and supporting siblings cannot be underestimated.

There are specific difficulties when two children in the family are affected with the same condition. The way they both cope and manage their condition may of course be very different; even their experiences of this will differ. In some families, a tremendous camaraderie and closeness can develop between siblings. Problems may arise, however, if one child encounters difficulties that the other child may predict happening to them, for example, in brothers with Duchenne muscular dystrophy, when the first brother requires a wheelchair. The second child might be faced with having to learn the realities of what is to come before he is ready to accept this information.

Constructions of Professionals

Children will form their own impression of doctors and health care professionals, based on their direct experience of them, and the way they see other people, such as their parents or other children on the ward, relate to them.

Some children feel very angry with health professionals and blame them for not making things better. One girl screamed at her mother that if the doctors and nurses really were any good, then why was she still no better? Another child, suffering a recurrence of his condition, refused to talk to the doctors, whom he perceived had lied to him. They had indicated that he would be made better by their treatment. However, in his eyes, being made better meant forever, without any possibility of recurrence. Understandably in this context, credible reassurance that the child was once again recovering after treatment was very difficult.

Children may find it difficult to show their frustration or rage directly to doctors, especially if they feel dependent on them for further care and are wary of the consequences of not being liked by the doctor. Some children feel responsible themselves if their treatment fails. One young man, who was in the terminal stages of cancer, was very keen for a message to reach his radiotherapist that he was thankful for her help, and sorry that he had not got better despite all her effort.

Many children have very positive and important relationships with particular professionals, and this becomes a valuable protective factor in the very challenging and stressful aspects of their care. Children may say that the professional is honest with them, listens or talks to them (and not just their parent) or even makes them laugh. What is apparent, however, is that this professional has shown interest in them, has enabled confidence and trust to develop, and has demonstrated a willingness to help.

Continuity of care with a known and trusted doctor and paediatric team is very important, and the transition to an adult service after many years in the paediatric department may be a considerable loss for the young adult (see also *Chapter 9*). Some children have literally grown up, living in and out of hospital, and the ward or clinic staff have become like extended family members. These professionals 'hold a history' about the child, and the child can often feel known and very special. It can, therefore, feel very alarming to contemplate moving to an adult department, to strangers, where the process of getting to know people will have to begin again, as well as the process of people getting to know them and their particular needs or preferred ways of doing things. It is difficult to leave behind the security and specialness of paediatric life.

The reality is often that the adult department will be considerably busier, so that less time is available for the young adult. The implications of this are that there will be less flexibility in terms of accommodating individual needs, and less follow up (chasing) if the young person has missed appointments or not adhered to treatment regimes.

The adult unit may have its own particular routines or preferred ways of doing things, and the young person may have to accept changes in management, such as the size of the needles used, the frequency of clinic appointments, or the strictness of diets or tablet-taking required. Changes in treatment can further challenge confidence in the new unit, which may be perceived as less expert than the paediatric service.

Some young people are physically and/or emotionally delayed in their maturity, and although remaining in a paediatric setting is not necessarily appropriate, there are often concerns as to how they will cope in an adult environment. They will also find themselves confronted with seeing the long term implications of their condition, such as visual difficulties or older adults with amputations in diabetic clinics. We will consider ways of preparing young people (and their families) for the transfer to adult services in *Chapter 9*.

Some young people view the transfer very positively. Although the 'family' of paediatric staff can be very supportive and caring, they can also find it difficult to see the young person as anything other than a child, and may not treat him or her as an adult. This can be particularly true for children who are short in stature or are delayed in terms of puberty, since they may feel as though they are being treated the same as younger children. Some teenagers have described how perplexing it is for them on the one hand to be dating, drinking in pubs and seeing adult films at the cinema, and then to be in hospital entertained by a clown, having Disney characters around their bed, or the nursing staff insisting on supervising their medicines and making sure they wash behind their ears! Some teenagers have also spoken about the relief in being able to leave behind some of the more traumatic and distressing childhood memories, which for them are triggered by places, sights or staff in the paediatric unit. It is hard to even contemplate the memories that some of these young people hold, and the move on to an adult unit can be a fresh start for them.

The age of transfer to an adult department appears to vary amongst specialities and professionals. An accepted transition point is when children finish statutory education. However, it can sometimes be as difficult for the professional to 'let go' as for the young adult, and there are reports of particularly challenging or favoured patients continuing to attend paediatric services well into adulthood.

Constructions of Treatment

Children's constructions of treatment will be dependent upon many factors, including their understanding of the nature and course of their condition (and therefore influencing how important and useful they perceive treatment to be); the way treatment affects them personally –

that is, how unpleasant, invasive or painful treatment or the side effects of treatment are; and the impact socially in terms of how restrictive, disruptive or time-consuming treatment regimes are to social activities and routines. Co-operation and adherence to treatment regimes will only be reached when perceived benefits outweigh perceived costs or disadvantages of treatment.

Some children are in no doubt of the necessity of treatment, accurately believing that they will be very ill or even die without it. Other children may believe the treatment is life-saving simply because they are aware they 'have' to do it. For example, one young boy believed that if he did not catheterize to empty his bladder, he would 'blow up like a balloon, burst and die'.

Although it is hoped that children would be given appropriate explanations of their treatment, this may be very difficult when the treatment is complex and when there are no immediate or apparent benefits from the child's perspective. A further difficulty arises when parents have withheld information about the seriousness of the condition because they feel the child cannot comprehend or cope with it. For example, encouraging the child with cystic fibrosis to co-operate with physiotherapy or inhalation therapy may be even more difficult when the child does not appreciate the seriousness of the condition and perceives only limited benefits from treatment, for example. Other treatments, such as vitamin or mineral supplements in renal replacement therapy, may seem unimportant to a child as they do not affect how well he or she feels, whereas other tablets (such as for blood pressure) have more evident consequences if not taken as prescribed.

Even if children are aware of the necessity of their treatment, the treatment process or regime may be very complex and not well understood. As a result, children and families may develop idiosyncratic styles of carrying out treatment. One mother, for example, after discharge home, insisted on giving her child his medicine at precisely the time it would have been administered on the ward. She required her child to stop whatever he was doing at precise times, and became very anxious if she was even a few minutes later than the 'drug round' time. One 12-year-old girl needed to take eight different tablets, in total requiring 22 tablets daily, some before food, some after, some once a day and some twice or more times each day. In addition, she was following very stringent dietary and fluid restrictions. Given the complex and disruptive nature of her treatment and the limited knowledge she and her family had about the treatment rationale, the family decided to simplify matters by dissolving all the tablets in water at the beginning of the week, with the girl taking one tablespoon of medicine every day. As a result, at the beginning of the week, she was taking considerably less drugs than she needed, and was overdosing herself as the mixture became more concentrated towards the end of the week. Clearly children and families need to have appropriate understanding of the rationale, process and practical aspects of treatment.

For many conditions, long-term treatments are seen as tedious and intrusive on daily life. Many children are, however, able to meet this challenge by incorporating treatment regimes into their own daily routines. *'You've just got to think of it as part of daily life, like cleaning your teeth. You just have to get on with it and not worry about it.'*

Many treatments involve the child learning a complex set of skills. There is opportunity here for the child to achieve and feel positive about accomplishing these new skills, as well as this enabling greater independence and self-reliance. Difficulties arise when treatments do not become incorporated as part of the child's life, but when they take over and become the focus of the child's life.

Many of the treatments are very challenging and a continual pressure for children and their families. Children may feel that they get little appreciation and acknowledgement for everything they do have to do and do well. Instead, it becomes an expectation and is taken for granted. However, they feel that as soon as they do something wrong, they have a lot of attention, however negative. This might strike a familiar chord for many of us, who swiftly move on from children who are doing well to focus on others with problems. Reinforcing and praising the child's achievements, and not just focusing on areas of difficulty, is important, as is being interested in them, not just in their condition or treatment. In *Chapter 9* we will look further at ways of supporting children in co-operating with treatment.

School

For some children, school (hospital or community) can be the one place of safety, predictability and normality in a world which may feel unsafe, uncertain and chaotic. School is a familiar place in which children will be active and busy in a relatively predictable environment, where the role of the teacher is known, and where children know what is expected of them.

Similarly, for children returning to school after leaving hospital, it can be a very reassuring sign that some sense of normality is being resumed, both for the child and for other members of the family (see also *Chapter 9*). It allows the child some autonomy and independence from the family. Of course, the parents may also be able to resume something of their lives, and have autonomy of their own by returning to work or even just being on their own during the day. The child is also given much needed opportunities to be with and to be treated like other children. A good supportive school will always help children feel they have succeeded in terms of academic goals, if these are selected to suit the child and support the child's efforts. This can be particularly important for children who have lost confidence, or even previous abilities or skills as a result of their condition.

On the other hand, returning to school after prolonged or repeated absences is likely to create specific problems for children, teachers and the school authorities. Children may have difficulties slotting back in academically and socially. Schools may be unprepared or have inadequate support resources to meet the child's medical, social and academic needs. School authorities may also have significant concerns about the child's medical condition and whether they can be kept safe at school.

Children's cognitive functioning might be affected as a result of their condition. This may be due to the direct effects of the condition, such as memory or concentration difficulties following head trauma. It can also be due to the effects of treatment, such as medication or cranial irradiation for a brain tumour, or due to time lost from school. Even without these difficulties, children may be anxious about missing many aspects of the syllabus or concerned about not grasping the current topics. Children (and their parents) may have to adjust their expectations, or cut down the number of subjects they take, particularly during examination courses. With special dispensation, children are able to drop subjects which would otherwise be considered part of the essential National Curriculum.

After repeated absences, teachers may lose interest in the child or be less tolerant of areas in which the child requires special assistance. It is undoubtedly an additional burden of work for teaching staff when children miss long periods of time from school or are frequently absent. Children easily detect teachers who are not being supportive and this can make them feel very anxious and insecure about returning to school. One child was bluntly told by one of his teachers that it was simply up to him to copy up all the missed work as she did not have any more time to waste on someone who was so rarely at school.

Even when teachers *are* being supportive, as most of them are, it can still feel an enormous pressure on children to try to keep up with school work when they have missed so much and when they may not feel at their best. What can help is for a teacher or form tutor to go through and identify the important coursework which needs to be covered, and to give the child extra time to help them with this. However, children should not be expected to copy up reams of work as this is really not a good use of time, when work could be photocopied and read through instead.

Schools can also be instrumental in helping children assimilate information about their condition, feel accepted by others, and communicate with their peers about their experiences. One child chose to do his term project on epilepsy; this was so well received that he was asked to do a presentation to the school assembly. He clearly felt good about helping others understand his condition and was able to deal with their questions in a constructive way. In an infant school, the class teacher helped a young boy create a dialysis machine from cardboard boxes and elicited the child's skills to draw on the appropriate dials. This proved a very popular plaything for many of the children in the class.

For some children it is not possible to return directly to school after treatment and there may be a long period after leaving hospital when they need academic stimulation. In these circumstances children may greatly benefit from a home tutor, who can also be a good link with school and support children in the transition to school when they are ready.

Friendships

Socially, children may find it hard to fit back in with friends both in and out of school following treatment. Their peers may talk about everyday matters, local gossip, or what they watched on television, when children returning from hospital may have been contemplating their death, or suffering considerable discomfort or pain. Trying to communicate this and have these experiences validated by peers is very difficult.

Although some children return to school as a celebrity, the attention is often short-lived, even when the child still needs to talk about his or her experiences. Some children just find it very hard to be in an environment where they are not the centre of attention. In hospital they are well known and may be given a great deal of attention, and as a result, they may experience difficulties re-integrating and being part of a group. One teacher aptly described this as 'the faded pop star phenomenon'; the child wants to be special and craves attention, but the other children have moved on to the next interest.

Children may find that best friends have also moved on to new friends, and that they do not have the security of their normal social circle to support them. When conditions are unpredictable and severely disruptive, children can be helped significantly by having loyal friends who understand and are available to pick up the pieces again when the situation is more stable. Sadly, however, many friends lose patience and interest unless they are encouraged and made to feel involved and helpful by parents or teachers. Involving special friends in hospital visits can be beneficial, both in terms of the understanding these friends can develop and in the way they feel part of helping their sick friend. However, it requires extra effort and organization on the part of parents, who may be preoccupied with more pressing matters and not have the energy to arrange this.

Many children find themselves the target for bullying when they have either received special help or care at school. For example, this may occur if they are exempt from having to copy up homework, allowed to go to the toilet without asking permission, or leave the class to rest if they are tired. Bullying may also occur simply because there is something different about them. Children can be very unkind to each other, and they may insult, call names or ostracize a sick child. However, good friends around children make them less of a target for bullying in the first place and can even stand up for them and support them.

One girl had a very unhappy experience at school following a bladder condition, which made her incontinent during the day. Although her personal hygiene was scrupulous, one particular group of girls frequently accused her of smelling and went to great lengths to avoid walking near her or touching anything she had touched to the extent of refusing to lend her exercise books when she needed to copy up work. She was always the last person to be picked for any teams and no other girl in class offered to work with her as they did not want to be associated with someone so unpopular. It was only after the teacher dealt with the ringleaders of this bullying, and spoke to the class about the medical problems that any progress was made in terms of helping the girl feel safe and able to be at school.

Children with chronic physical or medical conditions may be quite restricted in their social contacts generally. This may be due to the physical constraints placed on them by the condition, or to long periods of time in hospital, where the child becomes quite institutionalized and used to interacting more with adults than with peers. It may also be due to difficulties with peers in school as we have discussed. However, another important reason is that many young people feel different, either as a result of looking different or through having such different life experiences. As a result they may lack confidence and the ability to initiate and maintain friendships, and therefore become isolated and even more dependent on their family or withdrawn. Clubs, groups and activities which integrate physically able-bodied and physically disabled young people, such as PHAB groups, are good resources for enabling social links.

Conclusion

Throughout this and the previous chapter, we have considered how different children construe their world of illness and the problems they actually face in adapting to it. Illness has implications for all aspects of their lives and the individual child's experience of this has to be considered in understanding adaptation. This is actually the starting point for help; it is only by understanding the way the specific child construes his or her world that one can help.

Summary

❑ Children's perceptions of their family, professionals, school and friends were explored, because these are all important aspects of a child's life and will, in part, determine their adjustment to their condition.

❑ Children's experiences are varied, illustrating the importance of individual meaning and the necessity of listening carefully to them in order to make sense of what they feel is happening to them.

❑ Their perceptions of others and relationships generally, can change quite significantly following diagnosis of chronic medical condition.

❑ Within the family, children can gain considerable help from parents and siblings in managing the social and psychological challenges of their condition.

❑ Conversely, areas of conflict can be exacerbated by the demands of the condition and the child's dependence on family members.

❑ A relationship with healthcare professionals can be a valuable protective factor. Continuity of care and sensitive handling of any transfers in care is important.

❑ School can be a place of safety, predictability and normality for the child. It is important for school staff to be responsive to children's emotional, social and educational needs when supporting the child's return to school after periods of illness.

5

The Aims and Process of Helping

'Why can't they understand that taking even more tablets [steroids] doesn't help? I can't even bear to look at myself when my condition flares up, let alone be seen out anywhere. I just want to scream at the doctor when he hands me yet another prescription and says he will see me in a month's time. He knows the tablets don't work and I don't bother taking them half the time. No one understands or asks me what I'm going through – I'm just told to be a good boy and take my tablets. I feel an absolute freak.'

These exasperated comments from a teenager with chronic inflammatory disease indicate his frustration with his condition and with the level of communication between his doctor and himself. Effective help will involve more than using drugs to try and manage his physical symptoms. His overwhelming need is for his experience and frustration to be understood, and this could easily happen if his doctor listened to him and explored the nature of his distress. On this basis it would be possible to plan, in partnership, how to manage the symptoms. With appropriate information and support, the doctor would be able to help this young man develop more adaptive strategies for dealing with his situation.

Good communication skills are the basis of any helping relationship, whether they are employed by healthcare workers or skilled counsellors. Such skills are required by all those in direct contact with children and their families, and need to be viewed as an integral part of the clinical approach to working with children. The provision of emotional care and psychological help should not be seen as separate, less important, or an extra to medical care. It should be incorporated as part of the total care package.

Before we consider the specific skills of communicating effectively and helpfully with children about the issues addressed in the last three chapters, it may be useful to provide some basic frameworks that underpin these skills. Helping is potentially a very complex process, and it is therefore useful to provide clear models as a guide. The basic elements to consider are:

1. The aims of helping.
2. The relationship between the child and helper.
3. The process of helping.
4. The basic qualities and attitudes of the helper.

Being clear about each of these is likely to facilitate effective work with children, and we will consider these in turn, although in reality they are very much interrelated.

Aims of Helping

Essentially, helping is about enabling children (and members of their family) to develop adaptive strategies to meet the challenges of their situation, and by so doing, to prevent or ameliorate the difficulties they face.

As the needs and coping resources of different children inevitably vary, the specific objectives of the helping relationship will also differ from child to child. In most cases however, it will encompass some or all of the following:

1. To enable children to feel that someone is listening to them and taking their experiences and feelings seriously.

2. To maintain or increase their self-esteem, so as to help children feel good about themselves.

3. To increase their feelings of self-efficacy and sense of control, and to facilitate their own coping strategies.

4. To help their adaptation by clarifying problem issues, giving appropriate information as necessary, and correcting unhelpful misperceptions.

5. To help children be clearer in communicating their needs to significant people in their environment, such as family, friends, or the medical team.

6. To help them acquire appropriate skills to do with the management of their disease, including, for example, specific strategies for pain management.

We will take each of these aims in turn and consider them in more detail.

Enabling the child to feel heard

Although we have moved on from the Victorian era where children were supposed to be seen and not heard, there are still many occasions where adults find it difficult to listen to children. The child's communication may be perceived by the adult as being nonsensical, irritating, perplexing, ill-timed and unanswerable. The much-loved children's book, *Not Now, Bernard* (McKee, 1980, see *Appendix B*), illustrates this wonderfully. It is the tale of a boy whose parents are always too busy to listen. They respond to all his attempts to attract their attention (even when he is telling them about the monster in the garden) by the phrase in the title, striking a chord with both adults and children!

A child may feel significantly relieved and unburdened just by being able to talk to someone about their experiences or worries. Sometimes children have simply not been given the opportunity to do this, as carers (family, friends) have not recognized their need to do so. It is a very common occurrence for children to hear parents or other adults talking about them. Parents may be heard to stress how the adults feel about certain aspects of the illness or treatment, or talk about the child's difficulties, without giving the child the opportunity to speak. However, even if opportunities have been given for the child to talk, there are several reasons why they may not discuss their problems fully, including the desire to protect their family from distressing worries so that they will not upset or burden them.

Children may be equally silenced by the reluctance of people to hear anything negative, distressing or angry. They may receive a strong message to just get on with life and not talk about the difficulties, because talking about it is seen as synonymous with feeling ungrateful or sorry for oneself. Repeatedly telling children how brave they are, or how lucky they are not to be more seriously affected, are also very potent silencing mechanisms. Children may become guilty that they feel so upset or angry about their situation, when faced with worse examples. They may think that they are going crazy, that no one will be able to understand them, or that people will consider their worries and fears petty or ridiculous. As a result they are quiet and worry alone. On the other hand, feeling able to say these things out loud can lead to a different and less frightening perspective.

Increasing self-esteem

Self-esteem is a crucial aspect of adaptation, and influences all areas of our behaviour. It refers to the extent to which one feels valued and important. Having serious problems makes one vulnerable and can easily undermine one's sense of value, and this must always be considered an issue in helping anyone.

Children's self-esteem may be raised by an adult taking an interest in them, respecting them enough to ask them about their experiences, achievements and interests, and not just about their condition. This can make them feel valued and special. Illnesses easily take over, and it can become easy to forget that the child is, nevertheless, a child first and foremost – a child with spina bifida, rather than the spina bifida child, for example.

In conversation it is always possible to feed back something positive to the child; perhaps about their smile, the way they have spoken to you, or something about their name or appearance. It may also be possible to identify something the child feels good about doing, or something they have been able to manage, which they or others have found difficult. Watching children's faces when they are genuinely complimented or praised is a real pleasure.

Increasing self-efficacy

Self-efficacy is an important aspect of all people's ability to cope with whatever happens to them. It is a belief or construction that they can manage, can deal with situations and can cope. Without such a belief, the world becomes a frightening place, full of threat and danger.

Encouraging children to identify their own solutions to difficulties is a fundamental aim of helping and a way of increasing their sense of control and self-efficacy. Solutions that children work out for themselves are far more likely to be put into practice, and will develop the child's self-esteem and confidence in their abilities to cope. As in acquiring any skill, it can be a very positive and self-affirming experience to overcome or be involved in overcoming a previously insurmountable problem oneself. It can empower children to develop and apply their own coping strategies in the future, rather than being dependent on others to find solutions.

Although there are many aspects of disease and treatment over which the child has no control (for example, the result of an operation), ways can usually be found to capitalize on areas over which they *do* have control, to increase their sense of efficacy. The first step is to identify and acknowledge with the child the areas of their lives over which they have control (either partially or wholly) and the areas they do not. Giving this acknowledgment rather than pacifying, glossing over or giving false reassurance can be helpful in its own right. It may then be possible to look more objectively at what use is being made of the control that is available. For example, although the need to take a number of medicines throughout the day cannot be changed, there may be some choice and control over the way they are taken, whether as capsules, tablets or liquid, or crushed and blended with other food. There may also be some flexibility as to the time they are taken, in order to fit in better with the child's daily routines. This kind of exploration in itself may increase children's understanding of their situation and, therefore, help them to develop skills for coping with uncertain, more difficult situations. It will enable them to predict problems more effectively and this allows a greater sense of control over their lives generally.

Clarifying problems and providing information

Children who are ill may be distressed, overwhelmed and confused, without being able to articulate or understand why. Giving them an opportunity to explore their situation can help them clarify areas of difficulty or confusion, and make these less frightening (see *Chapter 7* for a fuller discussion of exploration). Opportunities to discuss experiences can also allow children to identify unhelpful thoughts or strategies currently being used, and encourage alternatives to be developed. Simply helping them to name their feelings or distress can go some way to dealing with this.

Clarification may be achieved, of course, by the helper providing appropriate information, and this is common and sensible practice. However, in doing so, it is important to establish initially what the child already knows and is conceptually able to understand. The aim is then to give the information required in ways that are understandable to the child, and correct any misperceptions. (We will discuss this in more detail in *Chapter 8*).

Some children may not feel that they have a problem at all and may be responding to pressures from parents or other healthcare workers to get help in the first place. They may construe the reason for people being concerned about them in very different ways, or may articulate their concerns differently. For example, children who are asked why they are not taking prescribed tablets may feel people are cross and fed up with them. They may fear that they are going to be told off, whereas the adult talking to them may actually feel very worried and frustrated and be desperate to understand the problems which are preventing the child from taking the medication.

The basis of all this is good communication. Effective communication skills are necessary to clarify how the child perceives the problem and helping situation, for the helper to understand the child's behaviour and decide how best to help the child, and for the child to understand the concern and response of other people.

Helping the child communicate their needs more effectively

It is important for children to be able to communicate effectively, and this is a major area in helping them. If they are clear about their situation, they will be in a much better position to express their feelings and describe their symptoms, difficulties and needs. As a result, adults will be able to understand them more clearly and be more able to provide appropriate and effective help.

Skill teaching

There are a number of skills that may be useful for children to acquire. These include social skills, pain management and relaxation techniques, or skills associated with specific treatment regimes. These will be considered in detail in *Chapter 9*. However, although the aims are to help children deal more effectively with their situation, such skills in themselves have a number of other possible positive outcomes. In particular, the child is likely to become more involved in the treatment process, understand it better, feel more in control, more effective, and have greater self-esteem.

The Helping Relationship

Children with any special physical or medical needs will come into contact with many professionals and carers whose intention will be to help in a variety of ways including those just described. However, the achievement of these aims, and effective help more generally, is dependent on the relationship which develops between the child and helper. If children do not trust the helper sufficiently to communicate openly, then there is no way that the helper can understand or respond appropriately to the individual child's needs.

It is useful, therefore, to be very clear about the nature of an effective helping relationship with children. Before doing this, however, as much of the work undertaken with the child is carried out through the parents, with the parents, or, at the very least, with their co-operation and consent, it is first necessary to consider the relationship between the helper and parent.

The partnership model

There are a number of models which can be used to represent different helping relationships (a comprehensive discussion of this can be found in Davis and Fallowfield, 1991). These vary in the balance of power between the person to be helped and the helper, and the degree of participation and responsibility taken by both for decisions and resultant action.

The partnership model is widely acknowledged as a useful and satisfying model for working with adults (Davis, 1993). This model suggests a close and co-operative working relationship, in which open and honest communication and mutual trust are central elements. Aims and goals for change are negotiated and jointly agreed, and each partner is valued as bringing a different but complementary expertise to the relationship.

This model may describe an ideal situation, but it is one to which all healthcare professionals could usefully strive. By way of contrast, however, the expert model is more frequently observed in healthcare settings. This is one in which the helper assumes expert status and takes on the responsibility for solving the person's problems. This is often done by giving advice or instructions, but may fail to take account of the fact that there are many possible reasons why the advice may not be followed, including dissatisfaction with the way the professional communicates.

In helping children, a partnership should ideally exist between parent and professional. This would involve an exploration of the needs of the child and a discussion about ways of possibly meeting these needs in the context of the different expertise and knowledge which the parent and professional bring to the relationship. The parents know their child better than anyone else; they know the changes that have occurred, the problems they and their child are facing; the context in which they live and their value system. The expertise of the professional includes the knowledge and skills of disease diagnosis and treatment. A successful partnership, therefore, is very much dependent upon careful integration of the knowledge and skills of both.

Partnership model applied to children.

Such a relationship between the professional and parents needs to exist if the child is to benefit. However, within this context, the relationship between the child and professional can develop along the same lines as the partnership model. This essentially means attempting to form a close relationship in which children are respected for themselves and their expertise. The child is assumed to be able to give valuable opinions, to be able to negotiate and agree aims, and to be able to take some measure of control. Honesty and mutual trust are again central elements. However, there are key differences from the adult relationship.

Responsibility.

The relationship cannot be entirely equal as the adult helper holds *some* responsibility for the child, either legally or morally. These responsibilities may vary, but all have concern for the child's safety and welfare. As stated in the Children Act (1989), the child's welfare is paramount and the adult must take all appropriate steps to safeguard this. Healthcare professionals are particularly concerned for the physical well-being of the child, and for providing appropriate medical care, but this certainly does not negate responsibility for promotion of the child's cognitive, emotional and social development.

Issues of privacy and confidentiality in particular are different in the adult–child relationship. Total confidentiality cannot be guaranteed. It may be important for certain information to be passed on to parents or other health care workers in order to ensure the child's well-being. This may be contrary to the child's wishes, and the reasons may have to be carefully explained, so that the child's knowledge, if not consent, is obtained.

As an example, one girl was reluctant to let the doctor know she had a pain, as this might have meant another needle or a further stay in hospital. The nurse, to whom this information was confided, *had* to inform the doctor, but she explained the reason for this to the child, helping her to understand why this information had to be passed on, even though the child was still not keen to do so. This discussion also gave the nurse an opportunity to explore the child's fears about needles and hospital and she was able to start to help with both these.

Possibly the most important area in which knowledge cannot be kept between the child and helper is when self-harm or abuse of any type is suspected. Guidelines for procedures for sharing concerns and informing others in these circumstances are given in *Chapter 11*.

External constraints on the relationship. The relationship with the child will differ from that with an adult in the constraints placed by others on the relationship. For example, parents may sabotage or undermine help offered to the child, if they do not have confidence in the helper, or if they feel their own needs are being neglected – particularly if they feel anxious or excluded from the relationship between child and helper. This may be quite subtle in terms of the parent not making the meetings a priority and always arriving late with their child, or interrupting sessions. One mother returned to her daughter's session after 20 minutes, carrying a hot lunch for her child, saying they had not had an opportunity to eat beforehand! On the other hand, the sabotage can be quite evident, as in the case of parents who openly question or deny the need for the child to talk to the professional. One girl was challenged in this way by her father on the grounds that it did not change anything. Her response was to articulate very confidently that the person listened to her and understood her. However, not all children are able to be as articulate as this or to withstand negative comments which undermine this kind of work. Even though children may wish to bring a total commitment to the relationship, they may be faced with a dilemma over loyalties. This can mean, for example, that children may be anxious about disclosing information, if parents give children the message that they will be inconvenienced, angry, let down or even get into trouble as a result of what is said.

At a practical level, adults outside the helping relationship may place constraints on the relationship, if the child is dependent on them to travel to the sessions, for example, or to have permission to miss school. Therefore, the negotiated agreement with the child's parents or carers may be as important as the agreement with the child. This is also true of any suggested plans of action or change. For example, one could not help a child develop more confidence and independence in taking their prescribed medications if this was not carefully negotiated with the parent also, in order to gain their support both practically and emotionally. In some instances the child's views can be ascertained and noted, but it is likely to be the parent or other carers who ultimately make the decisions or implement change.

Developmental considerations. As with all relationships, it is important to be able to communicate meaningfully, and this entails a good understanding of the cognitive abilities and knowledge base of the other person. This is particularly relevant with children, who are still developing intellectually and will vary considerably in their ways of understanding events. The notion of equality in the relationship is not really feasible, given the fact that the adult will usually be able to process information in a far more sophisticated way than the child. A greater flexibility is, therefore, required to accommodate their needs and understanding, in terms of the pacing of work during sessions and the medium used for communicating and sharing information, using verbal and non-verbal modes.

Partner contributions. To summarize this discussion, it is possible to consider the relationship between a child and an adult helper as having characteristics of a partnership. There are differences, however, between the child and helper in terms of what each brings to the relationship. The adult helper is likely to bring the following if the relationship is to be successful:

- A desire to help, clear aims and a coherent model for helping.
- Personal qualities or attitudes that enable the helping process.
- An intention to understand the meaning and experience of the condition for the child.
- Skills for communicating with the child and providing information in a meaningful way, taking account of the child's cognitive abilities.
- An adult and therefore mature frame of reference within which to view the overall needs of the child, taking into account cultural, moral and social perspectives.
- A general understanding of the developmental needs and cognitive abilities of the child, and an understanding of the child's condition and treatment.
- Some degree of responsibility for the child's safety and welfare.

Children bring:

- Their own unique experience of their lives, and a unique set of constructions, including those concerned with their medical condition, and the impact this has on all aspects of their world.

- Expectations or preconceived ideas regarding the relationship with the helper, and their views about what they would like to happen.
- Their own repertoire of coping strategies and communication skills.
- A desire to be understood and possibly a desire to change or be helped.

The child and helper bring different but complementary expertise to the relationship. Although the relationship is not equal, this does not preclude one from having respect and valuing the child, and acknowledging the contribution made by the child.

The Process of Helping

In order to achieve the aims of helping specified earlier in the chapter, a process is initiated, and this can be construed as a number of stages or interrelated tasks. The first of these must be to establish a relationship with the child of the kind discussed in the previous section. It is only when the child has acquired a basic trust and respect for the helper, that further tasks in the helping process can be considered and negotiated successfully.

It is therefore important to have a clear and useful model of the process of helping, and a number of different models are available. Here, we will describe a model based largely on Egan's (1990) problem-management approach, which provides a clear, practical and skill-based framework. The advantage of this model is that it can encompass other approaches, including cognitive-behavioural work (Hawton *et al.*, 1989), personal construct theory (Kelly, 1991), and ideas from Carl Rogers (1965), all of which have influenced what we have to say.

The model describes the helping process as a sequence of stages or tasks which include: *relationship building; exploration and clarification of problem areas; establishing and agreeing goals; formulating a plan of action to meet the goals; implementing the plan;* and subsequently *evaluating the effects.* Although we will follow this sequence in describing these tasks, in reality the situation may be more complex. Not all the tasks will be relevant to all children, and the sequence will be dependent upon the complexity, type and number of problems presented. For example, one might have to go through the sequence several times when there are multiple problems, or backtrack in a particularly difficult issue.

Throughout the process it is important to work at the pace of the child, without hurrying and being intrusive. Some children will take longer to be able to trust an adult, or be hesitant at particular points about disclosing information or moving on to the next stage or task. The process of helping is about giving opportunities and facilitating, and not about pressurizing, imposing or forcing. It is also important to acknowledge that although we are considering the process of helping in terms of a direct one-to-one relationship with the child, there is a very wide and complex network of people involved in the child's care. Good communication with appropriate and sensitive sharing of information, strategies or plans is therefore important, in order for the most consistent and helpful management to occur, and for children's experience of being helped to be meaningfully integrated rather than disparate from the rest of their lives.

Each task in the process will be described briefly here and elaborated in the rest of the book in relation to the skills and qualities required of the helper working with children.

Relationship building

As mentioned earlier, the first step is to establish a relationship with the child, as this is a prerequisite of all else. If the child dislikes, distrusts or is threatened by the adult, then nothing further can occur. However, a meaningful relationship takes time to develop and does so within the context of the whole process of helping. The aim is to establish a relationship in which the child feels comfortable disclosing and sharing information about themselves, and this assumes that the adult helper is to some extent trusted and liked. The ability and length of time required to establish this relationship will depend on a number of factors, including: the child's personal characteristics (for example, natural shyness); previous experiences of relationships with adults (for example, being let down or rejected, loved and valued); preconceived ideas they have formulated about the current helper; the way they perceive the behaviour and attitudes of the helper; and the purpose of the contact. However, the relationship will be enhanced considerably by valuing the child above all, by courtesy, and by listening carefully to him or her (see *Helper Attitudes* at the end of this chapter).

For children to be relaxed and able to talk openly, they need to feel they are valued and liked, that what they are saying is important and is being taken seriously, and that the adult can be trusted to take care of them. For younger children, this trust might include the notion that the adult is not going to hurt them, and for the older child, that the adult will protect their interests and not pass on sensitive and intimate information about them.

As children may be totally unfamiliar with the situation of talking in this way, it is very important to explain clearly the meaning and purpose of meeting them. As with most unfamiliar situations, there is a degree of anxiety and tension which will need to be overcome for the child to feel relaxed. This will be compounded by any distress or embarrassment about the problem area itself. A great deal of this anxiety may be alleviated by explaining expectations or rules about the meetings.

Children possibly need more guidance about this than adults, because of their lack of experience of contact of this type and the likelihood that they have not initiated the process or even asked for help.

The child needs to be involved in the process and not just be the passive recipient of someone's good intentions! This necessitates the helper explaining the purpose and model of the helping process in a way that is most meaningful to the child. It is important to introduce yourself to the child in a way he or she will understand. This should include your name and what you do. You should be as explicit as possible about your understanding of the purpose of the meetings, usually after you have given the child the opportunity to express his or her understanding. It is then important to begin a discussion regarding a shared view of the aims and areas of work to be done.

Exploration and clarification

Although an initial relationship may be established quite quickly, it will continue to develop throughout contact with the child. Nevertheless, with the process of relationship building initiated, one can quickly move on to explore the child's situation, and help him or her to derive a clear understanding of his or her difficulties. The aim is for the helper to find out how children see their problem, what sense they make of it, and their explanations, all from their own perspective (see also *Chapter 7*).

It may be helpful to make explicit the assumption that there is usually more than one way of construing a problem, with some ways being more helpful than others. Theories about the causes of problems can be explored with alternative explanations put forward for the child to consider. These should always be put forward in a respectful and tentative way, without children feeling you are correcting them for being wrong, but merely putting forward another viewpoint for them to consider.

The child may be able to tell their story with minimal prompts from the helper. This may involve a few open-ended questions, with occasional, more specific, questions to clarify information or to check what the child is saying (see *Chapter 7*). Younger children, or those less able to articulate their story, may need more structured questions to help them explore their situation. Some children may choose to say very little, but may illustrate their situation either by drawings or by their play, which can be the basis for exploring the child's thoughts and feelings.

Using the child's account, the helper can work with him or her to identify key issues and discuss likely explanations. The helper may also be able to identify areas of misconstruction, which are clearly unhelpful, and may enable the child to correct them. Part of this work will be to help the child break down the problem area into different parts so that the various aspects of the problem become more manageable.

If children feel the helper is listening and supporting them in this process, they are more able to face their difficulties and therefore gain a better understanding of them. Children may challenge unhelpful assumptions or misperceptions themselves at this point, just by thinking about the situation.

An example of this is Susan, who was 14 years old and had coeliac disease (gluten intolerance). Her main problem was that she did not comply with her gluten-free diet. Her mother had approached her doctor in a very distressed state. She asked him to talk to Susan, as she had tried everything, but could not persuade her to keep to her diet.

Susan was initially very unimpressed at being asked to speak to the doctor. She assumed that it was her mother's way of punishing her by having to admit to the doctor what she was doing, and also her mother's way of washing her hands of her. However, the doctor began by clarifying with her the purpose of the meeting, and by doing so was able to help her see that her mother was not punishing her, but was trying to help. Exploring her situation in this manner enabled the doctor to gain a better understanding of the difficulties and conflicts Susan and her mother had been having over the diet and to explore with Susan her own concerns about the restrictions caused by her condition.

Setting goals

Once the relevant issues have been explored carefully and a clear understanding of the problem established, the next stage of the helping process can be tackled, namely the formulation and negotiation of goals. The task here is to encourage the child to set clear aims and devise realistic goals so that plans can be made to achieve them. The aims of treatment indicate the general directions to pursue (for example, to be more socially active) and goals suggest specific and concrete outcomes (such as to meet with friends at the weekend, to phone and ask a friend round to tea). The more explicit, specific and concrete, the more likely it is that their achievement can be assessed when evaluating outcomes.

It is important to take the time to explore what the child wants to achieve and to set goals carefully, as this determines all the following steps in the process. The temptation to rush in with solutions or suggestions without fully exploring the situation or negotiating the goal should be resisted.

Although some aims may need to be negotiated with the adults involved with the care of the child, joint and agreed aims need to be established with the child. It is the role of the helper to recognize the important issues put forward by the child, and yet also to deal with other areas which are in the best interest of the child. For example, one teenager wanted the doctors to acknowledge her fear and just give her sedation to cope with a small medical procedure. However, given that she also had to face a series of other procedures, it was thought to be more beneficial for her to develop general strategies herself for dealing with these situations, and for communicating her anxieties about them to the doctor.

It is also necessary to guide the child to set realistic goals, that are achievable within a reasonable time frame. One has to consider what is possible to accomplish over the time of seeing and supporting the child. Goals such as attending school all day, every day, for a child who is frequently too tired, is clearly unsuitable. A more helpful goal might be that the child goes to school every morning and reviews the situation at midday, or attends on alternate days, perhaps for a time-limited period, until the plan is reviewed. The goal of losing 20 kilogrammes over the next two years would also be unhelpful. It would be more helpful for a dietary and exercise programme to be set up, with shorter term goals associated with carrying out aspects of the programme daily. In addition to being achievable, this goal is far more concrete and assessable in terms of success. It is far better to limit the goal and achieve it relatively quickly; once achieved, a new goal can be set, building a little further on the existing achievement.

The process of setting goals will often involve helping the child to set priorities in the context of complex or multiple problems. When there are lots of possible goals in relation to multiple problems, an attempt must be made to decide what one should do first, perhaps beginning with the goal which is the most accessible and manageable, or the most immediately needed. One young man decided to concentrate on establishing an exercise and activity routine around his home, before tackling other goals of arranging appointments with the careers advisory service and resuming membership of various social and sporting clubs.

In the earlier example of Susan, with coeliac disease, the goal she decided to pursue was to understand the nature of her condition more fully. This was thought to be important so that she could make an informed decision herself about whether she felt it was necessary to stick to a restricted diet. Only then was she able to consider further goals, such as keeping to her diet.

It is not surprising that the aims of the child may be different from those of the parent who originally requested help. For example, Lisa was a bright six-year-old girl with spina bifida. She required intermittent catheterization of the bladder to help her keep dry. This involved inserting a tube or catheter into the bladder to remove the urine safely. Although her parents and doctor felt she was capable of learning to do this herself, Lisa flatly refused to take any part in learning the technique and became increasingly unco-operative when her parents tried to do it for her. She would ask for her mother if her father was helping her, or her father if her mother was free.

When help was sought in resolving the problem, the aim her parents set was for Lisa to learn to catheterize herself independently. Their specific goals were that Lisa should spend time with a trusted nurse to discuss any worries about the technique, and for the nurse to work out a graded programme in which Lisa would gradually take on responsibility herself.

In contrast, initial discussion and exploration of Lisa's situation indicated that learning to catheterize was far from her first priority. She was much more concerned about her parents' frequent rows and threats to divorce. Lisa was most concerned about what would happen to her, if her parents divorced, because she believed she would have to choose between them, when she felt that she needed them both. Lisa's demands for both parents to help her was her way of trying to keep the family together.

In summary, it is important to spend time in the helping process to formulate appropriate goals. They need to be negotiated with the child, with constructive guidance in terms of selecting and prioritizing appropriately. An attempt should be made to make them specific, concrete, clear, realistic, achievable and time-limited. The more successful one is in doing this, the more the helper and child will be able to evaluate the extent to which they have been achieved.

Planning action

Once goals have been decided and agreed, the next step is to formulate a plan of action. It is important to encourage children themselves to think of ways of achieving their goals and to help them think of all the possibilities, with the helper adding his or her own contributions and suggestions. Essentially here, as throughout the whole process, the child is being involved in the attempt to find solutions, because this will improve their commitment to the strategy and foster their image of themselves as competent.

A brainstorming approach, where as many ideas as possible are generated, is helpful. It should be done in a way that frees the child to generate any number of ideas without fear of suggesting something silly or wrong. When a list of possible options is prepared, each can be considered for its merits. This would include thinking about the relative costs of the option as well as the benefits in achieving the goals. It is also important that any predictable problems in implementing the plans are discussed, so that strategies for dealing with them (or avoiding them if possible) are considered. The role of the helper throughout is to facilitate this process rather than feel they have to provide all the answers.

Helper: *(recapping)* *'So one option you have is to fight this lad and all his mates who are teasing you. Another option is to carry on missing school, and the third option we have just been discussing, is to talk to your form teacher to get his help. Which of these sounds most promising to you? Let's think what might happen with each of your options . . .'.*

Implementation

Following the agreement of a clear plan of action, there may be certain tasks for the child to complete independently, and strategies that are dependent upon the action of others. For example, in the situation of children being bullied at school (as above), the agreed plan may be for the child to tell his or her parents and form teacher what is happening. Subsequently, there may be the need for a meeting at school to discuss how to deal with the bullying, and the child may require help to feel more confident with peers at school.

Whatever the actions, children will need support throughout the process. The helper's role is to monitor how the child (and relevant others) are getting on, to praise the child for success and to provide encouragement when the child is feeling discouraged. This monitoring and support may be maintained in the form of regular meetings, telephone contact and feedback from other adults such as school teachers and parents.

Evaluation

The evaluation of any plan is an on-going process, which begins as soon as a solution is specified. Any suggestion is evaluated immediately in terms of predicting how likely it is to be successful. However, once one begins to implement strategies, it is important to have a way of determining how successful they have been in practice. It is helpful for the child to acknowledge which of the strategies were most helpful and to understand what factors contributed to this success. This may be particularly helpful in situations where there are a series of strategies which are dependent upon one another for success.

Good evaluation enables one to reformulate the problem, set new goals and devise alternative plans, which would themselves be evaluated subsequently. Useful information can be derived even where plans have not been successful. For example, it could be that the co-operation of other people has not yet been obtained or that other factors need to be considered for the plan to work. In the case of the child being bullied at school, if acknowledgement of the bullying and support for the child are not forthcoming from the teachers, a school-based plan is unlikely to succeed.

Basic Helper Attitudes and Characteristics

Having considered the stages or tasks involved in the process of helping, we shall now go on to discuss which attributes of the helper are necessary to establish a good relationship. Perhaps the most important considerations in developing any successful helping relationship are the attitudes and characteristics of the helper. Carl Rogers (1959) has probably had most influence upon current thinking and appreciation of the desirable qualities in the helper. He proposed a number of conditions that constituted the 'necessary and sufficient conditions of therapeutic personality change'. Although this statement has been challenged in research, the attitudes to be discussed are nevertheless important factors in instituting, maintaining and developing an effective relationship. We use the term attitude here to indicate a general stance that permeates the whole of the helper's behaviour towards the child.

Empathy

This is often described as the ability to step inside someone's shoes and experience the world from their perspective. Carl Rogers defined it as 'the ability to experience another person's world as if it were one's own without ever losing that "as if" quality'. We can never totally achieve this or fully understand how another person feels, but we can try to reach a fairly accurate view of the other person's model or way of conceptualizing the world.

To be effective, empathy has to be conveyed to the child, and this requires being able to communicate some understanding of the child's thoughts and feelings back to them. It does not necessarily mean agreeing with the child, but involves trying to put aside one's own views and feelings and to focus one's thoughts on the experience of the child. Coming to an understanding of a child's world can be difficult for an adult; the child's world might contain dragons, witches and magic. The helper needs to be able to put their own knowledge of the world to one side to be able join the child in his or her world. It is a cynical adult who dismisses a child's fear of monsters as silly, or non-existent.

Respect or unconditional positive regard

This attitude involves the helper in thinking positively about the child he or she is trying to help, regardless of cultural, religious or any other differences. It means deeply valuing them and showing respect for them at all levels. It also involves a deep belief in children's strengths, abilities and resilience to cope with whatever happens to them. This positive regard is not conditional or dependent on them saying or doing what the helper values. The helper should be non-judgmental, thereby enabling the child to be able to share their feelings without fear of criticism or of them being trivialized.

Although the child's knowledge and experience may be significantly more limited than that of the helper, this does not diminish the respect held for the child and for the skills and problem-solving capacities that the child may bring to the relationship. If the helper is able to convey this and not instruct or talk down to the child, the child will feel more able to work at the problems and take seriously the help offered.

Genuineness

This implies that the helper is not acting, being pretentious or defensive. It refers to an acceptance and openness about oneself and one's experiences. In working with children, it implies being open to their experiences and being willing to explore these and make sense of them using their framework. It does not mean holding pre-conceived ideas about his or her experience, or distorting them because of prejudice, personal interest, defensiveness or to fit one's own framework. It is important to behave with spontaneity, to respond freely and naturally to children, rather than being artificial, or unavailable to them.

Honesty is essential in establishing trust in a relationship. Promises which cannot be kept should not be made. Issues of confidentiality are particularly relevant here; promises of keeping information private cannot be made if there are child protection concerns. It may be necessary to tell the child that although conversations with the helper are private, it may sometimes be necessary to share parts of that information with other people who may need to know in order to help the child. The child should be reassured, however, that if this need arises it will be discussed with them before other people are involved.

Humility

This refers to helpers having a realistic appraisal of what they are and are not able to do, and even feeling comfortable with the notion that it is not necessary to have all the answers to be helpful to others. We must all recognize our skills, but also our limitations and areas with which we may need help or advice. In working with children, the desire to make everything right for the child (sometimes called the 'rescue fantasy') can be particularly strong. However, we all need to be able to stand back a little from the situation and recognize what we can and cannot do, what we need to allow the child to do, and when to approach others outside the relationship.

Enthusiasm and positive thinking

Children are particularly sensitive to cues they pick up from the helper about how they feel about them. Working with children can be very challenging and yet very rewarding. It is important for the helper to maintain a positive outlook on their work with a child, recognizing that although it is not possible to make everything right, there is a great deal one can do to make things a little better. It is important to be enthusiastic, to enjoy the child and to have confidence and respect in children's resilience and ability to make use of a trusted relationship in order to make changes in their lives.

We all make decisions about who we will talk to and trust with private information about ourselves. Children are far more likely to talk freely and disclose private information about themselves when they like and trust the helper, and this is closely related to them feeling accepted, liked and cared for by the helper. These basic attitudes, therefore, are likely to facilitate the development of a trusting relationship. They are likely to set the conditions for the child to explore their problems and to work effectively with the helper. These basic qualities therefore underlie the whole process of helping outlined earlier in the chapter. They are, however, in themselves very powerful therapeutic tools. If children are honestly and genuinely respected by an enthusiastic, positive adult who is seriously trying to understand them, then they are likely to be influenced by this alone. They are likely to feel valued and will be more able to value themselves, to feel better about themselves and to have greater self-esteem, which is a major aim of helping.

Summary

❑ In general, the aim of helping is to enable children (and members of their family) to develop adaptive strategies to meet the challenges (physical, social and psychological) presented by having a chronic condition or disability, thereby preventing or reducing difficulties.

❑ More specifically, the aims are: to enable children to feel listened to and valued; raise self-esteem and self-efficacy; to help them clarify their situation; to communicate more effectively; and to facilitate coping and problem-solving strategies.

❑ Helping is most successfully achieved within a relationship which respects the child and the skills and abilities they contribute to the relationship, and which works closely with the child to produce mutual aims and an agreed plan of action.

❑ Ideally this relationship may be characterized as a partnership, although special considerations when working with children include the responsibilities which the helper may have for the child, external constraints on the relationship, and the need for awareness of developmental issues.

❑ As a flexible guide, the process of helping is described as a series of stages or tasks, which include: establishing the working relationship; exploring and clarifying the situation; formulating clear aims and goals; setting a plan of action based on these goals; implementing the plan; and evaluating the outcome.

❑ There are fundamental attitudes or qualities of the helper that are likely to facilitate the development of the relationship and subsequent helping process, as well as helping to achieve the aim of increasing children's self-esteem. These include empathy, respect, genuineness, humility and enthusiasm.

6

Engaging the Child

We have described in some detail the problems faced by children with chronic medical conditions and have begun to suggest ways in which all who come into contact with them can help by communicating effectively. To aid in this, we have outlined the aims of providing such whole person care and have suggested a model of the process of helping. We have also described general qualities of helpers that will enhance this process. Our concern now is to consider the skills of the various stages of the helping process in more depth. We will begin by looking at the organizational aspects of meeting with children and then consider the skills required in engagement and relationship building with the child.

Setting the Scene

Before meeting the child and family, it is important to be very clear about the purpose of the meeting and how best to facilitate this. Careful thought should be given to who needs to be present and the length of time available for the meeting. All relevant notes or information should be at hand. Such planning will involve making sure you are not interrupted for the time you are with the child. If you carry a bleeper this should be handed to a colleague for the duration of the meeting, and meetings should not be constantly interrupted by phone calls.

Good preparation also includes consideration of the setting in which the meeting is to be held. Ideally, it should be welcoming, comfortable and non-threatening for the child, but what is particularly important is that it offers privacy. Little useful work can be done in places that are noisy, busy, offer little or no privacy, and where there are likely to be interruptions, as in corridors, the middle of busy wards and waiting rooms. On occasion, in exceptional circumstances, the helper may have less control than desired over the setting, as when the child needs to remain in bed. However, some preparation and organization of what is available will still prove useful. If the helper is well-prepared, it is possible to be more focused and responsive to the needs and experience of the child in this imperfect situation, rather than be so distracted by the situation itself.

Clinic room

If a clinic room is available and the child is likely to be seen a number of times, it is helpful if the same room is used, as familiarity with the room may promote feelings of security in the child.

Ideally the room itself should be designed specifically to accommodate children of a range of ages, with the intention of providing an inviting environment within which the child can relax, communicate and/or play. There should perhaps be a small table and chair for very young children and a number of adult-sized comfortable chairs. In terms of toys or other accessories, account should be taken of the age group, abilities and ethnicity of the children likely to be seen, and the reasons for having toys. For example, you may wish to have toys to entertain children so that you can talk to the parent, or to use the toys to engage and communicate with the children. You may want to use them as an assessment aid, or as a distraction for use when examining the child.

A selection of puzzles of graded difficulty, picture books, a family of dolls, some toy animals and a friendly, furry handpuppet, are a few ideas. For children of all ages, having access to paper and pens is very useful. Other items specifically relevant to hospitals may also be useful, such as the Playmobil hospital kits (ambulance, ward, operating theatre and dentist's surgery), special needs figures (reflecting a number of disabilities), or other toy medical equipment. This might include real syringes, butterfly needles (minus the needle) and bandages. Toys which are inherently noisy or require a lot of movement around the room should be avoided for obvious reasons! One further useful item is a box of tissues; it is very embarrassing to be tearful and have a runny nose, and accessible tissues can make this far more manageable.

Although many children feel quite comfortable just to sit and talk, some, particularly the younger or more anxious, will find this difficult. Consequently it should be possible for them to move around in the room to explore and use the toys. If possible, the room should be structured in such a way that children in a wheelchair or on crutches can also move about comfortably.

In terms of the position of the furniture, sitting behind a desk should be avoided by the helper. If access to a desk is necessary, it may be possible to position your chair to the side of the desk rather than directly behind it. A desk is a real barrier to developing a relationship with children; it clearly reinforces the power and superiority of the helper. It also obscures the child from your view, and means that you lose valuable observational information about the child.

If possible, chairs should be of a similar height, so that the helper is not in the position of looking down on the child. The chairs should be positioned at a comfortable distance of about one metre from each other, and angled at about 90 degrees. If the child is being seen with other members of their family, it is useful to angle the chairs in a curved or circular format, so that all members can see each other, and are not lined up in front of the helper!

It is important to consider how a child might perceive the room; equipment and accessories we take for granted can be very alarming to a child. It might be helpful, therefore, to introduce items in the room which might catch a child's eye. This is a way of breaking the ice, and beginning to talk, but it is particularly valid if you are using a room which is used for treatment procedures. It is always important, however, to consider and note children's reactions to a new environment and ask about any worries they may have.

If it is necessary to examine the child physically as part of the session, the examination should be seen as separate from any important discussion about unrelated problem areas. It is a vulnerable position for any of us, to be lying down partially clothed with someone standing over us. This is not the time for discussing emotive issues either with the child or with the child's parents. Consideration needs to be given to protecting the child's privacy and it should not be assumed that the child is comfortable about removing clothes or being examined in front of other members of the family or other people present in the room. If tests or procedures are not the purpose of the meeting, it is important to state this clearly, so that the child understands that you will just be talking or playing and is not warily anticipating the examination or procedure.

The child's bedside

If contact with the child has to occur at their bedside, it is important to be aware that you are entering the child's space, and this needs to be done with consideration and respect. For example, you might like to ask the child if you can pull up a chair and sit and talk for a few minutes, or if you can sit on the bed to talk. Never assume you can do what you wish. You might also like to ask children if they would like a little privacy by pulling the screens around them.

Although this is not the ideal way of enabling privacy, one has to make the best of the situation if the child is confined to bed. If you are going to talk in this setting, it is important to consider who may overhear and be distressed by the conversation (especially other children), as well as the privacy of the child to whom you are talking. It may be possible to move the child in the bed to another room, or to a quieter part of the ward. This can be a very powerful message to children that you are taking them, their problems and their need for privacy seriously.

It is also important to consider what is, for the child (and for yourself), the most comfortable position in which to be talking. If the child needs to lie flat, a carefully positioned mirror may still allow him or her to see the helper's face, without the helper having to loom over the child's body. It may also be necessary to position yourself on a particular side of the bed to allow visibility over equipment.

Less than ideal settings

It may be that initial contact with the child occurs in less controlled settings, such as a corridor or busy clinic waiting room. It is not really possible to talk about personal issues in such a public place, although there may sometimes be a safety aspect to it for children. A nurse once had a very important chat about monsters and ghosts and what happened when baby sisters died with a seven-year-old child, while sitting on the rather cold floor of a hospital corridor. This felt safer for this very worried child than going somewhere more private. It enabled him to keep an eye on what was happening to his sister, without actually having to be in the same room with all the activity going on, or feeling totally removed from it. Although the corridor was very quiet, the odd noise provided a relaxing distraction and talking point. If the corridor had been more public or busy, it might have been preferable to suggest, at a suitable point, that they went somewhere a little quieter.

Generally corridors and busy places should be avoided. If a child initiates a conversation with you here it can be helpful to acknowledge that what he or she has raised is important and it might be easier to talk in a quieter and more comfortable place. This also enables the helper to regain a little control over an impromptu conversation and to set some boundaries with regard to time, for example.

Home or school visits

It may be possible to see children in their own homes or at school. This has the obvious benefit of helping children to be more relaxed and feel more in control, as they are in familiar environments. However, this also has drawbacks such as loss of time through travelling, and there may be difficulties in securing a private place with no intrusions. It is also sometimes more helpful for children to be able to go to talk somewhere special, which is physically separate from home and school. This may enable them, in one sense, to leave some of their distressing thoughts and feelings behind in this special place before returning to deal with everyday life at home or school.

It may be possible to take children on an outing in order to develop a better relationship with them and subsequently enable them to talk more openly. In this case, it is important to give children the reason for the trip, so that they do not come to expect regular treats/trips from you, or come to associate this time as the only time they can talk to you. Although it may be considered a great treat for a child to be taken to McDonalds or similar places, these are not therapeutic situations in which children can easily talk about personal or distressing events. They may choose to divulge private information or ask important questions at these times, but it is usually quite difficult (or inappropriate) to follow through these conversations.

Basic Skills

Before considering the initial meeting and ways of engaging children, we will look first at the basic skills for communicating with them. Basic skills involve close attending and listening to what children are communicating, demonstrating empathic responses to these communications, and helping them explore their problem by gentle prompting. These skills are particularly necessary at the first stages of helping, for forming the relationship and exploring the problems. However, they remain the basis of effective communication at each and every stage of the relationship.

Attending and listening

Listening in this context is not a passive process of absorbing information. It is a skilled behaviour requiring considerable concentration and attention, not only to what is being said, but to the way it is being communicated, and the way it makes the listener feel. Attending closely conveys the fact that you are listening carefully; being able to focus one's attention fully on the child is perhaps the most fundamental skill required. When children feel someone is listening carefully, they will be encouraged to start talking and be able to explore their situation. They will also feel valued and this will contribute significantly to the development of a trusting relationship.

The helper is active in the process of listening in continually looking for what the child means exactly and finding ways to check the accuracy of this. The aim is to build up as precise a picture of the child's constructions or internal representations as possible. Listening/attending requires intense concentration and interest. However, a variety of factors may interfere with this, such as distractions in the room, other things going on, feeling tired, worried, preoccupied, or uncomfortable. It may also be that the child's comments may trigger memories from the helper's own past. It is important to try not to get distracted by such extraneous thoughts. In the case of personal memories being evoked, great care needs to be taken in relating the child's experience to one's own. You are not the same person as the child, and assumptions should not be made that any experience is the same. In addition, there is a danger that if as a helper you have formulated your own ideas or solutions, you will stop attending fully to the child, or perhaps only selectively attend to information which supports your view.

Disclosing any personal experiences in order to suggest possible solutions to difficulties faced by others needs careful consideration. It is important to allow children the opportunity to reach their own conclusions and possible solutions, because these will be more meaningful to them and will make them feel more competent in working through issues themselves. Children are unique individuals, and what works for one person may not be appropriate for another. There are, however, occasions where appropriate self-disclosure about experiences or past difficulties can be helpful. It may be useful in making a stronger or more meaningful link with a child. However, great care needs to be taken that the self-disclosure is intended specifically for this purpose, rather than to entertain or revel in anecdotes as is commonly the case in everyday conversation.

Demonstrating attending.

To be effective the helper needs to demonstrate that he or she is attending. This is mainly conveyed by the helper's non-verbal behaviour such as eye gaze, facial expression, body posture and bodily movements. It will also be communicated through accurate empathic verbal responses to what is being said.

Gaze.

The most evident sign of listening is the direction of our gaze. Characteristically, people do not look at each other all the time when conversing. The person listening looks at the person who is talking most of the time, whereas the speaker has a more variable pattern, which corresponds with what they are saying – looking back at the listener at key moments to check understanding and attention. The speaker tends to make less eye contact if the material being discussed is very sensitive or distressing.

Children may choose to engage in another activity while talking to you, finding this a more comfortable way of not making eye-contact at these times. They may also appear totally preoccupied in another activity, such as drawing or making figures from plasticine, but will have been listening intently. They will often surprise the helper with a comment, or will even correct a parent's answer to a question!

Sensitivity to the child's needs for reassurance and carefully noting points in the conversation when the child looks away can reveal useful information. If possible, the helper should not break eye contact at difficult moments in the conversation, for example if the child says something emotive or looks tearful. Children may interpret this as embarrassment or the helper feeling uncomfortable, and this can prevent them from disclosing more of their feelings.

Facial expression. Interest and enthusiasm for the child can be conveyed by facial expression, and sensitivity to the child's emotional state should be reflected in this. Changes in the child's facial expressions during their play or conversation can reveal something of the meaning and intensity of feeling the child has for that subject. Commenting on their facial expression can convey the attention you are giving to them, and something of your understanding of their communication.

Discrepancies between children's facial expressions and what they are saying are particularly significant. For example, in one case it was very important that the teacher noticed that a girl had a fixed smile and tears in her eyes while saying she was not bothered by the teasing comments made about her appearance at school. Other children may look very puzzled and vague, but say they understand what they have been asked to do. If this happens it should be picked up and addressed, for example, by saying, 'You are looking very puzzled?'.

Bodily posture and movements. If possible, position yourself at the same height as the child. This clearly conveys the fact that you are working with them and are involved and interested. Squatting down to the child is better that leaning over him or her, even if it is a little wearing on the legs! A relaxed and open body posture in the helper will encourage the child to relax and feel at ease in the session. Arms and legs which are tightly crossed, or, at the other extreme, a slouched posture with head propped up by one's hand do not indicate a readiness to engage in any meaningful discussion or an interest in the child. Leaning slightly forward in the chair can convey interest, but most important is to adopt a comfortable, relaxed yet attentive position. Although it is natural to move during a conversation, the helper should not fidget or do anything which could be distracting or suggest inattentiveness or boredom, such as checking your watch.

The posture of the child will also give clues about whether they are tense or relaxed. Notice should be taken of the child's body movements. Restlessness could be the result of: the topic being discussed, particularly if this is anxiety provoking or boring; the child not understanding what is expected; a need to go to the toilet; or a concern to get home in time to watch the next episode of their favourite soap opera! Commenting gently on this may enable the child to disclose pertinent information about their situation or how they are feeling about the meeting with you.

Thought should be given to the need to take notes within a session. If information needs to be recorded, this should be kept to a minimum to avoid distracting and interrupting the child's comments. It should also be explained to the child what you are doing and why.

Mirroring the child's language

Active listening can be conveyed by many non-verbal aspects of the helper's behaviour. However it can also be demonstrated by closely mirroring the child's language, in terms of using similar sentence structure and vocabulary, since this will be more meaningful to the child. It is helpful to use the child's own words, providing you have grasped their meaning. For example, in discussing a young girl's involuntary muscle spasms, the nurse used the terms 'funny' or 'wobbly', because these were the words the girl used when talking about her legs. Children may use words which are idiosyncratic to them or their family, particularly for private parts of their body. They might use terms like 'twinkle', 'percy', 'happiness' and 'wee wee hole', for example. They may also have very limited vocabulary for naming emotions or pain experiences: 'feeling weird', 'being fed-up' or 'bored' can cover a wide range of feelings.

Demonstrating empathy

We have already talked about empathy as being a fundamental attitude, underpinning the whole process of exploring the constructs and experience of the world from the child's perspective. For this to be useful to the child, the helper needs to be able to communicate understanding. This can clarify for children what they are feeling or thinking, and it also demonstrates that you are listening carefully.

Demonstrating empathy is more than saying, 'I understand' or, 'I know how you feel'! The reality is that you *cannot* ever know exactly what the child is feeling. The skill is to reflect back in a simple statement your understanding of what you think the child is feeling or thinking. Any attempts to reflect back feelings should be tentative, to allow the child to deny, modify or agree with the helper's comments. Examples follow: the words underlined are what make the comment tentative:

'I <u>wonder if</u> you sometimes feel your relapse was somehow your fault?'
'It <u>sounds as if</u> your brother really hurts your feelings when he says you should grow up and not spend so much time with your mum?'
'It <u>seems as though</u> you don't feel anyone could understand how difficult this is for you?'

It is important not to feel you have to prove your skills by over-interpreting the child's behaviour or comments. This can feel rather persecutory, as if you are imposing your view on them. Sensitive feedback is usually preferable and more acceptable to hear. For example:

'What you have just said makes me feel sad for you', or, *'You were so looking forward to that trip'*, may be better than, *'You are depressed about not being able to do what you would like to'*.

It is also important to make the feedback to the child meaningful in terms of the child's level of understanding. Children are unlikely to disagree or try and modify something they have not understood. Demonstrating empathy is useful for checking that your understanding is roughly on the right track. If it elicits a response from the child, it will enable both the child and you to develop a more accurate understanding. Even though demonstrating empathy cannot directly take away distress or in itself solve problems, it can help enormously in indicating to children that something important about them has been understood, that in some way they are 'known' by someone who cares and is willing to help them.

Empathy can also be demonstrated by commenting on the child's non-verbal behaviour. For example, if children suddenly pause and break eye contact when they have been talking, you might comment that whatever they are saying seems quite difficult for them to talk about. You might wish to suggest tentatively why you think it might be difficult. You might also comment that it is difficult to think about upsetting things as they sometimes make us feel sad and upset. If appropriate, this could be followed by a comment reflecting that the child looks a little sad and wondering if he or she feels upset at that moment.

Just as it is possible to comment on the child's non-verbal behaviour, as in the previous example, you might also choose to comment on other activities in which the child engages within the room. If a child is playing out a scene with dolls in hospital, you might tentatively suggest how a particular doll is experiencing the event and follow this up by asking if he or she ever feels the same. For example, you could say one or more of the following:

'This young patient of yours has needed lots of needles and treatment. I wonder how she is feeling under all those drips and bandages' ... *'I wonder if she is feeling pretty fed up at the moment? What do you think'* ... *'I wonder if you ever feel fed-up at times with your treatment?'*

The First Meeting with the Child and Family

Unless one is working with older adolescents, it is very likely that the first contact with the child will be with members of their family. In most instances, following parental consent, a preliminary discussion is held with the parents to establish their concerns and to think with them about the best way of approaching and talking to their child. The helper must be sensitive to the parent's feelings about someone else talking to their child. As already emphasized, it is necessary to support the parents so that they do not feel undermined or excluded from their child's care.

Letting the parents know you talk to many young people in this situation can reassure them and ease the process a little. It may help to suggest that it is sometimes very difficult for family members to talk when they are worried, and that it may be easier to talk to someone who is a little removed from the situation. It is, however, also important to establish that you will keep parents informed about progress, which is *not* the same as reporting back everything that is said. The aim is not to replace the parent as the child's confidant, but to help bridge a gap where communication has broken down, or to help the child communicate better with family members.

Introductions

If the child is in a waiting room before you meet, going to collect the child personally can be a very positive start to the meeting. It can convey to children that you are expecting them and are pleased to see them. It also means that you consider them important enough to come to greet them in person. The walk from the waiting room to your clinic room also gives a few moments in which to talk about neutral issues or to prepare the child for who or what is in the room.

Although initial introductions will have already been made, perhaps in the waiting room or other public place, it is helpful to repeat this again in the privacy and quiet of the room. It is easy to mishear or forget in the first few anxious seconds when meeting someone. When introducing yourself to the child, give your name and profession in language meaningful to the child. Children may be familiar with the role of doctors and nurses, but not with many of the other child health professions. It might be helpful to ask the child if they have met anyone from, or know anything about, your profession, and then based on their answer, fill in any pertinent details. For example, as psychologists, after checking what the child already knows about psychologists, we might say that our job is to talk to young people to help them think about what is happening to them and to try and sort out any worries or puzzles they might have. For some children who are receiving a great deal of medical care, explaining that our job is to look after their feelings and not do anything to their bodies can be a very safe introduction. In a hospital setting, children may be expecting painful tests and this will put them at their ease by informing them what is going to happen.

In many hospitals it is considered good practice for staff to wear name badges. This can also be very useful in helping the child remember who you are. If one considers the large number of people a child may have contact with in hospital, having a clearly visible name on a badge and introducing yourself by name will make remembering easier. Although uncommon, one adolescent did actually ask to see an identity badge before agreeing to leave the ward and talk to a member of staff. In this instance, the boy's behaviour was partly to test out his power in the relationship. Nevertheless, it raises the importance of children knowing to whom they are talking and feeling safe with them.

Some wards and clinics have adopted a 'rogue's gallery', a collection of photographs of all members of staff. This is a good idea, because it helps children identify and remember significant adults in their environment, as well as understanding their place in the organization.

As well as helpers introducing themselves to the child, it is important for children to introduce themselves on their own terms. Getting the child's name right may seem to be common sense, but people frequently get it wrong, even though it is very important for the child! If necessary, check with the child how they pronounce or spell their name, or what they prefer to be called, if their name abbreviates. This can be a useful ice-breaker in starting the conversation. It can also be useful to ask the child to introduce you to the other members of their family since this may enhance the child's feeling of being important and an active part of the meeting.

The meeting

As part of the greetings and introductions at the start of the meeting, it is very welcoming to smile at the child and to say something positive. It may be that you compliment them on their name, clothes, hair, eyes, smile, or on something you have heard about the child. It may have the same effect saying that you have heard a little about them and that you are very pleased to meet them.

The child may immediately wish to bring to your attention his or her concerns, but usually there is an opportunity to help the child relax into the session by asking a neutral question. You might begin perhaps by enquiring about their journey, or about their school uniform, if they are wearing one, or anything which helps them settle down.

The next task is to clarify with the child the reason for the meeting. Parents may have already fully discussed with their children the reason for the meeting, or may have told them little or nothing about it. Children may have asked for help, or may be surprised, relieved or dismayed to find themselves with you. If they have come because someone else suggested it, you might ask them why that person thought it would be helpful, or why they thought their parent had brought them along to meet you. You might also ask them what they think about the idea.

If they reply that they did not want to come, it may be entirely appropriate to say you are pleased they did come and then to ask what they thought would happen. This may enable the helper to allay any unrealistic fears about the meeting, and to let children know that it can feel quite strange to be expected to talk to someone they do not know. It can also be a first opportunity for the child to realize that you are interested in their views and are able to listen to negative comments or their concerns, and take them seriously. If children have made the request to meet, it may just be useful to ask them to say a little about what they felt they would like to talk about, and then follow the child's lead on this.

At this point, the helper may wish to explain or clarify his or her own understanding of the reason for meeting. It may be that the helper explains his or her role as getting to know young people (and members of their family) a little better to see how things are going at home or school. If a problem focus is apparent, then the purpose can be stated as helping them think about ways of dealing with it. In this case, the problem should be framed in the least threatening and most positive manner possible. For example, instead of saying that you have heard the child is being very naughty and disobedient, you might say that you have heard there are some difficulties about the diet, school or physiotherapy exercises.

The helper can then go on to explain a little more about the meeting, including what it might involve and the rules of the meeting, including confidentiality. Children can be reassured that they will not be expected to say or do anything in the meeting against their will. It may also be helpful to say that the first meeting is really about getting to know one another better. This might dispel any myths about anything necessarily being resolved or magically sorted out right away. It can also relieve children of feeling under pressure to say anything they feel uncomfortable about revealing so early on.

Depending on the preferred method of interacting with children, you may wish to say that this meeting is a special time, just for them, where they can think about or do whatever they like. Children tend to use this overture in sorting out their problems very well.

Once the reason or aims for the meeting have been established and the format of the meeting discussed, it is useful to be clear how long you have available and also how much time the child and family have put aside. If the child is uncertain of the time, pointing to a clock on the wall and indicating that the session will end when the big hand reaches a particular number may be helpful. If time is limited, you can tell the child that although you have just twenty minutes at this particular time, it will be possible to continue the conversation the following day or at another specified time. It is inappropriate to have to end a conversation abruptly or to become distracted because you are running late for another appointment, especially if children disclose something sad or frightening. They may be left with the feelings raised by the discussion, without having the opportunity to deal with them. They may also misperceive the helper to be leaving because he or she is unable to cope with what the child has disclosed.

Following an initial exploration of the area of difficulty, some form of agreement can be drawn up with the child about what happens next. The aims or expectations should be made explicit, even if this is only to decide the next step, such as talking to the doctor to get more information or deciding when to meet again.

Ending the session

The end of the session should be clear and anticipated by the child (in terms of a few minutes' warning). This allows them to prepare for the ending, and plan what happens next, including the time of the next meeting. If possible, central themes or aims should be repeated, any plans explicitly stated, and the conversation lightened to end on a positive note. It may be useful to ask children if there is anything they would like to say or ask before they leave or to ask what the one, most important part about them they would particularly want you to remember. It is also good to negotiate what information will be passed on to parents or shared with other staff.

One very good way of ending the session is to be positive with the child about how you have found them during the meeting. For example, if the child has played imaginatively with the toys and helped to put them away, this could be mentioned. They can also be praised for the open way in which they have been able to discuss matters with you. They might need to be reassured that they did well in the meeting, as well as acknowledging how difficult they found it to talk. Children may be very uncertain about what was expected from them and whether you are pleased with them. Their need for reassurance is as great, if not greater, than when an adult seeks help.

It may be helpful to have written on paper or on an appointment card exactly who you are and how you can be contacted, as well as details of the next time you have arranged to meet if appropriate. These details can be given both to the child and to their parents.

Difficulties in Engaging Children

Difficulties in engaging children occur in a number of situations. These include when they have not requested help, but have been persuaded or forced; when they are not clear about the purpose of the meeting; when they are very anxious or unfamiliar with adults focusing attention on them in this way; and when children feel they are in trouble or likely to get themselves or others into trouble.

It is important not to feel you have a mission to discover something important about the child, or feel a failure if the child has not felt able to open up to you on the very first occasion. It is also important not to make children feel they have failed or that you are angry with them. If the child is reluctant to communicate, it is important to consider carefully the purpose of the meeting and the possible difficulties which may be preventing them from talking openly. Once the reasons are clearer, then one can be creative in working out a more helpful approach to the child.

It may be that the timing or setting for the meeting needs to change, or even that the child may respond better to a different person. If it is considered that the child is somehow emotionally frozen or there are concerns that the child is very withdrawn or depressed, a referral to a more specialist psychological or psychiatric service may be indicated. We will consider assessment and referrals of this nature in *Chapter 11*.

It is, however, important to remember that even children who do not respond in the way you might predict may derive some help from the session. For example, one girl was a cause of concern to the nursing staff as she persistently lay in bed with her eyes closed, pretending to be asleep, as a way of cutting off from everything around her. One of the nurses sat and chatted to her for nearly ten minutes, letting her know of these concerns and thinking aloud about the sorts of things she might be worried about. In doing so, she reassured the girl that all of these were important to sort out, and that she, and others, wanted to help. Throughout the very one-sided conversation, the nurse noted the child's body and facial movements, which, although minimal, did indicate she was following the comments. After a while, the nurse let the child know she would have to leave in a few minutes, but asked if she could come back and talk later in the day. The girl, still with her eyes closed, whispered 'Yes', and seemed visibly more relaxed.

Difficulties in Communication

Children may not be able to communicate in words for a number of reasons. This might include when they are intubated (requiring a tube to assist breathing) or have weakness of oral or facial muscles preventing clear articulation. Use of communication boards, sign boards or written/drawn signs will greatly aid communication. If you are unclear about the child's level of understanding or their language skills, it might be useful to request the help of a speech therapist who will be skilled in assessing and facilitating communication.

Children who have hearing impairment also require special considera-tion. If their articulation is difficult to understand, it is important to care-fully 'tune in' to their verbal style, and allow enough time to habituate to it. It may be important to be clear with the child that you are going to listen carefully but may need their patience, if not their help, when you miss something or need something repeated. If children are reliant on sign language to communicate, it is important to access the help of a skilled sign interpreter. It is also important to be very explicit about the aims of the meeting and any communications to be made. The subtleties of com-munication are often lost in translation.

If children have serious visual impairment, thought needs to be given to how they experience the conversation with you. If it is an unfamiliar setting, they may like you to describe what is around them in the room or (more likely) may wish to investigate for themselves. They will prob-ably be more reliant on vocal indications that you are following what they are saying, as non-verbal cues such as facial expression and eye gaze will not be seen.

Language and cultural issues may also result in difficulties in com-munication. When the helper and family are not able to speak the same language fluently, it is important to assess whether each party is able to make themselves sufficiently understood, or whether the services of an interpreter will be required. It is not usually appropriate to carry out therapy or counselling through an interpreter (although some interpret-ers are taking futher training in counselling to develop their skills in this area), but for meeting and communicating information or eliciting questions or concerns about treatment, interpreters can be invaluable.

Summary

❑ Engaging children and developing a trusting relationship with them are important prerequisites to helping them deal with problems.

❑ Careful preparation should go in to the first and all subsequent meetings with the child, so that the helper is clear about the purpose of the meeting and has thought about how best to facilitate this.

❑ Ideally, the setting in which children are seen should be private and undisturbed by telephones, bleepers or people. It should be accessible, comfortable, and child-orientated.

❑ Appropriate equipment should be available, including paper and pens, graded puzzles, picture books, puppets, appropriate toys. Their functions include aiding communication, enabling assessment, entertaining the child, relaxing or distracting them.

❑ It is helpful to be explicit about the length of time put aside for the meeting.

❑ Important basic helping skills include: attending/listening and demonstrating empathic responses to communication.

❑ Listening is an active process, with the aim of making sense of what is said, the way it is communicated and how it makes the listener feel. The aim is to build up as accurate a picture of children's experiences as possible.

❑ Attending is communicated by non-verbal behaviour, such as eye gaze, facial expression, body posture and bodily movements, as well as through empathy.

❑ Empathic responses are demonstrated by tentatively reflecting back in a simple statement your understanding of what you think the child is feeling or thinking. The child can then think about this, and deny, modify or accept the comments made.

❑ Communicating with children involves sensitivity to how they experience their meeting with you and communicating your readiness to listen and try to help.

continued

continued ---

❑ It is important to be as clear as possible with the child about the purpose, expectations and rules of the meeting.

❑ During the initial contact, an agreement needs to be reached about what might happen in any following meetings, or the next step, if no further meetings are planned.

❑ Some children will be reluctant to talk or form a relationship with the helper, and careful thought must be given to the child's understanding of the meetings, the timing, setting and format.

❑ If necessary, an alternative helper or referral on to a more specialist mental health professional may need to be considered.

❑ It is important to plan a comfortable ending to the session, giving the child warning towards the end, and using the closing minutes to summarize main points, deal with any final questions and reinforce any plans.

7

Exploring the Child's Experiences and Understanding

Having looked at the basic skills for engaging and developing a relationship with a child, we will now turn to strategies used in exploration, as a means of further getting to know the child, to explore his or her experiences and understanding, and to assess the areas of help required. In the following chapters we will continue to look at ways of using this understanding to help the child, whether in terms of giving the child information (*Chapter 8*), or strategies for dealing with a particular challenge or event (*Chapter 9*).

Getting to know children and exploring their experiences of events is perhaps the most important part of the process of helping. It is through exploration and coming to a shared understanding of the child's experiences that the relationship between the child and helper can develop. This will enable the child to relax in the sessions and to develop trust, because of the powerful message that you are interested in them, and not just in their medical condition or problem.

Exploration is an essential pre-requisite for helping, as one has to come to a shared understanding of needs and the areas of difficulty before any plan of change or helping strategies can be implemented. A good assessment of this kind will also enable the child's experiences or difficulties to be placed in the context of their life generally. Sometimes talking through one's experiences or problems is sufficient to make sense of them and help children address issues that were previously too overwhelming. It can also enable a more helpful perception of events, which may be perceived as less distressing, less out of control, or less persecutory.

Getting to Know the Child

In getting to know the child, it is helpful to begin by exploring more neutral topics about their home, friends, interests and school. As discussed earlier, it can feel very uncomfortable for children if you focus too early on talking about problems or areas of distress; it is first necessary to engage children and help them feel more relaxed with you. Children can be asked about the names, ages and occupations (or schools) of family members. It may be possible to engage the child in drawing a family tree, depicting all family members, and even pets! This activity can be very useful in terms of understanding the family context to the child's difficulties, since many children offer comments spontaneously about members of their family whilst engaged on this task.

Other neutral areas may be about children's activities, what they like doing and with whom they do these things. It is useful to build up a picture of the child's social life both at school and home. Children can be asked if they belong to any clubs or groups, or have friends who call for them to do things together. It can be revealing to ask if they have a best friend or a group of friends, who they sit next to in class and what they do at break-times; whether they are with others or on their own. If they mention a social group, it is useful to ask if these are the same friends as at school, or whether school and home friends are very separate. It may be, for example, that children mainly do activities with members of their own family, or are not allowed to go out with friends.

With regard to school, children can be asked about their favourite and least favourite subjects. The latter may be particularly revealing in that we rarely enjoy subjects or activities at which we are not very good. It can be useful, for example, to ask them where they would place themselves in terms of ability (towards the top, middle or bottom of the class) and how this feels for them. Children can also be asked about ambitions and what they would like to do when they are older.

When the conversation flounders or begins to feel stuck, it may be useful to get a sense of what they might like to change in order to discover areas of difficulty for them. For younger children, one can ask what they would do if they had three wishes and could ask for anything in the whole wide world. Many children will be able to use this opening to say something important about what they would like to change. They might say, for example, 'I wish that my brother would let me play with him and his friends', or 'I wish I could go on holiday with my mum and give her a rest'. Any wish of this sort can be explored and can give further understanding of relevant issues for the child.

Another helpful opening is to ask how things might be different for them if a particular thing changed. For example, one might ask what would be different if they managed to get a working transplant, if they had a best friend, or their hair was to grow back right now. This can free children to explore what is difficult for them to manage currently. It can also be revealing to ask children what has changed for them and their family since their condition was diagnosed.

Exploration of children's experiences involves engaging children, listening carefully to them, asking questions to clarify their understanding, and facilitating thoughts and discussion by making observations about their play or other communications such as their drawings. We will now look at some basic verbal and non-verbal exploration skills. These techniques may be carried out with the child individually, or (as is more likely initially) with the child and family together.

Verbal Exploration Skills

Children should be asked for information in a non-threatening way. They should not be made to feel they are being tested or accused. They should not be made to look silly if they do not know the answer or make a mistake. If children feel anxious, or 'put on the spot', they are more likely to say they do not know rather than risk getting an answer wrong. Other reasons for children saying they do not know an answer when in fact they do, include feeling shy, upset, confused by a complex or badly structured question, or being asked something they consider odd or unusual.

There are a number of ways of prompting children to talk: these include the skills of enabling children to open up and start talking, to keep them talking once started, or help them move in a particular direction. There are a number of different types of questions and other facilitating comments including empathic responding which can be helpful in this process.

Open questions

The most often used prompts are in the form of open questions, which serve as an invitation for the child to talk freely, without being limited in their responses. One might, for example, start a conversation with questions such as:

'Can you tell me a little about yourself/family/school?'
'How have you been getting along?'
'I wonder if you could tell me why the doctor and you felt it might be helpful for us to meet today?'
'What do you think all these tests are for?'

Some children may need a little further encouragement to begin telling their story, and a facilitating statement before an open question may be useful:

'Some children feel very fed up about having to keep coming into hospital..how do you cope with this?'

'Many young people have told me about the worries they have in start-ing this treatment. I was wondering what you might have been think-ing and feeling?'

None of these can be answered by a 'Yes' or 'No', or a single piece of information. They do not constrain what children can say, and it allows them to decide what they wish to mention. Consequently, most ques-tions used to explore children's experiences will be open, enabling them to tell their story in their own words. Open questions can also be help-ful in ascertaining children's understanding of any information they have been given about their condition or treatment.

'What does diabetes mean to you?'
'Could you let me know what the doctors have said about your legs?'

Closed questions

Questions which do not give the child a free response (that is, closed questions) may be used to follow up an open question, for example, where the child has been unable to answer or where clarification is sought by the helper:

Helper: 'How have your headaches been since taking the medicine?'
(open question).
Child: 'Pretty bad!'
Helper: 'Are they any better at all?' (closed question)
Child: 'Yes, a little.'

Closed questions should be used sparingly, as they can make the conversation become rather one-sided, and more of a verbal test than a discussion. Care needs to be taken about closed questions which lead the child to a specific answer, because younger children will be particularly influenced by what they believe they are being asked to say. These so-called 'leading questions' may not fairly represent the child's views. Examples are:

'You are always so good about your tablets. You must have just forgot-ten these. You won't forget next time, will you?'
'Did you feel guilty that you made such a fuss and screamed at your poor mother?'
'The most sensible plan is for you to do this. Do you agree?'

It may be difficult for any child to disagree with such loaded or pointed questions. Alternatives might be for children to be asked open ques-tions about what happened with the tablets on the previous day or to ask what the upset with their mother had been about, or to explore what plan the person had already considered for themselves.

Multiple choice questions

Another form of question which may be used to prompt includes multiple choice questions. These are more concrete, and offer the child a choice of answers. They are particularly helpful, if the child finds it difficult to generate an answer, or is saying that he or she does not know. For example:

Helper: 'How did your meeting at school go?'
Child: 'I don't really know.'
Helper: 'Were you able to sort out all of your questions or are there other points you would like to deal with?'

Another example might be:

Helper: 'How do you feel at the moment?'
Child: (No answer)
Helper: 'Do you feel better, the same, or worse, than when I saw you this morning?'

Multiple choice questions can also be used to elicit the frequency or intensity of an occurrence. For example:

'Does it bother you all the time or just some of the time?'
'Are you more tired, about the same, or less tired, than usual?'
'Is it a daddy bear pain, a mummy bear pain, or a baby bear pain?'

This last example is obviously idiosyncratic to a particular child. However, one must always try to use vocabulary which will be meaningful to the child.

Another use of multiple choice questions can be to determine the child's view of the likelihood or probability of a particular occurrence, such as the outcome of treatment or how frightened they are about what will happen. For example, one might ask:

'How long do you think it may take for you to feel better ... one week, one month, or one year?'
'What do you think are the chances of your headaches stopping after this surgery ... around 100 per cent, 50 per cent or 10 per cent?'

Multiple choice questions are definitely not the same as asking multiple questions. The latter can overload children so that they are unable to follow or comprehend:

'Are you feeling really fed-up with all of this, or are you just pleased the worst part is over? You must be feeling really tired now. Were you really scared when it was happening? Tell me how you are feeling?'

Facilitative responses

The most powerful facilitative comments are empathic statements or responses, and these are discussed more fully in *Chapter 6*. At the simplest level, they involve reflecting back significant words, ideas or statements which communicate an involvement and attempt at understanding the experiences being spoken about. At a deeper level, reflection may be more about the unspoken message, concerning the feelings or thoughts behind what has been said. Both are very helpful in encouraging the child to explore, think about, and communicate further. For example, following an interview with a mother and her child, the child became progressively less engaged as the mother talked about their difficulties, to the extent of turning away and curling up on the chair. The response from the helper was to say:

'You have curled up as if you are sleepy, but I wonder if you are just tired and fed-up of hearing about the problems with your illness?'

At this, the child gave a wry smile and replied that it was just very boring, but added more seriously, that they never seemed to talk or think about anything other than hospitals anymore.

Responses such as nodding, smiling, saying 'Yes', or 'Uh huh', are normal parts of conversation and serve to keep the child talking, conveying interest and reinforcing the speaker. Pauses in the conversation can also encourage a response. For this reason, it is important not to jump in too quickly to fill pauses in the conversation. Short pauses can allow time for children to think about what has been discussed, and to make their own sense of it. However, care must be taken to ensure that silences do not become persecutory for the child. If there has been a pause, you may like to acknowledge that you have asked a tricky question. You might also want to encourage the child to respond by saying it is an important point, and you are interested in the child's views.

Structuring

Once children have begun to talk, it may be necessary to help them tell their story in a coherent way, so that it becomes clearer for both the child and the helper. Structuring may be required for children who present a muddled picture or have difficulties sequencing their story. This may frequently occur for younger children, but also for children who are distressed or unused to speaking in this manner. For example, it may be necessary to ask questions to clarify when, how, to whom something happened, and what happened as a result.

If the child has a limited concept of sequencing or time, it may be necessary to talk them through their account stage by stage. For example, 'What happened after that?' Younger children may get confused with past, present and future tenses. It may be helpful to use concrete markers such as after dinner, before school, before their birthday, or after swimming, to clarify times. For children familiar with the freeze frame on a video, it can be helpful to ask them to use the pause button to stop their story, just so you can clarify what is actually happening, who is involved and even what people might be saying, thinking or feeling.

Sometimes children are quite vague about the way they present information, and it may be necessary to ask them to clarify what they have said by giving an example. It may be helpful to focus the child by asking them to think back to the last time this happened and to talk you through events. For example:

Child: 'My brother is always moody with me.'
Helper: 'Moody? In what way?'
Child: 'Just moody. I hate him!'
Helper: 'Can you think back to the last time he was moody with you?'
Child: 'Yes, this morning! I asked if I could borrow a book to read on the train coming up here, and he said no, that mummy's little boy had everything he ever wanted and just needed to look sick and ask Mum and she would buy me my own book!'

Non-Verbal Exploration Strategies

There are a number of strategies for exploring children's experiences, in ways that both complement what the child is saying and facilitate communication when the child is unable to speak freely. This might be due to language limitations because of the age of the child, developmental delays, physical difficulties (for example, dyspraxia, cerebral palsy) or it may be due to the emotive or abstract nature of the material, making it too difficult to put into words.

Using pictures

Most children enjoy drawing and this can be a very non-threatening way of starting a session and beginning to get to know children. You can suggest they draw a picture of themselves or of their family, for example. It might also be suggested that while they are drawing, you would like to talk to them so that you can get to know them a little better. Drawing is usually a relaxing, fun activity for most children, and talking to them about their pictures can be very revealing. You might ask them what or who they are drawing and their replies may be followed up with gentle exploratory questions such as 'Do you ever do that?' or 'Do you ever feel like that?' In this way children may be helped to communicate fears or feelings which have been too difficult to verbalize previously. Although there is always an opportunity to comment on pictures the child has drawn, it is far more helpful to encourage children to tell you about their picture themselves first of all and then to pick up useful cues to explore further. One young boy drew a futuristic weapon, which he explained was the special weapon of Terminator, half man, half machine. He continued by saying the weapon would only be used against bad people who hurt or teased him. He had required the use of a wheelchair for many years, and had experienced considerable teasing about his disability. As a consequence, he felt very vulnerable with his peers. His picture enabled a discussion of both his feelings towards others and his feelings about his dependence on his machine, his wheelchair. One teenager, with very limited mobility and movement, drew a very revealing picture of herself, depicting a large mouth, relative to the rest of her body. When this was commented upon, she described her mouth as being her most powerful weapon, as it was only through this she could stand up for herself and feel on equal ground with others.

The butterfly picture in *Figure 7.1* was drawn by the sister of a child who had been in hospital for several months, with the comment that it was to cheer up her sister. The helper stated that the butterfly was indeed beautifully bright and cheerful in colour, but asked the girl about the pattern on the wings. She replied quite shyly that the pattern looked like tears, and this led to a discussion about how hard it was to be the sister of someone who was so poorly, and how everyone told her how helpful she was in looking after and cheering up her sister, but how sad and worried she really was.

As indicated in this example, children's pictures can be used to explore how they are feeling about themselves. *Figures 7.2 (a) and (b)* were drawn by a young boy with a recently diagnosed progressive

Figure 7.1 Picture of a butterfly, drawn by sibling.

Figure 7.2(a) Picture drawn in the initial meeting with the child.

Figure 7.2(b) Picture drawn by the same child after explanations had been given to the child, family and school about his condition.

muscular condition. As the pictures suggest, he had very poor self-esteem and a low self-image, which was certainly not helped by the constant ridicule and punishment he received at school because of his clumsiness and poor written work. The first picture was drawn in the initial meeting, and the second after explanations had been given to the child, family and school about the condition and associated difficulties.

Drawings can also be useful in exploring children's understanding of particular tests or investigations, as in the following example, which illustrates the predicament facing Fiona, a seven-year-old who was very anxious about learning to catheterize (that is, insert a tube into her bladder to enable her to urinate). Fiona's anxieties appeared to centre around the fear that she would hurt herself, despite knowing that the procedure did not hurt her when adults did it for her, and that she was obviously competent to carry it out.

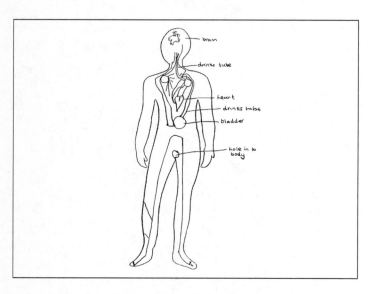

Figure 7.3 Picture of child's perception of catheterization.

Fiona described how 'all liquids' moved around her body in tubes, which travel around her heart. Her picture (*Figure 7.3*) shows the hole where the tube enters her body and the bladder, which she has drawn near her heart. She described how the catheter went into the bladder and took away her wee, but the picture enabled her to articulate her greatest fear which was that she might accidentally make a hole in her bladder with the tube. The consequence of this, she thought, was that her wee would leak, making her heart wet, and that this would give her a heart attack, from which she would die. Through exploring and coming to an understanding of Fiona's current knowledge, it was possible to see what information was needed to correct her misperceptions and offer the necessary support and information for her to catheterize safely.

Pictures can also be used to communicate particularly frightening or distressing experiences. For example, children may prefer to draw a picture to represent their bad dreams rather than tell you about them. Again, it is appropriate to explore what is happening in the picture carefully with the child and use this as the starting point for dealing with the anxieties. It can also be useful for children to draw a resolution or happy ending to their nightmare so that they can remember it the next time they have the same dream.

Some children need a little more encouragement to draw, or may prefer to be engaged in a joint activity with the helper. A useful icebreaker for getting children to relax is the 'squiggle game'. This involves making a random mark on a piece of paper or on a chalkboard and asking children to finish the picture. They can then tell a story about the picture, or take on the role of one of the figures or objects in the picture and say what is happening or how they are feeling. The game can be continued by the child drawing a scribble for you and then taking turns.

Using play

Children often find it easier to talk while they are playing. Like drawing, play can reveal interesting insights into what the child has understood, is worrying about or feeling. A child who turns the doll's crutches into imaginary machine guns and massacres the doctors may be communicating highly significant feelings! Watching children give a pretend injection to a doll or adult can tell you what they think of someone who tells them it will not hurt. Although one girl was heard to tell the 'patient' confidently it would not hurt, the expression on her face and the ferocity of her actions certainly suggested otherwise! This play can give an opportunity for the adult to explore the child's previous experience, and to plan ways with the child of helping to deal with future needles or tests.

In *Chapter 6*, we discussed useful play materials and many children are able to use the Playmobil hospital kits very imaginatively to work through frightening and painful experiences. As with drawing, it can be very revealing, if tentative enquiries are made by the helper about what is happening and how various patients and family members are feeling or thinking at various stages of the play.

One child with a severe form of epilepsy continually played with an ambulance which ran over everything (and everybody!) in sight to get to the hospital. The doll he used as a patient was then thrown out of the ambulance and the process repeated. When the nurse commented on this, the child explained that the ambulance had gone as fast as it could, but the child had died before reaching hospital. This startled his mother and opened up a discussion about the mother's fear that her child would die (as he had nearly done on one previous occasion) if he did not get to hospital fast enough when suffering a seizure. She had not been aware that he had picked up her concern, but this realization enabled her to make sense of his very clingy behaviour and extreme fear about coming into hospital for investigations.

If children have had a great deal of experience in hospitals, playing with pretend equipment can sometimes be very tedious. However, using real equipment, such as syringes, swabs, and butterfly needles (with the needle removed), can be more interesting for them. For a skilled needle crafts person, it is possible to make soft rag dolls for hospital play. They can be made with removable organs, and with openings in the nose or limbs in which to place tubes, syringes or other equipment that will be used.

Using handpuppets

Young children in particular can be fascinated by the magic of handpuppets which in practised hands enable them to suspend disbelief and to talk and interact with the puppets as if they were real. They may become engaged in a conversation with a puppet or doll and explain to a worried puppet who is about to have a similar test or investigation, what it is for and what happens. This is illustrated in the following example of a child referred because of chronic soiling. The child was difficult to engage in conversation, but was delighted when the handpuppet shyly admitted he was a little scared and asked the child why he was here. The young boy said it was because of his poohing and not to worry, these people were going to help them! This enabled the doctor to positively reinforce the child's expectations that people were trying to help and that it was possible for change to occur.

Handpuppets can be an excellent medium for exploring and passing on information to children who are suspicious or unwilling to listen to an adult. Jess, a little handpuppet puppy, is a frequent visitor to the children's wards at Guy's Hospital. She often talks to the children themselves, and asks them to explain things. She also asks the doctors and nurses questions about what this tube or that medicine is doing. Some children will even ask to hold and move the puppy themselves, listening intently to the information and even asking the puppy if she has understood!

More Structured Exploration Strategies

Having considered general ways of exploring children's experiences, we will now go on to look at more structured strategies that might be useful. Any of these can be adapted to meet the needs of children in specific situations.

Structured sentence completion

The technique here is to provide the first few words of a sentence and to ask the child to complete it orally or in writing. Providing a list of such sentences is potentially very useful in revealing how the child is feeling or what they are thinking about themselves and their world. It can also be helpful to repeat the list at intervals of a number of sessions to see what changes have occurred. Obviously such sentences can be tailored to the particular child, although a few suggestions are:

1. I hope that . . .
2. I get worried when . . .
3. My Mum/Dad would like . . .
4. The doctors and nurses say . . .
5. My condition means . . .
6. The most important part of me is . . .
7. I would never . . .

A variation on these sentences when exploring feelings with children is to divide a page in two and consider both positive and negative feelings. For example, 'Feeling happy is . . .' and on the other side of the page 'Being scared/unhappy is . . .' Children can either generate a list or draw the sorts of things which trigger these feelings for them. It was in a similar way that a mother helped her daughter to write 'The Big T', the very moving poem in *Chapter 2*. She asked her daughter to write a list of all the things which upset her and everything that made her happy. As a result, she was clearly able to think very creatively and constructively about her situation.

Incomplete sentence story

This is similar to sentence completion and can be carried out either with an individual child or as a small group activity. A story is told together, with each person finishing the previous sentence. The helper starts by saying, for example, 'It was a sunny morning, but Molly did not want to get out of bed because . . . '. He or she stops and allows the child to continue, taking up again where the child finishes. The value of this strategy is that the helper can introduce topics or issues at any point that can help children address difficulties or questions that are pertinent to them specifically. One helper added the following sentence to the story in the case of a boy who was being bullied at school ' . . . and after drinking the magic potion, he became twice as big and twice as strong. The first thing he did was to . . . '. In a group situation the teacher starts off the story and then children take it in turns to continue. This has been particularly useful in hospital school classes where the children not only reveal their experiences and feelings, but also their misperceptions. It is interesting to note, however, that in this context wherever the story starts and with whatever characters it involves, it invariably ends up in the hospital situation with them having a variety of tests and treatments. The following sequence of sentences are taken from a school session:

'The prince turned into a frog and hopped off London Bridge . . .'
'When the frog woke up it was in Guy's Hospital with broken legs and it had to drink some yucky bright orange medicine . . .'
'He had 100 tubes and lots of needles . . .'
'I'm going to die said the frog . . .'
'No you're not. Just be good and take your medicine.'
'OK, can I go home then?!'

Story books

Another technique is to help children to write a book about themselves. This has the advantage of enabling them to assimilate information about what has happened to them and can reveal to the helper what the experience has been. Children may wish to write or dictate the script or simply to use pictures or drawings to illustrate what has happened.

The book can be of any length and as elaborate as the child wishes. It can be done in the sessions with the helper or between sessions and discussed when they next meet. Whatever the situation, it will be unique to the particular child and as personalized or as private as he or she wishes. However, some children are happy for their books to be read by others, and some children show an interest in making their own book after reading the account of another child.

Writing a life-story book can give the child an opportunity and freedom to explore feelings and situations they have not felt able to in other ways. Children may also use this opportunity to explore 'what if' scenarios, for example, what if the surgery had not been successful or what if they needed to have more treatment. However, a more limited exercise of making up a scrapbook of their stay in hospital can be a very useful exercise for some children as a way of making sense of their experiences and feelings while recuperating at home. They might include photographs of particular staff or friends they have met on the ward, their identity bracelet, bravery certificates they were awarded for particular procedures, or the stitches they had removed.

Games and other resources

There are a range of games and other resources that may enable children to explain their feelings. These include, for example, the 'All About Me' games package which consists of a colourful board game in which the child and helper take turns answering questions written on a pack of cards and then move around the board accordingly. There are over 120 cards, each with a different design and statement, covering a wide range of issues. Some are very 'safe', for example, 'My favourite clothes are . . . ', enabling the child to relax and enjoy the game. Other cards explore feelings and the ways in which they are expressed. Examples of questions are, 'I get very embarrassed when . . .' and 'When I feel left out of things, I . . . '. This enables children and adults to communicate about all sorts of feelings in a supportive, non-threatening way, and is a helpful tool for developing a relationship with a child. This game is available from Barnado's (a charity helping children in need) and from the 'Being Yourself' company (supplier of reference and practical materials for working with children) (see *Appendix C* for details).

Similarly, there is also a very useful series of workbooks called *Drawing Out Feelings*, which is particularly helpful in working with children about issues of loss and change. These encourage the child to illustrate and/or write aspects of their story. For example, the child may be asked to describe their favourite memory, or to colour in an outline of a human figure using colours to depict what feelings are experienced where. Please refer to *Appendix B* for more details.

Some children have enjoyed using a simple adaptation of a formal psychology test to explore how they are feeling about themselves and others. Quite simply, a number of cards with different feelings written on them are posted into one of three boxes, labelled 'Like me', 'Not like me' and 'Not sure'. The descriptions of feelings can be provided by the helper or generated during the session with the child. The exercise of sorting the cards can be helpful in enabling children recognize and label feelings they experience. Discussing the cards further with children can open up a conversation about which situations prompt particular feelings, and how the child shows and copes with these feelings.

Using diaries

Most school age children will be able to keep some form of diary, which, apart from being a good assessment tool, also enables children to take an active part in the process. Depending on the situation, children can be asked to record a number of different events or experiences, such as feelings, activities undertaken, pain experienced and strategies used to cope with any difficulties.

Keeping a diary can be a very useful strategy in itself for structuring one's thoughts and being able to make sense of one's experiences. It can also enable a ventilating of painful thoughts or feelings, knowing they have been safely recorded and can be shared with the helper at a later point. Recording information in a structured (and therefore possibly more objective) way can even help the child develop a different perspective on their difficulties, thus facilitating change.

Children can be asked to keep an account of how they have been feeling, or how they have found a new experience. For example, a teenager recently implanted with a cochlear appliance kept a diary of her first few weeks with the implant. This enabled her to describe and communicate experiences that she would have found very difficult to have put into words (or sign language). She was very keen for her diary to be available to other children to help them to adapt to using their implant.

Diaries can also be used to help children work through distressing emotions. For example, a child who was being socially isolated and teased at school kept a record of all the day's events at school. For every negative comment or action towards her, she managed to write down firstly how this made her feel and then a comforting thought with which she could help herself. Over time, she added a further column to her diary, in which she evaluated how successfully she felt she had managed in these situations.

A child who was frequently getting into trouble by arguing and becoming aggressive also kept a diary of the day's events. When he had calmed himself after his outbursts, he recorded his step- by-step account of what had led to the altercation. In sessions with his helper, he was able to role-play some of the incidents and work out alternative methods of dealing with the situation. Just recording the events, however, gave him an opportunity to think in a more constructive way about what had happened.

Children who are feeling restricted or unable to engage in useful or enjoyable activities may become depressed and stop making plans to do anything for themselves, feeling there is nothing positive happening in their lives. Asking them to keep an account of what they have done during the day can be a helpful exploration of exactly what they *can do* and a starting point to helping them plan activities into their day. When a baseline has been established, the child can be encouraged to set tasks or activity goals for the day or week and to record how successful they have been in reaching them.

Some children will feel much more comfortable with diaries than others, but it is always important to establish the child's level of literacy and how much adult help will be required to keep a diary if written comments are to be recorded. In using diaries it is very important to take time in the session to plan exactly what the child is to do, as misunderstandings are common, and children will not necessarily remember the details of what they have been asked to do after a session. Care should be taken to be clear about what is to be recorded and when the child will be able to make time to fit in these recordings during their daily routines. If diaries are going to be regularly used, it is helpful to have a store of small booklets which can be given to each child. Taking away a proper diary book can raise the importance given to the diary, as opposed to using scraps of paper.

Rating scales, visual analogue scales and graphs

These can be used for a variety of purposes and may easily be incorporated into a diary. The type of scale can be negotiated with the child, using numbers, colours or pictures. The scales can be used to measure the intensity of feelings (happy, worried, upset), success in carrying out a task or achieving a goal, or as a measure of pain intensity. An example of this is found in *Chapter 9*. In addition to exploring children's own feelings, rating scales can also be used to indicate how the child perceives others to be feeling. For example, after a lengthy treatment for cancer, the doctors had suggested that Louise was well enough to get on with her life. Although Louise felt physically well, she was so anxious that she felt incapacitated and unable to do anything. This was compounded by the mixed reactions of others in their attitude and behaviour towards her. Because some treated her as though she were better and others as though she could still be ill, it was impossible for her to believe with any certainty that she really *was* well. Louise was asked to plot on a graph (visual analogue scale) how she thought others saw her, in terms of how well she was now, and the results are shown in *Figure 7.4*.

Louise realized how confused she was and how confusing she found the behaviour of others. She understood that some members of her family and her doctor felt that she was well enough to return to school, but her mother and teacher felt she was not. Through exploring how others saw her, Louise discovered for herself that it was not helpful to rely on everyone else to know how well she was and how she should behave. Instead, she decided she had to listen to herself and her own

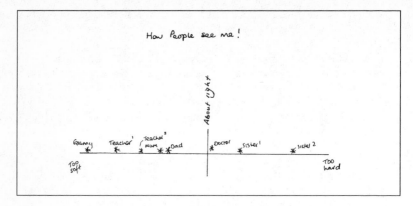

Figure 7.4 Louise's visual analogue scale.

body, and that she should assume she was well unless she felt (or medical tests indicated) something was wrong.

Concluding remarks

Getting to know children and exploring their worlds is perhaps the single most important aspect of the helping process and should therefore be an aim in itself. It involves all aspects of the behaviour of the helper in indicating respect and empathy for the child, but also involves specific skills of enabling children to communicate. A number of strategies are described here; for more details on therapeutic exploratory skills, please refer to Oaklander (1978). Exploring children's situations carefully and thoroughly not only enables the relationship between the helper and child to flourish, but also allows a clearer understanding to be gained. Such understanding, however, is not one-sided. It is not simply to enable the helper to understand the child; exploration as described here is very much a vehicle by which children's own understanding may be enhanced as a pre-requisite for empowering them to adapt and to help themselves.

Summary

❑ Getting to know children and exploring their experiences of events is perhaps the most important part of the process of helping.

❑ Exploration of the child's experience or problem is only possible when sufficient trust and openness have been established in the relationship between the child and helper.

❑ Exploration/assessment is a pre-requisite to enabling a shared understanding of the difficulty and required areas of change/help, and in implementing strategies for helping.

❑ Exploration is important in getting to know the child better and enabling the helper to put the child's difficulties into the context of his or her life circumstances generally.

❑ Exploration can in itself be of enormous value in facilitating change, by enabling developments in the child's understanding or perception of events.

❑ It also has important implications for the development of the relationship between the helper and child, enabling the child to realize that the helper is interested in her/him and not just their problem.

❑ Verbal prompts for facilitating exploration include open and closed questions, multiple choice responses, facilitative comments, such as empathic responses, and using questions which structure and therefore enable a more coherent and clear account to be given.

❑ The most frequently used verbal prompts are open questions, which enable the child to tell their story in their own words.

❑ Non-verbal modes of exploration include drawings, models/puppets and through play.

❑ More structured forms of exploration include the use of sentence/story completion tasks, books, diaries, rating scales and exploratory games.

8

Giving Information

In the last two chapters we considered the tasks of engaging children, establishing the basis for a working relationship and exploring the issues raised by them. At some point during this process, a decision needs to be made, preferably with the child, about what you aim to do together, before deciding how to meet these aims. One important aim will be to help the child acquire relevant information which enables a more helpful understanding of events and which may facilitate change or promote adaptation.

Information is central to preparing children for medical procedures, in order for them to develop realistic expectations and make sense of what is to happen. Being informed enables them to be actively involved in their own treatment, and to communicate their needs to others. Giving information is also one way of challenging or correcting misperceptions and inaccurate beliefs. In this chapter we shall consider some general issues which are important when giving information to children, and then extend this to consider the process and skills of communicating information about the diagnosis.

The Need for Information

Children acquire information from many different sources including other children and adults, either directly or as a result of overheard conversations. They learn from television, books, and from how they perceive other people, such as their parents, feel about the situation. It is clearly more helpful for them to receive important information in a planned and supported way. If information is not given, children will only be able to make sense of their situation by *ad hoc* information gathered in less structured ways, with less opportunities for worries or misperceptions to be addressed.

One 11-year-old child was very angry with her parents. She had been told that she was having X-ray treatment to get rid of a cyst. However, she could clearly read the 'Radiotherapy Department' sign in the hospital waiting room and knew a younger child who was on the ward and having radiotherapy as treatment for cancer. Following her own treatment, she continued to feel insecure, had terrible fears about cancer, and did not feel comfortable discussing these with her parents.

Children's imagination and fantasies about what is happening to them can be more frightening than reality. Giving them information in the most helpful and supportive way can go a long way to making the situation feel more manageable. It can help children make sense of experiences which are bewildering. It can reassure them that they are not mad, that there is a good reason why they are feeling the way they are, or experiencing the difficulties they are facing.

A teenager with a neuromuscular condition remembered being taken back and forth to the doctors for check-ups and investigations without ever understanding why. During his school years he became increasingly aware and fed up of how clumsy he was compared to other boys, how he was never picked for sports teams as his legs gave way when he ran. He also had painful memories of being frequently told off for his scruffy handwriting, no matter how hard he tried. It was not until he was nearly 12 years old when a doctor explained to him that he had a muscle wasting condition (Charcot Marie Tooth) that he was able to see himself as something other than lazy, clumsy or stupid.

Children need to feel they can trust the adults who are caring for them. Children with chronic illness or disability have long-term needs which are best met by having good relationships with staff. An important base for these relationships is trust, and this is dependent on honesty in the relationship, and in the information given. Children will certainly find it easier to trust those who have been honest with them. They can feel very angry and betrayed if they find out that information has been withheld from them, because they may feel that they have not been respected or taken seriously. They may fear that they will not be given important information in the future, and this can make them insecure and anxious.

In addition to good clinical practice which is sensitive to what children need, children have a right to information which concerns them and their bodies. They need this information to be able to be actively involved in their own care, in terms of making decisions and giving consent to treatment. This partnership approach between the child and health professionals will have important implications for long-term management and co-operation. In this relationship, health professionals are working with and for the child, rather than doing things to the child, making decisions for the child and mapping out the child's future according to how they themselves see it. With consideration to the child's developmental and cognitive maturity, the child is assumed to play an important part in the decisions made about treatment, and his or her views are respected and taken seriously.

Having considered a number of reasons for giving children information, it is important to acknowledge that parents or other adults may have very strong views about particular information being withheld from their children. This might include the seriousness of the diagnosis, for example, or that pain will be experienced. In most cases, the parents' views should be respected. However, many units, although respecting parents' wishes not to provide certain information, usually make it clear that they have a policy of being truthful, if they are asked a question directly. In certain instances doctors may even refuse to carry out procedures or tests if children have not been given adequate information, because preparation for a procedure or surgery, almost by definition, involves being honest about what it is going to happen.

Parents' reasons for withholding information are often to protect their children from distress. However, it is frequently the parents themselves who find the information intolerable and distressing, and in such cases they should be well-supported, and given enough time to think about the situation, to ask any questions, and to come to terms with the information to some extent. After disclosure of a serious diagnosis, for example, they should have time to compose themselves before moving on to discuss their child's informational needs. It is only when they have begun to adapt to the situation themselves that they will be in a position to support their child in receiving the information. At this point, it may be necessary to consider with them the benefits and costs for the child of either receiving this information or not, and most, with time and support recognize the importance of giving their child the information, although they may want to negotiate the timing of this.

General Principles for Giving Information

- Preparation and good communication between all those involved with the child are important. Everybody should be clear about who is taking responsibility for talking to the child, and all should be clear about what information is given, and should be consistent in all their communications. Children can be overwhelmed if information is provided by too many people, especially if it is presented differently or is conflicting. If the child has been told about a lump, it is important that everyone else refers to a lump and not a tumour, for example.

- Decisions about what information is most appropriate for the child should be reached by discussion between the parents and the medical team. In most cases it is appropriate for information to be given to the parents first, so that they can decide what their child should be told and the most supportive way of doing so.

- Information needs to be given as honestly as possible. The person talking to the child should be clear about what information is to be given, why, and what the response from the child is likely to be.

No easy ways exist for giving upsetting information, but evading or omitting it is not necessarily in the child's best interest.

- Basic information should be given as clearly and simply as possible, in terms which are familiar to the child and which match the child's level of knowledge. Subsequent information can be added dependent on the child's response, although the best strategy is to follow the child's lead in terms of answering all questions simply and therefore providing all the information he or she requires.

- Information can be given in many different ways. In addition to talking to children, one might use written information, simple diagrams, models and play situations. We shall explore these later in the chapter, but one needs to be creative in presenting complex information to children of a range of cognitive abilities or special needs.

- For situations where communication is difficult, as with children who cannot hear or speak, one might use, for example, communication boards or computers, or involve adults who are more used to the child's communications.

- Professional interpreters should be used when passing on important information to children and families who are not fluent in English. It is not sufficient to rely on other family members, especially children, to translate. Apart from the emotional burden this places on them, they will only be able to translate information they have grasped themselves, and this may be quite limited. It may also be difficult to know exactly what the child has understood and been able to translate.

- Good communication about what information has been given is also important. It might be useful, for example, to write in the medical notes what the child has been told. If the child is resident in hospital and is given information by one of the doctors, it is good practice for one of the nursing staff to be present. Nurses are likely to be approached to answer questions to clarify or confirm what has already been said. They will also need to inform others caring for the child about what was said.

Information Giving as a Process

Giving information is not a single simple event. It can be seen as a sequence of stages or tasks which are similar to the stages of helping we have already identified. These involve:

1. The fundamental skills and qualities of the helper in engaging the

child and the child's parents, so that an effective working relationship can be developed. Communicating effectively with them is dependent upon this, and has been discussed in previous chapters.

2. Exploration of children's needs or wishes for information, to discover what they already know, what would be helpful for them to know, and what they would like to know.

3. A negotiation with both the child and the child's carers regarding what information will be given, how and by whom.

4. Presentation of the information in a meaningful way, taking into account the developmental characteristics of the child.

5. Monitoring the impact and effectiveness of the information, in order to determine whether it has been understood and retained, and what it has meant to the child.

6. If there is a miscommunication or the child has not grasped the main points, then this can be remedied as necessary, by repeating the information, giving it in a different way, or explaining further.

7. Updating and revising information as necessary over time to meet the changing needs of the child.

Exploration of information needs and wishes

It is likely that children and helpers will be starting from very different knowledge bases when they first meet. For the helper to communicate meaningfully, both an understanding of how children acquire new information and a clear understanding of the knowledge held by the child are required. The first step in the process of imparting information is therefore to determine what the child already knows. As Davis (1993) says, it is impossible to give directions to someone for a journey, when you do not know the starting point.

The child is rarely coming from a position of *total* ignorance of a subject, and is likely to have some information, beliefs or thoughts, however accurate or helpful. To help children acquire information, we need to determine what is already known and build on this, rather than underestimate the child's knowledge or wildly miss the mark by giving them information which they do not want or which is beyond their reach.

A well-meaning doctor spent considerable time explaining intricate details of surgery to a young boy, who on questioning afterwards had understood very little. The boy had not heard of many of the body parts which had been mentioned by the doctor and held to his view that the doctor was going to mend a little hole in his tummy!

Establishing current knowledge and perceptions can also enable any misperceptions or omissions to be identified and constructive information given in its place. It would be of little benefit to give children elaborate, detailed information, if they had fundamental misconstructions of the basic information. In this situation, any new information would probably not make sense to them. Misperceptions can occur at any age, and are more likely if the child is anxious or has only partly understood something, as in the following example:

Simon was due to start radiotherapy for a tumour, following a recurrence of an earlier tumour that had been surgically removed. His doctor had talked to him about the radiotherapy, but Simon had appeared quite disinterested and had not asked further questions about it. His key nurse had noted that he was becoming more withdrawn as the radiotherapy approached, and suggested that they talk about what was going to happen, asking what he thought radiotherapy would be like and what it would do.

It transpired from this exploratory conversation, that Simon believed he would be paralysed as a result of the radiotherapy. This was not a realistic worry, but a misconstruction derived from a heated discussion Simon had overheard the previous year between his father and the surgeon. Simon's father had been dismayed at the loss of movement in Simon's legs following surgery. When further treatment had been recommended in the form of radiotherapy, he had responded angrily by saying that they had already half-paralysed his son with surgery, and that he was not going to let them 'finish off the job' with radiotherapy.

Although Simon's father had changed his view following further discussions with the doctor, this overheard comment formed the basis of Simon's understanding of what was going to happen to him. Merely giving information without exploring and addressing his beliefs would have been unlikely to allay his fears.

Exploration of children's knowledge can also challenge any incorrect assumptions the helper has already made about the child. It is possible, for example, to make erroneous assumptions about what knowledge a child has regarding their condition or treatment, either based on their age or how often they attend clinic or hospital. There is a myth that children who are regularly in hospital have already heard, seen or experienced everything and so will not need any further information.

David, a 13-year-old, received a successful kidney transplant when he was nine years of age, having been on dialysis for a number of years. Although his health was excellent, he remained very anxious at all his check-up appointments at the clinic. He was worried that if he had not taken good enough care of himself, he might lose his kidney and people would be cross with him. He believed that if he lost his kidney it would be his fault and he would go to the bottom of the list for children on call for a kidney. His theory was that the first kidney was found quickly, but if you were careless and lost it, you went to the bottom of the queue and could wait for ages for another.

In discussion with David, it was discovered that he had a rather limited understanding both of how kidneys might fail and the process of going on call for a new kidney. His rather punitive beliefs came as quite a surprise to the medical team who had cared for him for many years, and believed him to be quite knowledgeable.

Children who have been around a medical setting for any length of time may be very adept at using the correct medical terminology about their condition or treatment, without having any real knowledge of it. Not surprisingly, as in the example of David, this can lead to misleading assumptions being made by professionals. One child with a kidney transplant confidently talked of his creatinine levels (creatinine is a waste product used as a measure of kidney function and is obtained through blood analysis). However, when pressed for more information, he reported that doctors know the level by how red the blood is or by how many creatinine are present. He imagined creatinine as being greeny-brown spherical objects that float in the body!

Care should be taken that children are not just repeating back verbatim what they have been told by a parent or doctor without properly understanding it.

A young boy confidently said that he had severed T5 and T6 on his spine. On further questioning, he could not explain what this meant. His lack of understanding that these were in fact vertebrae, was revealed by the comment that he was relieved he had not broken his back, which he was aware his parents most feared. His misconstruction was in fact shared in this case by his parents, who had themselves not understood the terms used.

Similarly, it is important to explore children's explanations of terms or procedures, rather than to make assumptions. For example, although a group of children were all able to describe the practical steps involved in using a catheter and to report that the reason was to take away the urine from their bladder, more careful exploration involved asking what would happen if they did not use the catheter. Some of the group suggested they would get tummy ache and die, some said their veins would fill up with water and they would burst like a balloon, and others said they would wet themselves. Very few children understood that one of the most important consequences would be the risk of infection or kidney damage.

Careful exploration is also required of the child's wishes for information. They have the right *not* to know something, if they wish. It is important not to assume that they actually want to know, to be sensitive to any communications about this, and to explore this issue carefully. Some children will just tell you that it is all boring, and indicate they want to talk about or do something else. Others may avoid eye contact and appear to be disengaged. It may be important to comment on what you see and admit that you are not sure how much they actually want to know of the information you were able to give them. However, when children are showing no interest in what is happening to them, this implies that their natural curiosity has been overwhelmed by anxiety. In this situation, it is inappropriate to impose explanations on them, but better to attempt to deal with the underlying anxiety.

Giving information effectively

Once it has been established what children already know or understand, their need for information may be apparent. Misperceptions or omissions may be obvious, or the adults may be aware that other information would enable the child to cope better with future events. Considerable skill is then required to provide this information effectively. Factors which need to be considered in presenting information include: the pacing of information, using terms and language which are familiar to the child, structuring and breaking down complex information into manageable components, and, finally, being creative in using a variety of modes of presentation, verbal, visual, or structured play sessions. All these will of course be dependent upon the children in terms of what is meaningful and accessible for them.

Pacing. It is important to give information at a pace which suits the child. It may not be possible or appropriate to give all the information at once. Young children and those less able cognitively may be limited in how much information they can take in at one time and may take longer to assimilate information. If children are anxious or preoccupied they are likely to take in even less. Consequently, plenty of time needs to be made available, possibly over a number of sessions, for this important task.

Language and terminology. It is helpful to use words with which the child is familiar and to avoid using technical terms or jargon. Children will construct their own meaning of any words which are unfamiliar to them.

Matthew, aged four years, was about to be taken off his drip when the nurse explained that she was just going to use her forceps. Matthew became very distressed and pleaded with the nurse not to 'force it'.

Similarly, terms that are easily taken for granted by adults can be taken literally by children, and can become very frightening.

One young girl facing cardiac surgery was particularly anxious about blood tests, as she had heard the doctors say that she had poor veins which kept collapsing whenever they tried to take blood. She had heard that people could collapse and die from a heart attack and deduced that she could die from the blood test if her veins collapsed.

It is worth noting that much of the medical language that is used is suggestive of warfare. We talk of aggressive treatment or an aggressive tumour, invading organisms, or cells being destroyed. Children will make their own interpretations of these descriptions, and it is interesting to speculate what these might be!

Information which makes comparisons with familiar objects or events can facilitate better understanding. For example, a child who is struggling to learn a particular technique might be reminded of when they learned to swim or ride a bike. A child who is anxious about a new piece of equipment such as a neck brace or leg splint feeling strange, can be reminded of how a new pair of trainers or shoes can feel strange and need to be worn in a little. The experience of *petit mal* attacks in epilepsy may be likened to a brief break in programme transmission on the radio or television. After a brief 'blip', the programme (or world) carries on as usual, but a few seconds have been missed. A child with PKU (a metabolic disorder requiring a special diet) was helped to understand the necessity of his dietary requirements by likening his body to that of a car engine needing the 'special deluxe' type of petrol to run properly. Using everyday petrol would eventually harm the engine by clogging up the parts and not let it function so effectively.

Children may be able to come up with their own examples. One child explained the body's rejection of a transplanted organ as being like a 'new kid in school'; nobody knows or trusts him and because they want to get rid of him, the 'big boy' gangs come over and beat him up! The same child described being on call as a bingo game; if your number comes up, you get the kidney!

Structuring information. Information needs to be presented clearly and structured well. This necessitates being very clear about the aims of the information and what basic knowledge or understanding you wish the child to acquire as a result. It is helpful to start by making a short statement including the term or name to be used. For example, 'We want to take some pictures of your head using a PET scan, which is a special sort of camera'. This opening statement should not introduce other terms or unfamiliar words if possible. After a brief pause, a simple explanation or the next step should be outlined. 'This involves you lying very still while the PET scanner takes lots of pictures'. If the child does not react, then it might be helpful to prompt the child in order to obtain feedback on what has been understood, and to respond accordingly.

Plenty of opportunity should be allowed for the child to comment or ask questions, and there should be frequent checks by the helper throughout the meeting on the child's understanding of the information. In some instances, following initial information, any further information may be given totally in response to the child's questions or comments.

Other ways of giving information

Using books. There are many excellent books which can be useful both for giving children practical information about a condition or treatment, and for naming emotional responses to this information and facilitating discussion about this with the child. As with most books, there should be an opportunity to discuss the material with the child to check their understanding and to make oneself available to answer any questions raised. One cannot assume that children will make sense of everything they see or read, as in the following example.

One young boy was being shown a photograph booklet of children having a similar surgical procedure to himself, and then playing happily afterwards on the ward. This was intended to allay his fears of surgery. However, in discussing these photographs, he revealed extreme fear and distress over an 'instrument' he noticed in one picture. He was frightened about it and implied that it might be used for painful treatment. It was, in fact, a picture of a children's game and its accessories.

A bibliography of useful children's books is given in *Appendix B*. Some tell a story of a child or animal with a particular condition or experience, while others are more factual, but present this information in a child orientated way, such as in a comic format. Many organizations and societies produce their own pamphlets for families, with some specifically written for children. The addresses for these organizations can be obtained from the support organization Contact-a-Family (see *Appendix C*).

In general, the most useful books are those which are attractive and engaging for children, with photographs or colourful pictures and accessible storylines. Older children may be more able to relate to stories where the child or central character has particular difficulties and then demonstrates strategies for coping with and managing them. This is better than stories in which the character sails through without a worry or problem, since this does not reflect the children's real situation.

Photograph books are particularly useful, and can be tailored to the individual setting in which they will be used. In many hospitals and clinics, play specialists have produced their own information booklets using photographs of children who have already been through the procedure, ending on a positive picture of the child after the event is finished (that is, leaving hospital or completing the test).

Children can also be encouraged to make up their own books which can be used as a means of self-exploration and discovery for the child and a useful resource in explaining their condition to others. One girl was able to list a number of questions she had, and used these to supply her with the information she wanted to put in her book. These questions included: Where did my tumour come from? Why didn't you take it all out in surgery? What happens if it grows back again? Using the book, she felt confident to ask her doctor these questions.

Using drawings. The lesser known use of paper hand towels in hospital is for doing impromptu drawings on in order to explain information to children and their families! Many children have treasured the drawings they have been given for some time afterwards!

Drawings are familiar and non-threatening ways of giving information to children. They are also concrete pieces of information that children are able to take away with them. If explanations have been talked through step-by-step, using a diagram for example, referring back to this can help children to remember what they have been told.

Drawings should be simple, clear and well-labelled if this is appropriate. They enable the child to visualize the mechanics of what is happening, when words fail to conjure up meaningful pictures. Trying to visualize internal organs or bodily action is very difficult without this.

Play. A very good way of providing certain information is by giving demonstrations on dolls or models. This has the advantage of showing children the instruments to be used, and also what they do and how they are used. We will look at this in *Chapter 9* when we consider the process of preparing children for medical procedures.

Using videotapes. Videotapes which are tailored to the developmental abilities of the child, and which are meaningful in terms of the specific unit or hospital can be very useful indeed. However, considerable care needs to be taken in their production, taking into account all the general principles considered in this chapter. It is important, for example, that they do not present too much information or information that is too complex or not relevant to the child. One boy became very anxious when watching a film about the treatment for leukaemia. Although it explained what leukaemia was and how it was treated, it was over-inclusive and left him believing he was going to have to endure all the many tests and treatment options the film presented.

Monitoring impact and effectiveness

For information to be useful, it needs to have been understood and remembered by the child. It is, therefore, important to convey the principle that you are prepared to repeat information and that the child should feel free to ask questions at any time. Questions you may wish to use to prompt the child's comments or questions might be:

'Was there anything I said which you were surprised or puzzled by?'

'In thinking about what we have discussed, what do you consider was the most important part from your point of view?'

Quite often children find it difficult to ask questions straight away, but may be more able to do so after they have thought about the information or discussed it with someone else. You might suggest, therefore, that the child (and parent) have a few moments to think about the information together in a given session and then ask questions, or that they go away and think about it and return for another session to discuss it further.

The need to check what children have understood cannot be stressed enough. Simply asking if they have understood is usually insufficient, as children (just like adults) will often nod or say 'Yes', as it is too embarrassing to say 'No'. One direct way of checking is simply to ask them to explain back to you what you have just told them. This can feel quite testing, however, and a more subtle way is to ask them how they might tell their teacher, best friend or a family member about it.

Updating information

There is a tendency to neglect the changing information needs of children. The assumption is often made that once information has been explained, there is no need to go through it again later, as the child already 'knows'. In reality, the capacity for taking in more detailed information will increase with cognitive maturity, and the child's needs for information will also change. For example, a seven-year-old child might be most concerned with the way her condition restricts her from running around as fast as other girls. This same child at 13 might be more concerned about whether she will develop breasts or start her periods like her friends. Later in adolescence she may be preoccupied with whether she will be able to have children.

Providing opportunities for children's knowledge to be updated requires taking account of both the questions they raise themselves, but also areas which the helper feels might be appropriate. Young people will find it difficult, if not impossible, to raise personal issues regarding sexual development, for example, in a standard out-patient appointment. It may be appropriate, therefore, to use open questions to explore any additional informational needs the child may have. For example, you might say that there are many different questions that young people think/worry about and then enquire whether this is true for them. You may even wish to introduce a particular topic, saying that people of their age often have worries about keeping up with exam courses, dating, or starting periods, and you wondered if that was something they might like to talk about, either now or in the future.

Communicating about the Diagnosis and Treatment

Perhaps the most important (and certainly the most emotive) area of information giving is in the initial communication of the condition. However, there may be more than one occasion when important and sometimes very distressing news needs to be given. This includes the initial diagnosis, information about treatment or management options, the news that treatment has not been successful, or that further treatment (or no treatment) is now an option.

In recent years considerable attention has been given to ways of communicating the diagnosis to adults, and the effects this has in terms of their future adaptation (Davis, 1993; Ley, 1988; Buckman, 1992). However, very little attention has been given to this area in children. This is probably because historically children have been told very little, mainly in an effort to protect them, or because people have not been sure what, if anything, children should be told, and how this should be done. We will first turn our attention to talking to parents, as in many cases they will either be given the information first, or will play a central role in deciding what information is given to their children.

Talking to parents

It is often most appropriate that parents are put in control of the situation by being informed first, without their child being present. This enables them to have time to assimilate the information and plan how best to support their child in receiving the news. More often, however, parents are together with their child and need to leave the child on the ward or in a waiting room when they have their discussion with the doctor.

If the parents and child are to be separated at this key time for the doctor to talk to the parents alone, careful thought needs to be given to the message this communicates to children. Even quite young children who would normally be relieved to leave the room and play, rather than listen to adults talking, may pick up the gravity of the situation and the anxiety and distress in their parents. As a result, they may be unwilling to leave, placing demands for attention on their parents, or will be distressed and restless outside of the room.

Older children may also feel extremely anxious if they realize their parents are talking to the doctor and that they are not allowed to be present. Many children who have spoken about being excluded in this way admit to thinking the very worst, which is that they are going to die, but that no one will tell them. As a result, it can take considerable time to rebuild children's confidence in the doctor and in their parents. The following is a 15-year-old girl's account of how she remembered being given her diagnosis:

Following what seemed an eternity of waiting, Karen's parents were taken into a separate room by the consultant, for another eternity. Her father returned with the doctor to talk to her about the plans for treatment. Karen could see her father was pale and it looked like he had been crying. She wanted to see her mother, but was told that her mother was 'busy' and had popped out for a while. Karen wanted to scream out and demand to know what they had talked about without her, her unspoken fear being they had said she was going to die. Instead she was very quiet, she did not question anything and nodded that she understood the reasons for treatment. She was told that she was being very good and brave and that everything would be alright. Karen described this as one of the most frightening parts of her whole treatment.

There is no perfect solution to this situation. However, if the parents and child are to be separated, it is helpful to explain this to the child, saying this is how you normally do things, giving a rough idea of how long you will be and a clear indication of when you will come back and what will happen. It is certainly good practice for someone to be allocated to care for the child during the doctor's interview with the parents, regardless of his or her age. The carer's role might be to prepare the child a little for the interview to come, by starting to build a relationship with her or him in order to provide better support when she or he is given the information. At the very least, the carer will act as a companion, acknowledging that the child may feel anxious about what is happening but that he or she will find out soon.

Negotiations with parents

The process of communicating the diagnosis to parents has been described in detail by Davis (1993) and Lloyd and Bor (1996). On being given distressing news about their children, parents are likely to feel shocked, numb and/or confused initially. Very quickly, however, a range of extreme emotions may be felt and expressed. Parents may be angry, desperately upset and worried, and extremely protective of their child. Many parents have talked of just wanting to wrap their child in cotton wool or run away with them at this time to protect them from what is to come. It is difficult, at least initially, for parents to think as calmly and objectively as they would wish about informing their child. Nevertheless, parents are often most concerned about what they are going to say to her or him, or how to tell their other children.

We have talked earlier about working in partnership with parents to care for their children. Here, particularly, close support and working with the parents are essential. The task is to decide how best to communicate with the child, and the final decision about this must rest with the parents. They know their children better than anyone and will be able to give important information about what they already know or fear. They may also be in the best position to say how their children are likely to receive the news, what the most upsetting aspects might be, or which parts they may be able to take in their stride. They will also know the most supportive way for their child to be told.

Although healthcare workers may not have direct knowledge of the child, nevertheless, they will have experience of other children who have been given information about their condition or treatment. They can, therefore, use this knowledge to help parents decide how best to inform their child. By pooling their expertise, the health care worker and parents together are in the best position to make decisions about what information should be given, when, where and by whom. The possibilities to be explored include the parents telling the child themselves, with or without the doctor being present to give support or confirmation of the information. One mother felt she wanted to tell her daughter at home and at a time when her daughter could phone a best friend to talk. Another parent told his child in the clinic knowing his son would talk about it more easily during the car journey home. Other parents may wish their initial discussion with their child to be followed up with a joint meeting with the doctor to affirm particular points or give more specific information. Other possibilities are for the paediatrician or other healthcare worker to give the information with or without the parents being present.

Telling the children

Following the decisions discussed, the same principles and steps will apply for whoever gives the information. Good preparation is essential; the person should be clear about what they want to say and what words they will use. Whatever else, they should attempt to establish what the child already knows, thinks or feels, before giving this essential information. They may be able to anticipate likely questions and reactions from the child, but they should certainly follow the child's lead after the initial disclosure.

Naturally some information may provoke intense distress in the child, and so it is important for parents and professionals to have had an opportunity to think through how they will best care for their child at this time. Certainly, plenty of time needs to be given; children should be allowed to show their feelings openly and to be comforted appropriately by touching or holding if necessary. What one does here is to support the child and accept the feelings, but not try to stop them or take them away. It is important to respect her or his feelings and to listen carefully to what he or she says, responding honestly and calmly.

One should not try to communicate new information while the child is crying, but wait until he or she is more composed. It may be of course that this does not occur very quickly. In which case, one must either be patient or stop the session with care and pick up the issues as soon as possible at a subsequent time. Clearly this is much simpler to arrange if it is the parents who have decided to communicate the diagnosis or news.

If possible, the session should end with a clear indication of what is to happen next. This might include arranging the next appointment, but should involve information about the next treatment steps and who is to be involved. Whatever else it should involve a time to consider the implications of the news and answer any of the child's questions. It may be helpful, for example, to suggest that the parents and child develop a list of questions to be brought to the next session with the professional.

Informing parent and child together

For conditions which are diagnosed or occur later in life, it may be that the parent and child are in a position to be told the information at roughly the same time. This decision may depend on professional style, the information being conveyed, and the age of the child. However, the most important determinant is the expressed wish of the family. It is for the parents to decide how they want to hear the diagnosis, for example, and whether they would like the child to be there.

If this option is taken and the child and parents are seen together, it is important to ensure that explanations are at an appropriate level for the child, who should be engaged as much as possible in the discussion. The parents will be in a good position to see how the child is taking in the information and will be able to pick up important issues and discuss these with the child later.

The needs of all other members of the family must not be forgotten and it may be that it is the parents' responsibility to inform them. However, the professionals might offer to help the parents with this process. If this happens, then the principles, processes and skills described throughout this chapter should apply, whether talking to siblings, for example, or grandparents. It is important to consider the informational needs of *all* close family members, and not exclude them from opportunities to gain information. In many situations this can help family members feel more involved and enable them to be more supportive, rather than questioning or undermining what the child and family are saying about the condition.

Information Giving and Consent

Consent involves:

1. being comprehensively informed by someone competent to do so;
2. being sufficiently cognitively and emotionally able to understand this information;
3. being able to make a decision based upon this information.

The process of information giving is therefore a crucial aspect of consent both in terms of presenting appropriate information and in clarifying the child's understanding and expectations based on this. It is a negotiation and decision reached with the medical team and parents over what role and responsibility it is appropriate to give the child. There is wide variation in children's cognitive abilities and understanding, including, most importantly, their ability to contemplate the future (and future implications of their treatment) as well as their emotional maturity.

There is considerable debate as to whether children can be expected to be competent to give consent to surgery or treatment. The current legal position in the UK is that children are able to consent to having treatment, but they have no legal rights to refuse treatment. Child care legislation talks about listening to and respecting the child's wishes. However, for these wishes to be acted upon, they need to be considered by *adults* to be in the child's best interest. The area is very complex, as it is difficult to reach agreement on when it is possible to demarcate when children can understand the full implications of the consent they give or withhold. For that matter, how many adults are truly giving informed consent to their surgical or medical treatments?

In the midst of the debate over consent, there has been less attention paid to the process of involving children in their treatment. Consent is not something which should be bestowed on a child simply as a virtue of age or intelligence; all children should be made to feel involved in their care, part of informed discussions and part of the decision making process throughout. Please refer to Alderson's book *Children's Consent to Surgery* (Alderson, 1993) for a comprehensive discussion of this topic.

Summary

❑ Helping children acquire relevant information which enables a more helpful understanding of events can be one way of facilitating change and promoting adaptation.

❑ Children have a right to know information which concerns them and their body.

❑ Children also have a right *not* to know information they choose not to know.

❑ Information about their condition and treatment is helpful to make sense of what is happening and to challenge any misperceptions in understanding.

❑ Information is necessary for children to prepare for future events, and to be actively involved in aspects of their treatment such as decision making, consent and co-operation with treatment.

❑ Misperceptions and inaccuracies are common, particularly if children are reliant on *ad hoc* sources of information. Children's imagination and fantasies about what may be happening to them can be far more frightening than reality.

❑ Important principles to consider when preparing to give children information is for agreement about what information will be given and by whom, and for clarity and consistency of information to be achieved.

❑ Information should always be given clearly, simply and concisely and in the most honest and reassuring way possible.

❑ Creative ways of presenting more complex information including the provision of written information, using diagrams, models or videos and through play situations can help make this information more easily accessible.

❑ The use of professional interpreters is stressed when passing on important information to children and families who are not fluent in English. Children should not be expected to interpret for their families.

continued

continued ---

❑ Information giving can be seen as a highly skilful process with a sequence of stages or tasks. The first stage involves the skills and qualities of the helper in engaging the child and developing an effective working relationship. Subsequent stages involve exploration of current knowledge and of the child's needs and wishes for information.

❑ Giving information effectively involves consideration of the following factors: awareness of the child's emotional state and cognitive abilities, appropriate pacing of information, the language and terminology used and structuring the information systematically and clearly.

❑ Information should be given in the most accessible and meaningful way, taking into account the developmental capabilities of the child, ensuring that one follows the child's lead, checks for understanding and enables him or her to ask questions as necessary.

❑ It is important to provide opportunities for information to be repeated as necessary, with regular monitoring/checking that information has been understood and retained by children.

❑ Information needs to be updated to meet the changing information needs of the child.

❑ Information about the implication of any condition or treatment can be very distressing for the child. Good preparation both of the way information is given and the support offered to the child is very important.

❑ Generally a discussion with parents will precede information about the diagnosis or treatment being given to the child, and agreement reached with the parent as to the best way of supporting the child receiving this information.

❑ The information needs of all members of the family need to be addressed in a similar way.

❑ Good information giving skills are essential in working towards obtaining informed consent from children.

9

Specific Strategies for Helping

In the last chapter, we discussed the skills of giving information to children as a means of facilitating their adaptation. We also looked at the important area of disclosing the diagnosis or other news that might be distressing. In this chapter we would like to extend the application of these skills in supporting and helping children manage experiences which may be perceived as unfamiliar, painful, frightening or distressing. We will look specifically at preparation which enables children to develop strategies for coping with medical procedures, pain management, treatment adherence, and supporting children during transitions, including moving from paediatric to adult clinics and returning to school after a long absence.

Preparation for Medical/Surgical Procedures

General issues

Good preparation can help children organize thoughts, actions and feelings about an event, prior to it happening. It enables mental rehearsal (the 'work of worrying') to occur. This can enhance children's (and parents') sense of control of situations in which they often feel helpless, by mobilizing coping strategies and raising self-esteem. Most children benefit from appropriate preparation, which has been found to reduce both pre- and post-surgical distress, anxiety and pain (Melamed and Siegal, 1975). It enables them to cope more effectively with medical procedures and reduces the amount of pain relief they require. Even very fearful children are thought to be calmer before surgery if preparation has taken place (Peterson, 1989).

Preparation should be part of the routine care of children and families. However, the value of preparation is frequently underestimated and in busy clinics and wards, with severe time constraints on all staff, preparation is often neglected or inadequate. Sometimes, parents actively block preparation, feeling that the less the child knows, the less anxious he or she will be. Sometimes it is the child who will not co-operate with preparation, or simply does not wish to know what is going to happen, as this is her or his style of coping. In these situations, preparation is more difficult, but no less important.

The value of preparation needs to be considered in terms of short and long term benefits. For example, children who are poorly prepared and become very stressed and traumatized during a procedure may also become sensitized, and thereafter suffer increased anxiety levels whenever there is a need for further treatment. Children who experience repeated treatments or procedures, or who have experienced procedures at an early age, are particularly vulnerable in this respect.

Sometimes children's distress is not immediately evident to the medical team, even during a particular procedure. Children who are very passive or quiet and do not make a fuss may be just as terrified and traumatized by what is happening to them as those children who are able to verbalize or demonstrate their distress. They may have difficulties co-operating when further tests or treatment are required at a later point.

Good preparation requires:

- Preparation of the parents, as they may be the best source of support or information for the child. This is particularly true for young children who are difficult to prepare directly. Parents who are well-prepared and more relaxed will be able to support the child better.

- Sufficient time to carry out the most useful preparation with the child. This includes time for engaging and building a relationship with the child, careful exploration of what the child already knows, fears, needs and wants to know, and the presentation of new material in the most supportive, reassuring, meaningful and honest way possible.

- Taking account of the developmental and emotional capacities of the child, in terms of what, how and when information is given.

- Taking account of the child's previous experiences, and using these in the most positive way possible.

- Understanding the aspects of any procedure which are likely to distress children. Even procedures which are not painful can be distressing, particularly if the equipment is large and noisy (such as MRI or PET scanning machines) or the procedure is invasive (for example, tubes inserted into the bladder for urodynamic studies). For younger children, procedures involving being separated from parents may be particularly distressing (for example, radiotherapy). However, for any children, the actual test may be less anxiety-provoking than the expected results from the test.

- Giving children appropriate information, verbally or non-verbally.

This may involve information about the sights, sensations, or sequence of events likely to be experienced.

- Information to be given honestly, and framed in the most positive and reassuring way possible.

- Active participation of the child during preparation stages; for example, carrying out particular tasks (such as visiting and familiarizing themselves with the ward or clinic in which they will receive treatment) and learning skills or strategies for managing the procedure (for example, relaxation or distraction exercises).

- Planning and rehearsal of strategies which may be helpful.

- Praising and giving positive reinforcement to children about the skills and strategies they are practising or are already proficient at using.

When to prepare

Timing of preparation may need to take into account the child's age, emotional state and previous experiences of the event. It will also depend on what depth of preparation is aimed for and what is hoped to be gained by preparation. Generally, preparation should start well in advance of the event to enable sufficient time for children to assimilate information, clarify areas of uncertainty and mobilize coping resources. However, younger children will benefit more from preparation which is close in time to the event. They do not have a good concept of time and might be on a permanent state of alert and anxiety waiting for the event to happen if prepared too early. Just think how difficult it is for children to wait five minutes, let alone a few weeks! Timing needs to be related to concrete events for younger children to make sense of the information, for example, after dinner, or after three sleeps. Similarly, children who are very anxious may benefit from not being prepared too early.

It is helpful to negotiate with children as to how much notice they require whenever possible. It is also helpful to consider preparation as a process of giving some general information early on and building on this to cover specific areas in more detail as appropriate.

Using previous experience positively

If children have already experienced a similar procedure, it is useful to explore their memories and perceptions of the event, to build on the positive aspects, and to discuss carefully the parts they found distressing or difficult. Care needs to be taken that any preparation does not sensitize them to what is going to happen and increases their anxiety levels. It may be valuable to help them distinguish the aspects which they might control and change and how they might go about this.

Emma, aged 14 years, was told that she needed further surgery to remove another tumour from her brain. She was deeply shocked and upset, and remembered only negative and frightening thoughts about the previous surgery seven years before. One of her fears was of losing her hair, an event for which she had evidently not been prepared last time. In discussing the operation, the surgeon was able to acknowledge how important her hair and looks were for her. As a consequence, not only did he know that she wanted as little hair shaved as possible, he was able to agree with her exactly how much would be removed, and that this should be done when she was awake.

Judy had a distressing experience during a lumbar puncture, when although sedated, she woke up and moved. Her memory was of a number of unfamiliar adults holding her down tightly while the doctor completed the procedure. She said that she did not mind the sedation, felt no pain from the lumbar puncture and actually felt very well after the lumbar puncture itself as it greatly relieved her headache. The only distressing aspect was being held down and not knowing who was in the room. After careful negotiation with her doctor, the level of sedation required was agreed, as was the number of people who would be present. Judy and her doctor wrote out their agreement and put a copy in the medical notes. This was helpful in reinforcing the aspects of the procedure which she had managed, as well as agreeing a plan to change the parts that she had not. This discussion and plan enabled Judy to feel much more in control and calmer when she needed another lumbar puncture.

Those aspects which cannot be changed may be made better by carrying out particular strategies such as relaxation or distraction exercises. When children are particularly fearful and negative about the previous procedure, the helper can suggest some positive points, including the fact that the child did get through it, and that it only lasted a specific period of time. Additionally, the adult might mention something helpful the child did, such as keeping still, or something enjoyable that happened afterwards, such as going to McDonalds.

General preparation strategies

Although it may be of value just to talk children through a procedure, the use of visual or more concrete methods of preparation is likely to make the whole event much more meaningful. Having access to actual materials or equipment children will see or experience during the procedure is particularly useful. Allowing them to handle equipment makes it more familiar and less frightening, especially if it can be incorporated into imaginative and creative play situations. It is possible, for example, to create pictures using syringes full of paint, to make plaster casts for dolls and to paint masks used in radiotherapy. It is not unknown for syringes to be used for showering unsuspecting nurses or doctors with water!

In some wards, children are encouraged to form a relationship with a particular toy on which all the preparation occurs. They are given a teddy or doll on admission to look after for the duration of their stay – a responsibility that many children take very seriously indeed! The doll or teddy then experiences all the same procedures as the child, with each being demonstrated on the doll first, along with the appropriate drips and bandages the child will require.

Rachel, a four-year-old, required a portacath for intravenous chemotherapy. This is a device inserted under the skin which enables long-term intravenous access. She was prepared for it using a teddy who also had a portacath, so that Rachel could see where on her body it was going to be placed. The teddy, helped by the play specialist, talked to Rachel and was able to reassure her that the portacath would not stop her from playing or having fun. He told her that it was like a special friend who would be given special drinks of medicine to help her get better. Because of this, Rachel called her portacath Jenny, and all the nurses referred to the chemotherapy as Jenny needing her next drink. Rachel joined in the play by telling Jenny what a good girl she was after each drink!

The use of preparation booklets, including stories of children undergoing similar procedures, or a set of photographs depicting what is going to happen can also be very helpful. (Suggestions for appropriate books and their use are given in *Appendix B*.) Some of these can be read by children themselves whilst others are more suitable to be read by parents or helpers to or with children. Either way, there should be plenty of opportunity for discussion of issues or questions raised by the children.

Visual demonstrations can be particularly striking. In preparing a group of children who were on call awaiting organ transplants, the surgeon first put on his gown and then gradually put on the rest of his theatre clothes. As he did so, he described what was involved, and eventually showed them exactly how he would look when they came to theatre. This proved very useful, as although these children had experienced surgery before, they had all admitted to being alarmed when they did not recognize the surgeon in theatre as the person who had talked to them previously on the ward. One unforeseen benefit of this discussion was that the surgeon changed his practice, and removed his face mask when greeting the children in theatre, so that they could recognize him more easily.

Actually taking the child to see the clinic room or theatre, or seeing another child having a procedure, can also be an excellent way of preparation, but only after this has been carefully negotiated with both children and families. One must also be sure the child to be observed feels comfortable with the procedure and will be a helpful role model.

Preparation for coming into hospital

All the strategies already discussed may be used for preparation for admission. The event and surrounding processes should be described and discussed whenever children wish. Books may be used, relevant television programmes discussed, and specially prepared videotapes may be available from the hospitals themselves or from relevant support organizations. A number of hospitals organize structured pre-admission visits, but even if they do not, it may be possible to arrange a visit to the ward or clinic in advance as a way of preparing both the child and family. In some cases, an outreach or liaison nurse might visit the family home prior to the admission in order to meet the child and answer any questions about the hospital stay.

Preparation immediately before admission might involve younger children in helping to pack their suitcase or choosing particular toys or clothing to take into hospital with them. They might also be involved in making up their bed ready for their return from hospital, as a very concrete sign that they will be coming home again from hospital. Older children can also prepare by informing friends or teachers about their hospital admission, giving them a contact number and address, and possibly even asking for school books or work to take with them.

Pre-procedure preparation

Information about the surgery and what it will be like after the procedure is vital. One must be sensitive both to the likely anxieties a child may have, and to anxieties actually expressed by the child or parents. Young children may be particularly fearful of separations from their parents. Other common fears include being in pain, waking up during operations, or not waking up after the anaesthetic. Certain fears may be specific to one child or related to the particular procedure. For example, one young girl worried that the surgeon would not be able to stretch her skin sufficiently to sew her back together again after putting in a new kidney. One Muslim child was anxious that he might not be allowed to take the pre-medication, as he was told it would make him sleepy and assumed from this that it contained alcohol, which he was not permitted. Another young person, preparing for surgery on her chest, disclosed her fear of the surgeon cutting off her breasts.

For young children, preparation which focuses on sensory information (what is seen, heard, smelt or felt) is most helpful. This should include: who will be present (for example, Nurse Claire with the big smile, Dr. Jo who has the koala bear in her pocket, and Mum); what the equipment will look like and how it will sound, smell or feel. One child was told for example, 'You will sit on a comfy chair with Mummy and wear a special mask which might smell a little like pink candy floss and will make you feel a bit sleepy'. For older children, preparation which includes both sensory information and procedural information (the steps involved in the process and what the child is expected to do) has been found to be most effective.

Children need information which is as honest as possible. If a procedure is going to hurt, children should be given this information in the least threatening way possible. They should be told how long the discomfort will last and be given suggestions for how to deal with it. The way of describing likely sensations is important, preferably relating experiences to ones with which the child is already familiar. For example, a needle prick can be likened to a scratch or an insect bite. For children using EMLA anaesthetic cream, the sensation of the needle is often likened to a 'pushing' feeling under the skin. The whirring sound of a machine may be likened to the wings of a butterfly, or a louder sound to a motorbike racing along. An ultrasound of the stomach is commonly explained to children as 'jelly on the belly' because of the lubricating substance which is used to ensure good contact between the scan and the child's body. The sensation, which is perfectly painless, feels cold and slippery, like jelly!

It is important to be clear not only about the steps of the procedure, but also why it is being done and how the child will feel. It may be useful to stress that the procedure is necessary to obtain diagnostic information, or to help prevent or ameliorate symptoms, and is not done as punishment. Telling the child it is for their own good may, at times, feel very inadequate reassurance to the child, especially if they are likely to initially feel worse as a result. It is necessary therefore, to be clear about how it is going to help, or what benefits are hoped for, as well as giving some indication of how long any particular sensations will last and how long it will take to feel better.

Children also need to know what is expected from them. Although many people still insist that children need to be brave and not cry or make a fuss, it is perhaps more helpful to be explicit about what they need to do. For example, it may be more useful to say that they should stay as still as possible, rather than asking them to be brave and not cry. Some doctors tell children they can make as much noise as they like as long as they do not move. They may also explain that if they move, it will be harder to get the needle at the first attempt, or the pictures of the scan, for example, will come out fuzzy.

As we have implied, if children are undergoing surgery, it is important that they have realistic expectations of the benefits of the operation, even though there may sometimes be a fine balance between retaining a positive outlook and creating false hope. An example of this is where children with brain tumours are told that surgery is to take away the tumour and stop their headaches, when it is already known the tumour cannot be fully removed and will require other treatments. In other cases, children may have unrealistic fantasies about the outcomes – children with profound hearing loss may hold on to the hope that the cochlear implant will help them to hear 'like normal', or children with Duchenne muscular dystrophy, who have tendon- releasing surgery may believe they will be able to walk as normal. Sadly, normal hearing cannot be restored, and if walking is helped, this will only be a short-term benefit, and in many cases, very cumbersome and difficult. Children can feel very disappointed and frustrated with the results of treatment if they do not meet their expectations, which may have important implications for their co-operation with any rehabilitation or further treatment regimes. It is therefore important that every effort is made to prepare them realistically.

It is important, therefore, to explore what expectations and hopes children have and give ample opportunity for them to ask questions about the procedure and its effects. However, since it may be hard for them to know what to ask, the following questions might be useful. They were generated from a discussion with a group of teenage patients who had experienced renal surgery, who were asked to consider what they felt would be important for other children to know:

1. *What tests will be done before I go to theatre?*
2. *Can anyone come down to theatre with me? If so, who?*
3. *When and where will I be put to sleep?*
4. *Who is going to do the operation?*
5. *When I am in theatre, who is in there?*
6. *How big, and where, will the scar be?*
7. *Will I have any tubes? Where?*
8. *Where will I wake up?*
9. *What after-effects will there be (nausea, numbness, pain)?*
10. *What pain relief will I be given?*
11. *Will I be able to control the pain (for example, PCA (patient-controlled analgesia pump))?*
12. *How long before I recover from surgery and can move around and do things as normal?*
13. *How long will I have to stay in hospital?*
14. *How soon before we know if surgery has been successful?*

These teenagers felt it was particularly important to discuss pain relief options before surgery, as they felt it was difficult to do this so effectively in the early post-operative stages. The question about scars is perhaps not surprising, given the concerns young people have about their appearance and the number of scars some children with chronic conditions acquire. To deal with this, one young person requested that she have her next scar formed as a letter rather than an irregular shape!

Like all good teaching, preparation is best if children are actively involved. This is particularly true when they are helped to manage a given procedure by learning a new skill. This might include strategies for dealing with pain, or learning how to take their own blood pressure, pass a naso-gastric tube, needle themselves to administer insulin or growth hormone, or set up and sterilize the equipment used in the procedure.

A seven-year-old child was about to start radiotherapy, and had been observed to be very scared about being apart from his mother. He had visited the department and did not appear concerned about the equipment or about being hurt or in pain. However, he expressed considerable anxiety about his mother leaving him in the room. It was therefore agreed that he would practise lying still for five minutes on his bed at home and on the ward while his mother first talked to him from the doorway and then from outside the room so he could build up an experience of being alright when his mother needed to leave the room during his treatment. This child was praised considerably by his parents and the nursing staff for learning this new skill, which helped to develop his confidence and sense of being in control of a potentially very distressing and frightening treatment. He was also given suggestions for what he would think about while lying still and decided to sing a favourite song in his head. He tried this and found out for himself that the time went a lot quicker when doing something to keep busy.

Helping the Distressed or Anxious Child

Sometimes children will be very distressed, regardless of the care taken in preparing them for an event. Surgery is frightening, and many procedures, particularly the more invasive, are both uncomfortable, embarrassing and painful. It can be very upsetting for all concerned – child, family and medical staff – when children are made to undergo procedures forcibly. This may occur when they are essential for the child, but the child is unable or unwilling to co-operate. There are other procedures which can only be carried out if the child is co-operative, and the child may need considerable support to manage this. For some procedures, such as blood tests or administering insulin, children will need to be able to develop routine strategies themselves, as this will occur daily for the rest of their lives.

The most important aspects of helping very distressed or anxious children is the development of a close relationship with them, a careful exploration of their distress, and negotiation of the coping strategies which are helpful for them to try. It is important not to try to give information about a procedure when children are already very upset, as they will not be able to take in the information at this time and further talking may serve only to escalate their distress. If the situation allows, it may be better simply to acknowledge the distress and say that you should meet at another time to think of ways of making it a little better for them. It is also important not to direct any frustrations at the child's distress, or inability to co-operate, negatively at the child. For example, it is not helpful to patronize the child by saying that even the younger children can manage the procedure as this serves only to further undermine the child's confidence. It is far more helpful to acknowledge the child's evident distress and say that some children get worried or 'stressed out', but then to introduce some ways that other children have found helpful in dealing with it. Similarly, although it is important for children to be aware of why a procedure is necessary, it is not helpful to threaten the child with the consequences of their refusing or non-cooperation, as this serves only to make them even more fearful.

It may be helpful to explore with children and their parents any factors which may be contributing to the distress, including relevant prior experiences, or current stresses for the child. One should explore previous experiences for coping with new or potentially challenging situations, such as starting a new school, learning to swim or ride a bike. In this way, it can sometimes be possible to build on the fact that the child was anxious or felt that he or she could not do something in the past, yet managed to do it. Common coping themes are that they were determined to keep going and succeed, that they were striving for a reward, that they just made up their mind that they could do it, or that their parents kept encouraging them.

Sometimes this kind of help needs to occur over a number of meetings, as in the following example:

Clare was eleven years of age and suffered with an auto-immune condition called Myacenia Gravis. Treatment in the form of surgical removal of her thymus gland was felt to be in Clare's best interest by the medical team and accepted as such by her parents. Clare, however, became distraught at the idea. She cried so much when surgery was suggested that she almost made herself physically sick, effectively blocking any further discussion of the worries, distress or even the benefits of the surgery.

At a first meeting with the doctor, Clare was reassured that she was not going to be forced to have surgery. The doctor simply explained that he wanted to get to know her and her parents a little better and to make sure they all understood the issues involved and to be clear what she decided.

A separate meeting with Clare's parents revealed their own extreme distress at Clare's predicament and their concern about whether they themselves could cope with supporting her through the surgery. It became clear, therefore, that the parents needed time themselves to talk through their own feelings and concerns, so that they were well-prepared and could present a united, informed and reassuring presence for Clare.

At a second meeting with Clare, it was possible to engage her in a discussion about her life as it was currently, and how it used to be when she felt well. It was then possible to address what she would like to do if only she was feeling a little better in order to explore how life might be different if she had the operation. Again she was reassured that the discussion was simply to consider options and not to force her into anything.

Although Clare was still clear that she did not want surgery, or even to know anything about it, she agreed to help her mother and the play worker to think of the sort of concerns any young person might have about surgery. This was a collaborative exercise with her mother who was able to voice some of the anxieties she believed Clare might have. After a list was drawn up, it was possible to go through it looking at what could be changed and which concerns were based on incorrect information. For example, she was not aware that her parents were able to stay in the ward with her. Other distressing aspects could not be changed, for example, having to use the bedpan for the first few days, but this anxiety was helped by being reassured that, as her mother was remaining with her, the use of the bedpan would be as private as possible.

In this session, Clare's mother and the play specialist were able to praise her for being so helpful in thinking about her fears. They also said that the discussion had made it easier to help her and other girls who needed this surgery in future. For her part, Clare began to see that the decision to have surgery involved weighing up the realistic fears against the possible benefits. She agreed to find out a little more about what really happened to children in hospital, and, as a result, visits were arranged to the ward, hospital school and family's accommodation. Both Clare and her mother were visibly more relaxed and confident during each visit to hospital.

In a subsequent session with the play specialist, Clare asked questions about the operation, and she was shown a photograph booklet of a young person being admitted into hospital. At this point, she began to talk about having the operation and to plan where she would have a holiday afterwards to recover. Subsequently, Clare and her mother began their own preparation at home, cooking food for the rest of the family so that they would have good meals when the mother was resident in hospital with Clare. They made lists of clothes and supplies they would *need, including a TV so that Clare would not miss her favourite programme.*

Preparing or even engaging children who are already traumatized and who are withdrawn from adults can be very difficult. At Guy's Hospital we are very fortunate to have the services of C.H.A.T.A, an animal therapy service. The reassuring comfort, safeness and unconditional care offered by these therapeutic animals can build bridges with the child and help draw them into relating with others and being actively involved in events around them.

Post-procedural debriefing

Following any procedure or new event, it is important to give children an opportunity to work through their experience, in whichever medium the child is most comfortable. Although the physical trauma may be short lived, the emotional repercussions may continue for much longer and children need an opportunity to work this through for themselves.

Essentially the process is the same as described for working with children generally. The helper, preferably already well known by the child, explores the child's thoughts and feelings about their experiences. This might be done by talking, through play, by writing (for example, a diary of events) or by a scrapbook. The method has to be negotiated with each child, but the aim is the same of allowing them to express their feelings and thoughts, and to derive clear, accurate and helpful constructions of the situation. What is particularly important is to help children be positive, for example, in terms of their achievements within the experience.

Encouraging Co-operation with Treatment

We have already discussed in *Chapter 4* how children's adherence to treatment may be dependent on the child's (and parents') assessment that the perceived benefits of treatment outweigh the perceived disadvantages. Clearly there will be considerable individual differences in the way treatment is construed; therefore, the value of listening carefully and appreciating the child's unique experience (both positive and negative) is fundamental to any work in encouraging good adherence to treatment.

In considering how to support and encourage adherence to long-term treatments (many of which will be managed at home), all of the earlier points regarding good preparation are relevant. In addition, the following are important factors:

– helping children and families understand the rationale for treatment and the consequences of not having treatment;

– facilitating knowledge (and confidence) in children (and parents) carrying out the practical aspects of care;
– negotiating treatment regimes with children and parents and ensuring they are reasonable and manageable within the child (and family's) life;
– reinforcing and supporting the child in taking appropriate responsibility and control over his or her treatment.

The relationship between the child, family and healthcare professional will be the most significant factor supporting treatment adherence. This necessitates good skills in listening, giving information, and negotiating a workable treatment plan. There will obviously be considerable constraints placed by the nature of the treatment, but within this, it is helpful to discuss and agree a plan or regime which the child and family feel is manageable. This should include a discussion of how treatment will practically be incorporated into daily routines, encouraging the child and family to consider potential difficulties and to generate their own ideas as to how these might be overcome. It is helpful in further meetings to build in a review of how treatment is going, and to re-negotiate a working treatment plan as necessary. Encouraging feedback in this way enables problems to be shared and problem-solving strategies to be generated in a supportive way. It is also a powerful message to children that you are working with them, in partnership, and is therefore more respectful of the role and responsibility taken on by the child. When open discussions do not occur, children and families can feel that problems are insurmountable and that treatment plans are unreasonable and inflicted upon them, leading to resentment, reduced confidence and ultimately poorer compliance with treatment.

There may be many different reasons why children experience difficulties in adhering to their treatment and so it is not helpful to make assumptions that the child is just being lazy or unco-operative. Most children experience difficulties at some point during their treatments. It is important to help the child understand this, that it is not just the child's problem or fault – the problem is that the treatments are very challenging, and some discussion and new strategies may need to be tried to overcome the difficulties.

It can be helpful for children to self-monitor the way they carry out treatment, to help them understand what might be causing difficulty. One teenage girl kept a diary of the reasons why she did not take her tablets on the days where she missed them. Her reasons varied from 'too busy, too tired, got distracted and did something else' to 'I have been feeling so well this week, I thought I could perhaps do without them (the tablets)' to ' I failed to take my tablets this morning, so I won't bother tonight, I will start again tomorrow.' In sharing her diary, it was possible for her doctor to negotiate a plan of 'tablet-taking rules' to challenge some of her previous thinking.

Preparation for Leaving Hospital and Returning to School

Following careful exploration of children's experiences in hospital, it is usually helpful to elicit expectations and fears about returning home and going to school and to deal with these in turn. Although going home may be looked forward to for weeks or even months on end, when the day finally arrives, it can be met with much trepidation by both children and parents. The security of having experienced health professionals constantly available should not be underestimated. Children need to be able to build up confidence in local services, parents and their own ability to look after themselves, and so thinking through what they will do if they are feeling unwell or are worried about any aspect of care is important. In addition to the security provided by staff, hospitals can also feel a safe place where children's special needs and physical appearance are accepted and in some cases, considered the norm. Preparing for the reaction of others, for people looking, asking questions, or even not asking questions and not knowing what to say is important. Finally, preparation for the relative quiet and inactivity is also helpful. For children who have been in hospital a long time, there is often a social 'buzz' around wards, with constant activities in terms of events happening to the child or observed happening to others. Thinking ahead with children as to how they might structure their day and prepare their own activities is useful.

In preparing for returning to school, it can be constructive to anticipate the sort of questions they think a friend or classmate might have, so that they can prepare answers with which they feel comfortable. Questions related to changed physical appearance, taking tablets at school, frequently missing school and not being able to participate in the same activities are common areas to explore. Possible answers can be rehearsed in a safe way with a trusted adult in a role-play situation. The child can start by taking the role of the friend who asks the questions, and have examples of responses modelled by the helper. Other children will feel comfortable to try out their own responses, if asked questions in the role play. Children can also use this forum as an opportunity to practise taking control of the conversation with friends, asking questions about particular events or gossip at school, in order to direct the conversation away from themselves.

The school may also need to prepare for the child's return and re-integration. We have considered certain aspects of this in *Chapter 4*. Teachers may need to consider what information to give the class or form prior to the child's return. If possible, it is best to have negotiated this with the child directly, or, if not, the family and staff caring for the child. The child may wish peers to be informed by the teacher, health professional or wish to do it themselves. Of course, the child may not want any information to be given at all unless on a need-to-know basis, and this should be respected.

For children who have been away from school a long time, it can be helpful to institute a 'Circle of Friends' scheme, whereby a peer group of about six children is designated to care for the child, including them in social activities and generally being supportive and helpful for them. The importance of this role for these peers can be reinforced by their meeting regularly with the child and form tutor or teacher to discuss how they feel their work is going.

Preparation for Transfer to Adult Services

As discussed in *Chapter 4*, transfer from paediatric to adult services is potentially anxiety-provoking. In some areas, paediatric and adult departments work together to run an adolescent or young adults clinic; however, many young people will have to make this transition to an adult clinic either within their current hospital or by moving to a different hospital or clinic base. In asking a group of teenagers how much notice they felt they needed to prepare for this transition, they were unanimous in saying at least one year. During this time, they felt their aims were to gain more independence by taking on more responsibility for their care and by finding out about the adult service they would be moving to. Their specific tasks were to:

- Attend clinic appointments initially with parents present (but with themselves taking the lead in giving information or asking questions) leading to attending appointments without parents being with them.
- Taking responsibility for making appointments, collecting prescriptions from pharmacy and completing relevant forms, such as for travel reimbursement.
- Making contact with and getting to know the adult department. For example, finding out how to get to the new unit, visiting and meeting the staff, and even getting to know differences in treatment procedures so that they could discuss these beforehand.

Clearly it is not only teenagers who need to be active in this preparation process; for example, health professionals need to promote the attitude of involving young people more directly in their care and encouraging independence through attending on their own (or with a friend) at clinics. These particular teenagers also recognized a need for their parents to be part of this preparation, to enable them to 'let go' of the paediatric services in their own right and support their child in this process.

Pain Management

In all work with children who are chronically ill, pain is a constant theme and perhaps the most frequent worry for all concerned, so we will now look in some detail at ways of exploring pain and strategies for managing it. As with any experience, children's experience of pain will depend on a number of physiological and psychological factors, including developmental abilities, previous experience, emotional state, personality and coping resources.

It is not possible to separate out the effects of anxiety and pain as they overlap to such a considerable degree. Strategies for helping, therefore, need to take account of both. The general steps involved in the process have already been outlined at the beginning of the chapter. However, following engaging and developing a relationship, one of the most important steps is to explore children's experience of pain and come to a shared understanding about it. We will, therefore, begin by putting forward the current understanding of the physical and psychological experience of pain, since the next step in helping children after exploring their perceptions may be to share this model.

Gate control theory of pain

The influence of psychological factors on pain experience can be explained using the 'gate control' theory (Melzack and Wall, 1988). The theory proposes that sensations of pain are modulated by both physiological and psychological processes. Input from receptors in the nervous system is assumed to pass through a neural 'gate' in the spinal cord before being passed to the brain. The extent to which the gate is open is determined by activity in different parts of the nervous system and controls the amount of pain that is felt.

What is particularly useful about this model is that it helps to make sense for children of why their mood, focus of attention and expectations of pain influence their actual perceptions. It follows from it, for example, that children who are calm and feeling in control are likely to feel less intense pain than those who are highly anxious, expect the pain to be awful, and are unable to distract themselves. For example, when completely absorbed in an activity such as rugby or football, people completely fail to notice knocks and bruises that would otherwise be regarded as very painful at the time. On the other hand, being highly anxious that something will be painful will lead to increased levels of pain experience.

Exploration of children's experience of pain

All the strategies described in *Chapter 7* for exploring children's experiences generally are relevant here. However, pain is an experience that may be particularly difficult to verbalize adequately, even for adults, and therefore a number of alternative ways of exploring it may need to be used. The picture in *Figure 9.1* communicates very well a girl's experience of the intense pain of a migraine attack.

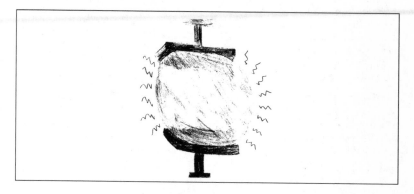

Figure 9.1 Picture of a migraine attack.

For children, especially those who are less verbally able, it can be extremely difficult and frustrating to try and communicate their experience of pain. They often feel misunderstood, ridiculed or dismissed by adults who have not listened carefully or explored fully their pain. Children may report pain which others find hard to understand, either as they think the child should not be in pain or the site of the pain does not fit the clinical picture. The feeling of not being believed in such circumstances can be very distressing.

The meaning of pain. Pain is not a unitary experience. Although usually distressing, it can mean different things to different children. It might signify a deterioration or recurrence of a condition or be seen more positively as, for example, post-operative pain following an organ transplant. The consequences of pain may be that children receive attention, comfort and special treats. It may allow them to opt out of particular activities, such as their household chores or homework. However, it may prevent them from being part of the activities they desire or make them fearful of doing anything which may exacerbate the pain. It can also make some children fearful of being parted from parents or leaving hospital, in case the pain recurs and they need help.

To explore these issues with the child, it may be helpful to ask them what is important for them to be able to do and what is currently not possible because of pain. They might also be asked to describe how their life might be different if they were not in pain. It is certainly useful to explore children's thoughts and feelings associated with their pain, and a diary can be one way of doing this. Thoughts or beliefs that are distressing or unhelpful can be discussed and challenged in an attempt to help the child alter them. Common constructions are that children feel they have no control over the pain, or that it is never ending. Other thoughts include the notion that they will never be able to do anything positive again, or that they might die. Some children can identify that they start the day in a negative frame of mind, because if they wake up in pain, they think that the day as a whole will be spoilt.

Particularly careful exploration is required in the context of so called 'psychogenic pain' where there appears to be no physical basis for the pain. Some children continue to experience discomfort months or years after a procedure or test. Other children complain of abdominal pain, headaches or pains in their limbs, yet no evidence of any problem is found on any physical scans or tests. In some cases, it may be evident they are under tremendous stress at school or home and their pain may be a message to others that they need more care or attention, or cannot manage particular pressures. In other examples, there is no clear evidence of psychological distress. However, whatever the explanation, the pain is real to the child and needs to be explored and taken just as seriously. In all pain experience, the role of psychological factors should not be underestimated, and when the child reports pain, it is important that they are believed. The challenge for the helper is in finding ways of understanding and managing their pain.

Specific strategies for exploring pain

Scales of pain intensity: Rating scales can be a useful measure of pain intensity. The type of scale can be negotiated with the child, using numbers, colours or pictures. Using numbers, for example, a 5-point scale can be drawn, with the pain meaning of each number explicitly stated for a particular child. This might involve both a description of the pain and what the child is able or not able to do as a result. For example:

1: No pain, with the child able to participate fully in activities.
2: Some pain or discomfort of which the child is aware, but which does not interfere with most activities.
3: Moderate pain from which the child can be distracted, and which does not prevent him or her moving around or actively doing something, but can interfere with concentration on more difficult tasks.

4: Severe pain from which it is difficult to distract the child in all but the most engaging of activities.
5: Extreme pain during which the child does not feel able to do anything and goes to bed.

Younger children may find visual pictures of faces easier to help them discriminate pain severity. *Figure 9.2* is an example of pain faces drawn by a nine-year-old to show how painful his legs were. One teenage girl devised her own pain chart with photographs of pop-stars, ranging from her most to least favourite.

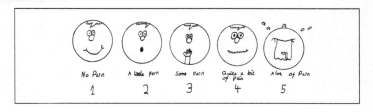

Figure 9.2 Pain scale drawn by a nine-year-old boy.

Colour coded scales have also been used to help clinicians understand the intensity of pain experienced (Eland, 1981). A further development has been the use of figure outlines of the body, which the child is asked to colour, selecting his or her own colours to represent pain intensity (Varni *et al.*, 1987). As there are significant individual differences in colours chosen by children to represent pain intensity, it is important for children to name what each colour means to them.

It is possible to use this to explore other sensations within the body, such as where the child has no feeling or movement or where they have abnormal sensations (for example, feeling tense or tight, tingling or very hot/cold). It can also be used to help a child illustrate changes they have experienced, for example, changes in sensation or movement in degenerative neurological conditions, to acknowledge changes with the child in the least threatening way possible.

Pain diaries. In addition to providing helpful assessment material, diaries are a useful way of encouraging children to be actively involved in the process. Children can be asked to keep a record of pain experienced over a period of time, either related to particular procedures or at arranged time intervals, using ratings if necessary. This can provide a record of the pattern of pain over time, and the way pain affects children's daily life. It can also be used to record change over time. For example, one might measure how painful a procedure is initially (a baseline measure), and then rate subsequent procedures as a way of assessing the success of strategies for dealing with the pain.

Measures of this kind can be a very positive and concrete reminder to children of the progress they are making, as well as giving feedback on their strategies. It may also be possible to detect patterns of when they are in most pain, and to identify and anticipate likely precipitants, such as trying to do too much in the day. One child was able to realize that although his headaches were incapacitating, there was a clear period of time leading up to them during which he could take preventative steps by being quiet or lying down and taking his tablets. This was a beneficial change from the situation of him believing he had headaches virtually all the time during the day and that they were totally out of his control. For other children it may enable them to test out the optimal time to take pain-relieving medication or practice relaxation or distraction techniques. Recording activities can also be a concrete reminder to children of the activities they still manage, given that chronic pain is wearing, and often leads to the perception that it prevents them from doing anything at all.

Strategies for dealing with pain

As already mentioned, giving children information to explain something about their pain can be very helpful in itself. However, there are many other strategies that can be usefully employed to help children deal with pain and we will outline a selection. Our general approach is to suggest to children that the task is to help them test out various strategies and find the most useful. Emphasis is given to the notion that they are learning a new skill that they can put into practice to help themselves. So much of the time children experience things as being done *to* them, and it may be a welcome change for them to construe themselves as being in control. The interventions described can be effective in dealing with painful or distressing procedures and can also be used or modified for use with children experiencing chronic pain.

Distraction techniques. The principle of distraction is simply to encourage children to focus attention on something other than the source of their pain. The most successful distraction techniques will, therefore, be those which are most interactive, engaging, and able to hold the child's attention. For younger infants, rocking, stroking and being sung to can be helpful. For older infants, blowing bubbles, or watching videos can be distracting. For older children interesting books with colourful pictures, or those involving finding objects (for example, *Where's Wally?*) (Handford, 1989, see *Appendix B*)) or pop-up books can be absorbing.

Jokes, games and puzzles can be very entertaining. 'Knock knock' jokes, however corny, require the child to concentrate and follow the speaker closely, as do verbal or mathematical quizzes. Stories can also be used very effectively for children of a wide age range. Familiar and favourite stories might be used, as well as joint story-telling, where children offer their own version of events. For example, at a particular point (for example, 'The prince then said to the frog . . .') the child is given free reign to make up what occurs next. Alternatively, the helper might make up a story for the occasion, using information which is particularly meaningful or enjoyable for the child.

An increasing number of hospitals are being offered the services of Clown Doctors (please see reference to the Theodora Foundation in *Appendix C*). In addition to their uplifting and hilarious role in visiting the wards, they can be a wonderful distraction and support for children during procedures. In addition to engaging and relaxing children, they also help to reduce stress in the parents and staff!

It is always important to use a technique which suits the child and which will absorb interest. Timing of the distraction techniques is important. It is not helpful to start these when the child is already highly aroused and agitated as they will simply not be effective. It is also not helpful to start the technique so early that the child has tired of it prior to the procedure occurring.

Relaxation. The basic premise here is that the more relaxed the child's body and muscles, the less the experience of pain. This works both at a physical and cognitive level. It is not possible for the body to feel relaxed and calm and to feel tense and anxious at the same time. Controlled breathing can be a very useful way of helping children relax. Asking them to take a series of deep breaths, each time breathing in slowly to a count of three, holding it for a count of three and then letting out the breath to a count of three, can help calm children and help them focus on something other than the pain.

The most commonly used relaxation method is progressive muscle relaxation, involving the tensing of all the body muscle groups in sequence and then the rapid relaxing (letting go) of the muscle group. Relaxation using guided imagery can also be very useful, but for younger or more active children, being physically involved in the process is more helpful. Details of the muscle groups which can be targeted are given in *Appendix A*. It is, however, important to adapt any relaxation schedule to the individual child, possibly needing to avoid muscle groups which are particularly sore or painful, or adapting the length of the relaxation schedule to suit the concentration skills of the child.

Guided imagery and hypnosis. Hypnosis as a term is probably best avoided because of the connotations this might have in terms of stage hypnotists who provide a very entertaining (and humiliating) spectacle of their subjects. Hypnosis can also be a potentially frightening thought for some children. It may be more helpful to talk in terms of deep relaxation and guided imagery, which Richard Lansdown (1996) calls 'directed daydreams'. Here children allow their minds to think of pleasant things, which help to distract them from the pain or procedure. While the child is relaxed, suggestions are made about images they might conjure up using scenes which they find pleasurable. This might include, for example, a visit to the beach or walking through a wood. For some children it may be possible to jointly create the scene they would like to enjoy while they are relaxed. Some examples children have given are: flying to Disneyland with Minnie Mouse, swimming with dolphins and having a tea party with Mary Poppins!

Desensitization. This is a technique usually used for dealing with extreme fears and phobias. Like the previous method, desensitization may require a few sessions to build up to the actual procedure itself. The basic principle is that while children are relaxed, they are encouraged to encounter whatever is feared in a graded, step-by-step way, beginning with something they can manage and working towards the most difficult situation. Children determine their own pace in working towards the final goal. This might be done in imagination, using suggestions and imagery, or by actually experiencing real situations. If the child is frightened of needles, for example, the first step may be to look at a picture of a needle or to play with one in a toy medical kit, then to look at a real needle, and handle one inside the plastic sheath covering. The next stage may be for the child to lay the needle across the skin and finally to allow the needle to be placed in the vein. A number of additional smaller steps may be added at points that children find difficult. Each step may be presented a number of times until the child can maintain a state of relaxation throughout the presentation.

Reinforcements and rewards. All children need to be encouraged and well-supported while trying these strategies. A particularly important and helpful principle is to ensure that children's achievements are rewarded immediately. For most of them this can involve plenty of praise, and this can be given for the efforts they are making and any benefits this has given them. Some, particularly younger children, will also enjoy more concrete rewards such as a star on a chart (for example, if they achieve the target of not pulling their arm away) or a more tangible treat or reward (such as sweets, stickers, crisps or a videotape). Bravery awards are also very popular, both in the form of certificates, which children can place near their bed for all to admire, or badges that can be worn.

Modelling. In general this means demonstrating what one is going to do, before actually carrying out the procedure. However, more specifically it can provide the child with a model of someone else going through the procedure and dealing with it effectively. For example, one might help/teach children to relax using desensitization and then show them a videotape of a child undergoing the same procedure and being praised or otherwise rewarded subsequently. Plenty of time should be available for discussion about the model, following the child's lead carefully in dealing with all questions.

Learning a new skill.

Learning a new skill. Children often report that doing something to themselves is less painful than when others do it. As a result, some children are motivated to learn a new skill such as passing a feeding tube down their nose or carrying out blood tests. There is an increasing move for children to take more control of their pain management following surgery, using a patient-controlled analgesia pump (PCA). This is a drip which is timed to give a continuous safe dose, and children as young as three years of age can press the pump when they need an extra amount.

The following example illustrates a number of issues we have looked at in pain management.

Martin was nine years old and had recently started haemodialysis three times a week in hospital. Although he tried to be as helpful and compliant as he could, he felt totally unable to cope with having the needles inserted at the start of dialysis sessions. His mother became very distressed and often left the unit in tears at these times. A typical scene was for Martin to scream and start wriggling as soon as his arm was prepared for the needle and the process could take up to an hour and require several attempts.

The dialysis team gave his key nurse the task of improving this situation if she could. To start, she began by reassuring Martin that no one was angry with him. She talked to him during a number of short sessions outside the treatment setting and tried to indicate her acceptance of his difficulty. Very quickly they agreed that they would work together to learn a way of dealing with the situation that would be better for him. They began by making a list of the things with which he found it most difficult to cope, and they explored which of the items of the list could possibly be improved or changed. This resulted in the identification of one area of distress which was that Martin always felt guilty about worrying his mother so much. Consequently, it was agreed that his mother would leave the unit prior to the needles being used, and use this time to get Martin his treat (a special lunch) for the day.

Martin and his nurse then explored a variety of strategies that other children had found useful, and Martin was asked what he would like to try. He chose to practise relaxation and decided to maintain this by slightly deeper breathing during the procedure. Martin was then able to practise this while imagining all the steps in the procedure verbally described by the nurse. He also planned a routine with her of all the things he would do on entering the unit. This included getting his tray with needles ready himself, and getting his school books ready so that he could work while on dialysis. The third step was to practise the breathing exercises before bringing the needle up to his skin (with the case on) so that he could just feel it. The final step was to remove the case, to press the needle against his skin and for the nurse to actually insert it.

Other suggestions that were considered included distraction techniques to be used during needling. However, after trying these, Martin found them unhelpful, as he wanted to see and be part of what was happening. Instead, the nurse just talked quietly throughout the procedure, reassuring him, praising and reinforcing how well he was doing with his breathing and trying to keep still. At the same time, Martin and his nurse kept a record of how still he was during the procedure and how much discomfort he experienced, rating each on a 10-point scale. As Martin was a naturally competitive child, he used his record to great effect, making a huge effort to break his record on each occasion. His nurse was also able to use the record to remind him on each occasion of how well he had tried the time before and what strategies he was going to use this time. In addition, Martin was reinforced by the praise and attention given to him by the nurses and his mother and the concrete experience of the needles becoming less awful.

Within a few sessions, Martin was able to deal with the insertion of the needles and the whole procedure very successfully. Although the individual aspects of the programme all contributed to its success, the fact that Martin was involved and in control of what happened was particularly important. Martin played a key role in developing his own programme and in assessing how useful or successful particular strategies were. As a result, the programme was specifically tailored to his needs, both in terms of the steps of the programme and the rewards offered.

Summary

❑ Good preparation can help children manage unfamiliar, distressing, frightening and painful experiences. It has been shown to reduce anxiety, distress and pain and increase children's ability to co-operate.

❑ Specific areas of help identified were preparation and support during medical procedures, pain management, treatment adherence and managing transitions.

❑ Preparation should involve parents/carers as they may be central in supporting the child.

❑ Preparation strategies need to take account of child's cognitive abilities, previous experience, beliefs and fears, and ability to co-operate.

❑ As with any work carried out with a child, engaging and developing a relationship is an integral part of the process.

❑ Children should be actively involved in preparation, thinking about and asking questions, carrying out tasks or learning new skills if appropriate.

❑ Preparation information needs be honest and given in the most positive and reassuring way possible.

❑ In preparing children for any event it is important to identify areas which are potentially distressing for each child, either by virtue of their uncertainty or unfamiliarity, or by anticipated or actual discomfort or pain.

❑ If these are discussed with the child, it is possible to set goals to try and make things a little easier or help changes to occur.

❑ When preparing for procedures, sensory information (what will be see, heard, felt) and procedural information (what the actual steps to the process are) are both necessary.

❑ Pain management techniques involve exploring the meaning of pain and planning strategies with the child to test out the most useful for them, and in so doing take more control of their pain and their body.

❑ Possible pain management strategies include distraction, relaxation, guided imagery (hypnosis), controlled breathing exercises, desensitization and cognitive behavioural methods.

10

Communicating about Death and Dying

In this chapter we will specifically consider communicating with children with life-threatening conditions and those facing death. In essence, the needs of these children and the skills for facilitating open communication are the same as we have already discussed. The aims of helping in this context are to promote the highest quality of living and to enable children to die with dignity and comfort. However, the death of a child is an extremely emotive event, and it is easy for helpers to feel overwhelmed and deskilled because of the profound anguish and helpless feelings aroused. The reality is that a helper who is known, liked and trusted will have a great deal to offer.

To be able to facilitate communication with children about death and dying, it is necessary to have a developmental context for making sense of their questions, thoughts and fears about death. It is important to be aware of the situations which may trigger children's thoughts or fears about death, and to be sensitive to the ways they might raise the topic both directly and indirectly, verbally and non-verbally. It is also important to be aware of children's emotional responses to the subject of death and how this relates to their understanding or coping strategies. For example, children who believe death is reversible may not be as distressed as those with more comprehensive understanding. However, children's emotional states and coping styles should be respected as they are strong determinants of what is accessible for the child to talk and think about. Some children with life-threatening conditions may be able to talk about the possibility of death, but for others, the denial of possible or impending death may be an important self-protective strategy.

In the following pages we will also consider the needs of other people affected by the possibility of the child's death, including parents, siblings and friends. The needs of the whole family are paramount at this time, and the helper is referred to Hill (1994) and Parkes *et al.* (1996) for more detailed accounts of family care. The emotional cost to helpers should also not be underestimated when working in this area, and important issues of support and supervision are considered in *Chapter 11.*

Children's Understanding of Death and Dying

Understanding of death and dying varies enormously from child to child. It depends on the child's cognitive abilities, cultural and religious beliefs, what the child is actually told, and any experiences of death the child may have encountered. This might be indirectly from school, books, television and friends, or from more direct experiences such as the death of a family member, friend or even family pet.

Given that death is such a taboo subject, many children will have been told nothing about it, and very few adults will have discussed the subject in detail with them. Instead, they will have heard a number of euphemisms and comments about death, from which they will make their own sense. For example, children may be told that the deceased is finally at peace, having a magic sleep, or has gone to a better place, to a place beyond the clouds, or to be with Jesus. Other less reverent euphemisms include 'kicking the bucket', or 'pushing up the daisies'. They may hear about heaven or be told that the deceased has become a star in the sky, an angel, or God's little helper.

Children may also be familiar with expressions such as 'You'll be the death of me' when they are being naughty, or hear that someone 'died of a broken heart', 'almost died laughing' or 'could have died from embarrassment'. They may also hear expressions like, 'I'll kill you if you don't behave' or be told to 'Drop dead' in a heated argument. When they hear of someone dying, they will attempt to make sense of the situation using this kind of information. Some children may take these statements literally, and they may develop totally erroneous beliefs that they may somehow caused the death.

Cultural beliefs and religious instruction have a major role in determining children's understanding, and in working with families from different faiths and cultures, one should be familiar with and respect their beliefs. The reader is recommended to read Jon Mayled's (1986) book *Death Customs*. Although it is intended as a primary school resource, it is nevertheless a clear and comprehensive introduction to the beliefs and customs of different cultural and ethnic groups.

Even if children receive no formal information (religious or otherwise) about death, they will still form ideas about death, often from stories and films. In the Walt Disney film, *The Lion King*, the father dies but returns in the form of a cloud-like vision to give Simba, the lion cub, advice. Older children may have watched another popular film called *Ghost*, where the central character is murdered but returns as a ghost to protect his wife. This film clearly makes suggestions about what happens when one dies, but it also gives a powerful message about the existence of Heaven and Hell. The murderer meets a terrifying end when he dies and is carried away by demon-like creatures amid agonized screams, whereas, at the end of the film, the ghost husband is seen walking towards a beautiful light.

From research on healthy children (Lansdown and Benjamin,1985; Kane,1979) it seems that children's understanding of death (like their understanding of illness) is not an all or nothing concept, but develops from simple ideas, to a partial and then more elaborate, understanding. At the same time, there is a move from concrete to more abstract and complex notions. Lansdown states that by the age of eight or nine years, most children have a fully developed concept of death. Nevertheless, children at a much younger age can have very good understanding, albeit somewhat different to that of an adult.

Through interviewing children, Kane (1979) identified nine components that contribute to a fully comprehensive understanding of death. Each of these concepts will be related to the ages at which they were reliably attained in her sample, since this might help in exploring with particular children their construction of death. However, caution must apply in making generalizations from this one study. It cannot be assumed that a child of a particular age will have *any* of these conceptions, and it is only by listening to individual children that an appreciation of their understanding is possible.

Realization

Although children as young as two years may use the word 'dead' in their vocabulary and therefore have some awareness of death, most three-year-olds realize that people die at some point. One three-year-old boy played a game in which he pushed his toy farm animals over, saying they were dead, and then picked them up again. One four-year-old girl, who was very impressed at the 'enormous' age of her 34-year-old mother, asked quite earnestly, 'You're very old Mummy. When are you going to die?' This same little girl had chatted in a matter of fact way about her granny dying and leaving her a little puppy as a goodbye present.

Separation

Almost all five-year-olds seem to have understood the notion that death involves being parted from loved ones. This is perhaps the most frightening and distressing aspect for children, as it is for adults. One child, talking about when he would die and go to heaven, repeatedly sought assurance from his parents that they would go to heaven with him as he did not want to be separated from them. Children may be concerned that they will feel lonely and upset, and may be worried that their parents will be lonely without them.

Immobility

The notion that when you are dead, you do not move around seems to be understood by most five-year-olds. This aspect was evidently understood by a very frightened six-year-old boy who woke up on intensive care following cardiac surgery, with numerous breathing, feeding and monitoring tubes. His first question to his mother was to ask if he was dead as he could not move his body.

Irrevocability or irreversibility

The fact that when you die, you cannot come back to life again is a notion available to most six-year-olds. The little four-year-old girl, who earlier commented upon her mother's age and talked about her grandmother's death, had evidently not grasped this aspect of death, since a few days later she began to ask repeatedly when her granny was coming. She eventually became quite frustrated at her mother's consistent response that she was dead and could not return. This may be to some extent a confusion of the notions of death and sleep, where one goes to sleep and then wakes up again. Death may also be understood in terms of a journey, where one goes away and then returns. One young girl was told her brother had 'gone far away', to which she responded by asking if he had gone to Spain, as this was the furthest place she knew. Another child was told by his family that his granny had died and gone to heaven. After a few days, he announced to his family that he was going to fly to heaven (like Superman) to find her, as she must have got lost. He said he would bring her back home, as mummy and daddy missed her so much!

Causality

The conception that there is always a physical cause leading to death is understood by most six-year-olds. Children who have not grasped this component may fear they have caused the death of someone by doing something or by wishing them dead. For example, the jealousy caused by the arrival of a new baby may lead to a sibling's wishful thinking that the baby will die or go away, and this can lead to terrible feelings of guilt and responsibility if the baby does die.

Lack of this concept was demonstrated by a five-year-old boy who was moved from one family member to another following the death of his mother, and subsequently his aunt, from AIDS-related illness. He became very upset at the thought of moving to yet another family. In talking to him it was evident that he believed that every move would be followed by a death, and that he was worried that he was somehow responsible for it.

There can also be very negative feelings towards the person who died, with children believing that if the person had loved them enough or had not wanted to die then they would not have gone away. Although anger at the deceased is not uncommon, or necessarily abnormal, the main difficulty is that children can develop quite erroneous reasoning about the cause of death.

Dysfunctionality

Most six-year-olds seem to realize that death means the cessation of all bodily functions. They have the idea that dead people do not eat, breathe, walk or talk, for example. One child was fascinated by visits to a graveyard, but became frustrated when she failed to see anyone who had died. She had imagined that dead people live under the ground, in the same way as the living exist on top. She kept waiting to hear or see her sister who had died, in much the same way as one would visit a living relative.

Universality

The notion that everyone will die eventually is grasped by most seven-year-olds. Younger children may believe that only the old or sick die, but they gradually develop an awareness that death occurs in all living organisms, including people, animals and plants.

Insensitivity

Most eight-year-olds seem to have grasped the idea that dead people cannot feel or be hurt physically. This can be important in children's understanding of burial or cremation, which could seem extremely frightening without this notion. Some children express concern, for example, about walking in graveyards in case they accidentally step on dead people and hurt them. Elizabeth Kübler-Ross (1969) talks of the body as being an overcoat for the soul (spirit), which is just discarded and not needed after the person has died. Her analogy of a butterfly (spirit) emerging and leaving behind the larval shell is sometimes useful to help children think about this.

Appearance

The notion that a dead body looks and feels different to a living body is grasped by most twelve-year-olds. The dead person does not look or seem asleep, for example.

Children's Concepts of Life After Death

Children who have grasped some, if not all, the components of death may have formed a view of what happens after you die, regardless of any religious instruction received. There is insufficient research to say how children's beliefs in this area develop with cognitive maturity, or whether children facing death may think differently about this than healthy children. What appears to be the case, however, is that it is virtually beyond most children's comprehension to think about not existing or not being somewhere in a recognizable form after death. Adolescents, however, with a mature understanding of death may be grappling with a concept of 'not existing' after death and may have profound and searching questions to which there are no absolute answers. Many children imagine themselves continuing to live in some form or another. One girl, raised in the Buddhist faith, talked of reincarnation and having a happier future life as she had suffered so much in her current life. Other children conceptualize a heaven-like place where they will continue to live after death. With this concrete idea in mind, children may ask (and compose their own answers) to many practical questions, such as what kind of place heaven is, where it is and how you get there.

One four-year-old girl was adamant that heaven is above the clouds and dead people are the stars which sparkle at night. While being pushed on her swing, she asked to be pushed up high so she could see above the clouds and see her brother in heaven. Children may tell you that you will get to heaven by plane, or spacecraft. Some will tell you that you grow wings and fly, or that you are carried up to heaven by the angels. Another four-year-old was told by her mother that a dead bird with a broken wing had died and gone to be mended by Jesus. Later her mother told her that the doctors could not make her leg better (she had an incurable spinal tumour). She happily told her mother not to worry as she would go to Jesus in heaven and he would make her better. Towards her death, she talked quite often about her bird in heaven, which seemingly enabled both the child and mother to derive considerable comfort and reassurance.

One young boy described a paradise with beautiful shimmering golden gates, and having many long tables where family members gathered, as if for dinner. His image was that as more people died, eventually all family members would be together around the same table. Some children assume that life goes on after death in much the same way as it does on earth. One boy had even made a list of the famous people he wanted to meet, including Ghandi and John Lennon. Others believe that people fly around with wings and just play all the time, or they take the form of ghosts and befriend or scare people.

One girl raised in the Catholic faith described how heaven was divided into many layers, depending on how good you had been when you were alive. Although other family members were praying for her dead mother to be exalted to the highest level of heaven, she was adamant that she wanted her mother to stay on the lowest level, so that her mother could watch over her better.

Children's questions about heaven reveal the careful thinking they do in an attempt to make sense of a subject rarely discussed or given a consistent or coherent response. One child wanted to know if her baby brother would grow up in heaven, or if he would still be a baby when she next saw him. Some ask who will be there to look after them: one child assumed that grandparents went to heaven to look after all the children there. Children may also be interested to know if there are toys in heaven, or if there is school.

One child wanted to know if you had birthdays in heaven. He was very satisfied by the answer from his vicar that everyone in heaven would celebrate his arrival and that would become his birthday. This same young man also wanted to check if there were both boy and girl angels. He had heard of the angel Gabriel and assumed this was a girl, so he wanted to make sure there were boy angels as well.

In contrast to the notion of heaven, many children will also have a concept of hell, or a place for naughty or evil people. This may, of course, raise worries as in one girl who was concerned to establish that she had in fact been a good girl and would go to heaven. Another girl was very distressed and worried that her mother (who had committed suicide) was not in heaven, as she had been told that suicide was a sin against God and she feared that her mother would not be allowed in.

Children's Reflections About Their Own Death and Dying

For healthy children it is not usually until adolescence that they begin to contemplate their own mortality. However, illness-related experiences may force a younger child to confront this issue or may advance awareness of the seriousness or life-threatening aspect of their condition. Many children think or worry about death far more than we might anticipate, whether they are in fact dying or not. Even if children are not expressing worries or asking questions, it does not mean they are not thinking about it. There are a range of situations or experiences which may trigger children to think about their death, which we will now describe with examples.

When children are very scared

Children who are traumatized and very frightened may fear the worst outcome imaginable, which is often that they might die. For example, feeling breathless or out of control, as in asthma or epilepsy attacks, is very frightening, and frequently provokes fears of death. Surgery is also very frightening, and many children admit to fears of not waking up after the operation. Children who have been traumatized by real or perceived 'near death' experiences, can be left with considerable fears. One teenager recovering from meningitis suffered severe anxiety attacks at night in the form of flashbacks of events in intensive care. She became fearful of sleeping in case these flashbacks occurred and she could not wake herself from them. Her ultimate fear was of lapsing back into a coma whilst asleep and dying. Children who are feeling overwhelmed by pain, may also believe they are going to die, including children having simple blood tests or those suffering severe sickle cell crises.

Children may also resign themselves to believing that as everything is going wrong it will continue to get worse. One girl who suffered kidney failure was plagued with the thought that if her kidneys had failed so suddenly, other parts of her body might also fail and she would die. On being told about necessary further treatment, a young five-year-old boy suffering complications from surgery asked in a very resigned fashion, 'Have I got leukaemia as well now?', expecting the very worst.

When parents are very scared or distressed

Children are very sensitive to the cues they pick up from parents, particularly if they are in unfamiliar or frightening situations. Children may fear the worst when they see their parents very upset or worried. This is especially true when parents try to conceal their distress or do not give a reassuring explanation of why they are worried.

Parents can be so overwhelmed with their own feelings that they become less sensitive and aware of their child's presence or emotional needs. For example, a distressed mother who was being consoled by her friend, started talking about a future holiday, adding that she only hoped her child would still be around to enjoy it. She was, however, quite oblivious to her nine-year-old daughter who was also in the room. The little girl stopped playing, looked inquisitively at her mother, but said nothing and asked no questions about the holiday.

Parents in the stressful situation of dealing with children who are unco-operative or refuse important treatment may sometimes resort to shock tactics to gain co-operation, saying, for example, that they will die without this help. However, if an opportunity is not taken to talk about this later, the child can be left with very frightening thoughts.

One teenager spoke of only casually heeding instructions for complete bed rest for a suspected blood clot, evidently not understanding the seriousness of his situation. He remembered being shocked when his mother screamed at him that he could die as a result of not resting. Months later he described a cold chill that paralysed him with fear when he thought about it.

On receiving the diagnosis

When being given the name of their condition, children's thoughts can turn to death, no matter how serious the problem. They are likely to already have their own understanding, correct or incorrect, of its seriousness. One boy with a slight heart defect assumed he would die, as he had known someone else who had died from a heart attack. On being given the diagnosis of diabetes, one young girl became inconsolable, believing she would die. Only later did it become evident that it was the gravity in the doctor's tone of voice which had led her to believe this. She had never heard of diabetes and knew nothing about the condition. One teenager felt that cancer was synonymous with death, and remembered silently sobbing as she was driven to the hospital to start treatment, whispering goodbye to her pets, home and village, believing she would never see them again.

Overheard or insensitive comments from others

Children can easily overhear or mishear information that leads them to believe rightly or wrongly that they might die. Children who are frightened or think that information is being withheld may be hypervigilant and make particular efforts to overhear their parent's conversation. Parents have been overheard to tell friends that their child could have died, or to break down and admit their worst fears that their child might die. Some children have inadvertently learned about the seriousness of their condition from television programmes or fund-raising leaflets. Others have been asked insensitive questions, as in the example of a girl returning to school after treatment for leukaemia being asked by another child when she was going to die. A second child was given a photograph of a beloved pet rabbit who had died, and was asked if he would look after it, if he died and went to heaven.

Children who have known another child who has died

Children can have very strong attachments to other children whom they perceive to be in a similar situation to themselves. As a result, there are emotional repercussions around a clinic or ward for children, families and staff when a child dies. It can suddenly increase children's awareness of the seriousness of their condition or make them realize that children with their condition or symptoms can actually die. It can make many aspects of their condition or treatment feel less safe.

One teenage boy with a non-degenerative muscle weakness, requiring regular monitoring but no treatment, experienced a number of panic attacks following the death of a child from a congenital heart defect. He was aware that his own heart was monitored every year, and this had always been a very routine and non-threatening part of his treatment. However, he now became very frightened, believing there was also something seriously wrong with his heart, since otherwise the doctors would not be monitoring him. He then began to fear that it was only a matter of time before he had a heart attack and died. One 11-year-old girl who had successfully completed treatment for a brain tumour came back to hospital with painful leg and back spasms, which were the prominent symptoms of her best friend who had died several months previously with a spinal tumour. In her own way, she was both coming to terms with the death of her friend and the fears this raised for her about the possibility of dying herself.

Children who perceive a change in their condition or treatment regime

Children may realize that they are not getting better with the treatment they are receiving. This may occur either through suffering a further recurrence of the problem or just not improving from the condition they have. They may be devastated with fears of requiring new treatment or having to go through previous treatments again. However, there is the additional fear that if it was not successful before, it might be even less effective this time. One child who was clearly frustrated and scared at his ineffective, and seemingly endless, treatment retorted to his mother, 'Are they just going to keep pumping these drugs in to me until I die?'.

Changes in the condition can involve more contact with the hospital or clinic and more drugs, or treatment. Alternatively, there may be a move from aggressive or active treatment to palliative care, which may involve less contact with the medical team at hospital and the introduction of a new set of health professionals such as community palliative home care teams. All such changes will be significant for the child, who will be considering the implications carefully.

Changes in attitude towards the child

Children are also likely to be aware of a change in people's attitude and behaviour towards them. They will detect a move towards being overly nice and generous or not making expectations or demands on them, such as working hard at school. One boy recounted an incident while shopping with his mother, when he became angry as he wanted two lots of sweets, which his mother had initially refused and then allowed. He admitted to feeling guilty for being so unpleasant to his mother, but was more disturbed that she had given in to his demands. Sometimes parents are so desperate to make their sick children happy that they remove the safe boundaries of normal and acceptable behaviour. Regardless of how frustrated children may feel about these boundaries or rules, they do nevertheless recognize and understand these limits, and may become very frightened at their new-found omnipotence.

For some children there will be great attention and gifts bestowed upon them. They may be overwhelmed with hundreds of cards and presents, receive visits from rarely seen relatives or superstars they had always wanted to meet, or be taken for a holiday of their dreams in Disneyland. However, they may become very suspicious about the reason for this and may infer that they are going to die. Make a Wish, one of the most respected wish-granting agencies for children with life-threatening conditions, takes great care to be clear the treat is for the *whole* family so that the sick child is not singled out. The treat is described as a support for families who have endured difficult times and not as the 'last wish' of the child.

We have discussed the different events or situations which might trigger a child to contemplate their own death, whether or not the child is in fact dying. For children with life-threatening conditions, there may be a combination of events which can lead to a dawning awareness of impending death. Stages in the concept of illness that contribute to an awareness of death have been outlined as follows (Lansdown, 1996):

1. *I am ill.*
2. *I have an illness that can kill people.*
3. *I have an illness that can kill children.*
4. *I am never going to get better.*
5. *I am going to die.*

In addition to the challenge of trying to adapt to their disease and treatment, children may also need to find ways of coping with the emotional consequences of the awareness of their own impending death. We will now go on to consider the possible emotional reactions of children who are dying, and how this might be reflected in their behaviour. We will then look at ways of supporting and managing children's behaviour at this time. For very helpful accounts of working therapeutically with children who have life-threatening conditions please see Judd (1989) and Soukes (1995).

Emotional and Behavioural Reactions to Life-Threatening Conditions

Children's responses to any life-threatening situation will vary considerably depending on their personality, understanding, actual experience and the point in the course of their illness. They are also greatly influenced by the emotional responses and behaviour of important adults caring for them. Although some children may find ways of communicating their distress or worries directly, for many their distress or emotional needs may be revealed by a change in their behaviour. It is impossible to say how an individual child will feel or behave, since there is no one pattern of reaction to coping with this situation; it is only by listening carefully and being sensitive to children that one can understand their experience at this time. However, we will present some common possible responses in the following sections.

Denial/blocking

For some children, the profound anguish, pain and distress of the condition may be so overwhelming that they can only use denial as a coping strategy, in order to bear each day. Problems can arise when children have unrealistic expectations of what they are able to do, and seem unable to accept reasonable or rational explanations to help them tolerate the anxiety or fury created when challenged.

For example, one child repeatedly demanded that his mother let him out to play with his friends. He coldly told her how much he hated her for stopping him, when in fact, he was so weak he could hardly sit up in bed, let alone go and play. Children who are in denial or are clearly blocking communication may also limit the support available to them, and have no opportunity to prepare for what is going to happen. Denial, partial or complete, was clearly the coping style in one family of an eight-year-old girl with cancer. Although she was told by her parents that she could die from her condition, she was later overheard telling friends that the 'stupid' doctors had said she might die, but of course Mummy and Daddy would not let that happen. Even though she was experiencing frightening nightmares, neither she nor her parents were able to think of anything that might be worrying her. Her eleven-year-old sister also thought that she was not going to die, as she did not look or act sick, but had a 'little worry' which grew every time her sister had to visit the hospital or when she received yet more presents from neighbours and friends. The parents felt they coped best by carrying on as if everything was alright, even to the extent of pushing their daughter to do 'normal', everyday things, even when she was tired.

Partial denial is illustrated by a 10-year-old boy who tried to bargain with his parents about his death. Although he had a very mature understanding of death, he insisted that he would be able to come back to the family if his parents had another baby when he died. He knew and accepted that he was to die, but he could not accept being parted from his family.

Anger

I am not God's little lamb
I am God's sick tiger.
And I prowl about at night
And what most I love I bite.
(from the poem *Little boy sick* (Smith, 1985))

Children may frequently become angry, and may particularly vent it on the restrictions their condition places on them at a specific time. This is so for all children, but can be particularly difficult for adolescents who are trying to forge independence and to do things without adult support or intervention. At times their comments can become hurtful, spiteful, or aggressive.

One girl was furious and frequently shouted at her parents when they tried to help her but did not do it exactly as she wanted. If they brushed her hair she complained that they were hurting her or that they had used the wrong ribbon. If they helped her move, she complained they had been deliberately rough or had placed her on the wrong side.

Such behaviour may seem to be deliberate provocation to test the parents and see how much they can bear. It can certainly be extremely distressing for parents (and carers) to be the brunt of the child's anger, when they need to be close to the child and to show their love. However, it is important for them to understand what the child is in reality doing and feeling, so that they can respond most effectively. For example, children may be using their anger to place a distance between themselves and those they have to leave behind, perhaps to prepare both themselves and their family for their death. Their anger and irritability, when their demands are not instantly met, may in part be due to a sense of urgency to get things done. It may also be a reaction to feelings of helplessness and powerlessness.

Depression

Children may fluctuate in and out of periods of sadness or depression, although clinical depression is not common. They are having to cope with an increasing set of losses: loss of autonomy, loss of physical (and emotional) control, and helplessness over their condition. Some talk of wanting to die or to kill themselves as they do not want to go on. For a number of these children, the knowledge that they are going to die, and the anxiety of not having control over when, can trigger thoughts of wanting to die 'now'. This relates to the fears of some parents that if their child were to know the terminal nature of their condition, they would become depressed and give up.

Anxiety/fears

Children may have very distressing fears about dying. Commonly these include being in pain, being alone, practical concerns, such as 'Who will care for me when I'm dead?'; 'Will I go to heaven?', and concerns for family members left behind. Uncertainty about when death will happen is also a major concern, as illustrated by one boy who, when asked where he would like to be 'right now', answered, 'In the future'.

Children who are very anxious and feeling overwhelmed may regress to an earlier stage of development, for example, wanting help with dressing, eating, and toileting, being clingy and requiring constant adult company, particularly during the night. Some may revert to wetting the bed. Any situation in which there is increased dependent behaviour may serve to draw adult carers closer to them at a time when they are very scared.

Some children can develop quite ritualistic behaviour as a way of trying to exert some control over what is happening to them. This may be relatively simple such as wanting to curl up to their favourite doll on their left side, or more elaborate in having to go through a set sequence of steps in the process of dressing, washing or eating for example. Some children may become very distressed if the sequence is not followed exactly, or they are prevented from carrying out the steps. Checking is quite common (under the bed, behind the curtains) or touching (touching wood or needing to touch a particular surface a number of times). For one young boy, demanding his pillow be turned every few minutes was a way of retaining control when he could do very little else but lie in bed.

Emotional and physical shut down

When children are nearing death, they can be in a weakened state and may withdraw. Some interpret this as a disengagement, as a result of acceptance of impending death, an 'anticipatory mourning'. However, although this may be true, it is an huge assumption, albeit comforting, in that it may suit carers' needs to believe the child is ready and accepting of his or her death. Children may be very tired physically and emotionally, and may not have the energy to take an interest in new information or events. They may also withdraw as a way of escaping from anxiety-producing situations. Many may only engage in a small number of favourite activities (perhaps the same video, or passage of a book), which is well known, predictable and therefore safe, and does not require too much energy or attention. They may not be interested in engaging in conversation, and in some cases, will withdraw from physical contact. One child turned to his mother and said in a tired and irritable manner, 'Your kisses are too hard, Mummy'.

Although special treats and events are often organized for terminally ill children, the timing of these should be very carefully considered. Sometimes they become a terrible strain, both for the parents who have such a great deal invested in the event being enjoyable for their child, and for the child, who may be under pressure to have a good time. This may not be what the child wants or feels able to do, particularly if it requires too much energy or concentration.

Ways of Managing the Child's Emotional and Behavioural Distress

There are three main elements when trying to support children in the emotional turmoil and distress in which they may find themselves.

1. Carers should be aware of their own needs and have access to appropriate support for themselves.

2. They should attempt to be sensitive and understanding of the child's behaviour and emotional distress.

3. They should try to facilitate open communication with the child and support him or her in developing more helpful and appropriate strategies for managing the distress.

Some of the child's behaviour at this time can be extremely perplexing and challenging, and may be perceived as demanding, negative or rejecting. Nevertheless, it is important that the behaviour, however frustrating, should be understood by those caring for the child as a manifestation of distress, so that the child does not get a negative response which results in carers being less close or available to him or her. It can be extremely painful for adults to feel pushed away or rejected by children at the very time they feel a tremendous need to be physically and emotionally close. Understanding what the child is doing and the possible reasons for this are very important in enabling the adult to withstand the pain of supporting a dying child.

Dealing with feelings

It is helpful to acknowledge and validate the feelings evident in the child's behaviour and then talk through more acceptable ways of dealing with them. In *Chapter 7* we looked at exploring feelings, both verbally and non-verbally. Children who are overwhelmed and confused can be very frightened by their feelings being out of control. One girl was terrified that she was 'going crazy', because she felt she could not 'think straight'. However, helping children to recognize and name their feelings is one way of helping them feel more in control. Talking of a 'knot' in their stomach, or likening swings of extremes emotions to a rollercoaster ride, are just a couple of examples.

Managing children's emotional distress or behavioural problems involves giving them an opportunity to discuss their fears or worries. We will address the issue of supporting children with some of the commonly presenting fears a little later in the chapter. However, the general approach is to listen carefully to what they say, to accept their feelings and not try to make them think they are not feeling what they feel. The idea is to contain their feelings and to make them secure in talking about them. At the same time, one should attempt to help them to be clear about what to expect and to let them know what are appropriate ways of expressing themselves.

Dealing with denial

Denial may be a very healthy self-protective strategy used when children do not have the emotional resources or support to withstand 'consciously' knowing. Denial can allow the child to absorb little pieces of information over time while carrying on with the tasks of living. If this is the case, it is only with great sensitivity and very good reason that this denial should be challenged. If it is challenged, it should be done with careful thought about what supportive resources will be available to contain the emotional response to knowing.

However, there is a problem in being certain about what is denial and what is actually not known or understood. This is an important issue because one might easily collude with what is assumed to be denial, perhaps because of our own pain and denial, when in fact the child is confused or ignorant. Denial is also a process that is subject to change, with the situation, the provision of new information, or the child's emotional state. Therefore what is accessible for the child to think and talk about may change from one day to the next.

The most helpful way of managing denial is by being sensitive to the emotional support needed by the child, and giving opportunities for discussion, following the child's direction and pace. Some children may even be able to tell you what support they want, if they have this opportunity. They may benefit from being reassured, that like any other girl or boy, they may have concerns or questions about themselves or their illness and that there is always an opportunity to talk about these.

Dealing with specific fears

Is dying painful? With advances in pain relief, there is no reason for children to be in pain and it is important to reassure them that death is not painful. It may be difficult for children to distinguish between physical and emotional pain, and so it is equally important that the child's emotional state and anxieties are managed as well as their physical state. Helping children to be active in their own pain management can be very important in giving them some control and reassurance (see *Chapter 9*). Children who have asked if dying is painful are often told that it is like drifting into a deeper and deeper, peaceful sleep. Although this may be very reassuring at one level, some children may develop fears about going to sleep at night. Unless death is imminent, it is important to put the time of dying well into the future, and perhaps say that they will be told when the time is getting near.

Fears of abandonment. Children may be very clingy and scared to be on their own. It is important to reassure them that they will not be left to die on their own. It may be possible to discuss with them who they would want to be with at the end. They may need explicit reassurance that they will not be forgotten, and some have been given considerable security by being told they will live on as memories, and will always be loved.

Worries about parents' coping. Parents may need to say that although they are going to be very sad when the child dies, they will be able to carry on and will manage. Some children feel extremely protective of their parents and need this reassurance. For example, one boy was preoccupied with how a recently bereaved woman (the mother of a child he had met in hospital) was coping; he kept asking about her and wanted to visit to see if she was alright. Another child felt under tremendous pressure to be strong, continually hearing what a tower of strength he was for his mother, who kept saying he was the person keeping her going.

In many cases, the child and family do not ever totally give up hope, and this needs to be respected. Whether or not children can fully accept their dying, it may be important for parents to be able to give their child permission to stop being 'the brave fighter' and to let them go.

Children's Indirect Communications About Death

Many parents have strong feelings about not wanting their children to know the seriousness or terminal outcome of their condition. The reasoning behind this is perfectly understandable: there is a natural desire to protect children from such devastating news in the belief that they could not possibly be expected to cope with such an intolerable burden. Parents may be afraid that their children will just give up, if they know the reality of their condition. However, many children know the reality without being told. This is not surprising given the situations which trigger children to contemplate death considered earlier, and the ease with which they pick up information whether explicitly told or not. In consequence, it is often a tremendous relief for children to be able to be open about their condition with their parents. It means they are able to share their fears and go through this part of their life supported by the adults they trust and with whom they feel safe. This is preferable to the situation of them protecting their parents while being uncertain what will happen, but also being aware that what is happening to them is so unbearable, that no one can share it with them and that they must face death on their own.

Nevertheless, children may find it difficult to ask about death directly or even to introduce the topic indirectly. They may detect that this is a taboo subject, which is not openly discussed, or they may themselves feel too scared to confront and talk about their worries. Children may also have direct experiences of being silenced when they have tried to raise the topic, by jokey reassurances like, 'Don't be so silly', a swift change of subject, an embarrassed silence, or overt distress caused by their comments.

It is important, therefore, to recognize the cues or overtures that children give as an indication of a need to talk. Sensitivity to these will help to keep open channels of communication at a difficult time, when relationships can be very strained. It will also help parents to accept that their children need to talk about death or dying. Their preoccupation or anxiety may be shown through play, drawings, dreams, or a change in mood or behaviour. They may also make indirect comments which give an opportunity to explore their concerns or thoughts. For example, one child introduced the topic by talking about a science fiction programme he had watched on television and asked whether dead bodies could really be frozen and returned to life later. Another teenager was interested in a memorial plaque on some equipment on the ward and asked the nursing staff about the girl mentioned on the plaque and whether she had died on the ward.

Children will choose for themselves the person with whom they feel able raise the issue of dying. When they do, the role of that person is not necessarily one of giving the child direct answers or getting into an in-depth conversation. Certainly the helper must give a powerful message that the child can ask questions, and that these will be taken seriously. However, an initial aim is to help the child decide to whom it would be best to talk, because the child's parents need to be involved either directly or indirectly in this. It is so easy for parents to feel undermined and powerless when their child is very ill, and it is important that professionals do not take over the intimacy of the parental role and exclude the parents.

Of course, not all children want to talk and many children die without speaking about death to anyone. If they are clearly blocking conversation or otherwise indicating they do not want to know, this must be respected. As Kübler-Ross (1983) says, ' Although all patients have the right to know, not all patients have the need to know'. In these cases, a clear message must be given that there may be questions they want to ask, either now or in the future, and that they can ask whenever they are ready. One might indicate that all young people in their situation have questions, although they may be difficult to ask. It may also be useful to discuss to whom they might usefully talk, should the need arise.

Talking About Dying

When children demonstrate either directly or indirectly that there are questions or concerns they need to discuss, there are a number of resources available which might facilitate this, such as Heegard's *Drawing Out Feelings* series of workbooks (see *Appendix B* for further details.)

Children may need specific information to help them prepare for death. They may want to know as much as is possible about when and how it will happen, and what it will be like. They will certainly have a number of fears to explore. They may also have particular tasks or ambitions they want to accomplish before dying, for example, completing a set of football stickers or swimming with dolphins, and will need to discuss this to determine what is possible and what is not. They may also want to make plans about precious belongings; they may want particular people to look after them or to have as keep-sakes. They may also want the opportunity to say goodbye to important people in their lives.

One of the greatest challenges for those directly caring for the child is in being able to provide this information in the most reassuring and honest way possible. It is important, because following death, many parents have derived comfort from having been able to talk to and support their child at the end of their life, by being open, honest and feeling a very special closeness to them.

In talking to children about dying, it is important to be responsive to what they are actually asking, so as to be very clear about what they want to know. The pace of giving information needs to be set by the child, and one has to be very sensitive to what is accessible to the developmental level, experience and constructions of the child. It can feel bewildering and frustrating to have conversations in which children on the one hand let you know some of their worries about death, and then suddenly change the tone of the conversation to tell you what they are going to do when they are better. The aim however, is to follow their lead and help them know you are able to listen to anything they want to say when they are ready. It may be helpful to say to children that part of them is trying to carry on as normal and to be positive and hopeful, but that another part is holding all the worries. One young man described a 'treasure chest of fears', which he had firmly locked up in his mind, so that he could carry on being happy some of the time. The nurse was able to acknowledge how effective this strategy was most of the time, but talked about the help she could offer in terms of looking at the fears one at a time in a way which felt safe.

Most, if not all, of the information given to children at this time should be in response to their questions. However, as with any information giving, a careful exploration should be made of what the child already knows, thinks or feels. For example, it can be very helpful to reflect questions back to check what they actually mean.

'You are wondering if the doctors can help make everyone with cancer better? . . . but I wonder whether you are really worried about yourself?'

'What do you think happens when someone dies?'

It is important not to jump straight in and answer the question asked, but to carefully consider the context in which the question has been asked and to explore with children what has led them to think about this now. For example, a girl on intensive care requiring further surgery to insert a more permanent breathing tube (a tracheostomy) asked her nurse what it felt like to die. The nurse might have gone into an explanation of how she did not really know, but believed it to be painless. She may also have (incorrectly) assumed the child recognized a deterioration in her condition and was asking if she was going to die. Instead, she told the girl that she was aware this was an important question, which she may have been thinking about for some time, and wondered what had prompted her to ask about it now. The girl was able to talk about how she had seen another child pull out her breathing tube in her sleep and had seen the considerable nursing and medical activity which ensued. She said she was frightened she might do the same when she was asleep and might die if she were not watched closely. In a reassuring way, the nurse was able to go through the steps of the procedure and how children were observed. She also continued by saying that many young people were frightened in intensive care, because they saw scary things, and they worried about how they would be. She did this to give the girl further opportunity to say that she was frightened of dying if this were the case. As a result the girl strongly and clearly denied being worried any more but the opportunity of following up this conversation was made by the nurse giving her permission to talk about it again if she became worried again.

When there are no absolute answers, it is important to be honest about the uncertainty, but perhaps use this to explore what the child believes. For example, a teenager, who had successfully been treated for a recurrence of his tumour, said to his doctor, ' Well at least it won't come back again', but said it in a tentative and questioning way. The doctor heard the implicit question and responded firstly by confirming that the scans were very positive. He then said that he hoped it would never return, but that he could not give any guarantees. He then asked the young man what he thought, and discovered that he believed the tumour would continue to come back, that it would be successfully treated another couple of times, but that when it returned yet again, he would probably die.

The question that many adults most dread is children asking when, or if, they are going to get better. As this question is so important and so emotive, it is important that parents and professionals plan ahead and prepare for what they are comfortable saying. If death is not imminent, or if active treatment is being used, it is perhaps best to be optimistic and act as if a cure is possible. It might be important to convey that the condition is serious, but stress that everything possible is being done and that everyone hopes it will be better.

'You have an illness that makes some children die, but the doctors are trying a special treatment and we all hope you are going to be alright'.

If the prognosis is poor and all active treatment has stopped, children's questions about dying should be answered clearly and simply. It is important to indicate that it is not always possible to cure disease, but that the symptoms can be controlled; for example, ' Sometimes although the doctors do everything they can, it is not possible to make tumours go away, and they cannot make you better. What they can do is to give you something for those painful headaches you have been getting'.

Lansdown (1996) suggests that children should not be told that they are going to die, but rather that they may die soon. Although this may seem to be avoiding the issue, the reality is that death cannot be predicted with absolute certainty. Just saying that the child is going to die can seem rather brusque and final and may leave him or her without the means to deal with the remaining time.

When they sense that death may be close, they will need confirmation with appropriate support and reassurance. A young man in the early stages of Freidrich's Ataxia had been almost incapacitated by the fear of dying for several months. He had, for example, insisted on sleeping with his mother and on her staying awake just in case something happened. Although he was appropriately shocked and distressed on hearing the confirmation of his worst fear, putting the event well into the future enabled him to reduce his fear and manage his current situation better.

Caring for Siblings

As already discussed earlier in the text, siblings of children with chronic medical conditions are often subject to 'benign neglect', where their needs and wishes are perceived as less important than those of the other sick or disabled child. The exhausting physical demands of treatment and the profound emotional demands of having a sick child can sometimes leave very little time or energy for the rest of the family. This is never more apparent than when dealing with a life-threatening or terminal condition. It is a time when siblings can feel particularly distressed, vulnerable and abandoned. A good model of care for the siblings at these times will incorporate the following:

1. *Recognizing the emotional needs of the sibling.*
2. *Keeping them involved in the care of the sick child.*
3. *Keeping their routines as normal and predictable as possible.*
4. *Continuing this care both during the illness and after the child has died.*

Recognizing the emotional need of siblings

Parents may have their attention so exclusively focused on their sick child, and be so devastated emotionally, that it is hard to even think about all the practical arrangements they need to make for their other children. They may feel worried or guilty about not being able to care for them and feel frustrated or irritated by the demands they place on them.

Siblings may be terrified by what is happening to their sick brother or sister, what is happening to their very stressed parents, and what is happening to their family in general. They may feel they are expected to carry on as normal and continue to work hard at school when in fact they cannot concentrate. They may experience nightmares or sleepless nights and feel tired and irritable with everyone else. On top of all this, no one may seem to be interested in them, and there may be a strong sense of feeling less important and possibly even less loved than the sick child. Even if they felt they wanted to tell their parents how they were feeling, finding a private or undisturbed time and fears of upsetting parents further can prevent this.

One eight-year-old girl, who had stayed in hospital for weeks helping to look after her dying sister, was invited to take part in some ward activities which were arranged for other patients. As part of the activity, she was asked to call out her name. She responded by giving the name of her sister. It may be she felt that she was representing her sister (who was too unwell to take part herself), or that as the well sibling she was not important enough to be part of the activity in her own right.

To offset these problems, particularly if communication between family members is strained, it can be of enormous benefit for an interested and involved adult to spend time with the siblings in order to help them make sense of what may appear to be chaos around them. The overall intention is to help them understand the situation and to cope with their feelings at such a difficult time.

A play specialist made a booklet with one sibling entitled *All About Gina*. This contained her story of everything that was important to her, including descriptions of family activities and pictures of herself and her family before and after her sister's illness. As well as providing a focus for attention on her experiences, the booklet enabled Gina to explore how things had changed for her and to make sense of how she was feeling. Gina also used the book as a talking point for both her sister, who was bedridden and unable to do very much, and her parents, who took a great interest in the work she produced each day. The book also facilitated communication about the good and fun things Gina was currently doing, as she had previously felt anxious about having fun or talking about it because she thought it might be painful for her sister to hear.

Involving siblings in the family care of the sick child

It is important to keep siblings appropriately involved in what is happening, whether the sick child is at home, in hospital or in a hospice. This can be done by keeping them well-informed and involved in family discussions and decision making. It may also be possible to include them in the physical, social or emotional care of the child.

A dilemma can arise in considering the different informational needs of the sick child and sibling. If siblings are close in age, or younger, difficulties may occur if they are given more information than the sick child. Firstly, this may place a terrible burden on the sibling who may have to hold distressing news and not be able to discuss this freely within the family. Secondly, the children may share a great deal between themselves without the knowledge of adults, so that there is the danger of information being exchanged at a time or in a way that is less helpful to the sick child.

These possibilities need to be balanced against the needs of the sibling to be fully involved, in order for them to cope themselves and to prepare for their brother or sister's death. They also need to feel comfortable with what information they give others about what is happening. Unfortunately, they are often the link between what is happening in hospital and concerned friends in the community. Apart from the irritation of always being asked about their brother and sister, seemingly without anyone being interested in them, children have also described feeling frozen with fear when asked how their brother or sister is. They may not know what to say, and often revert to saying he or she is alright, even if this is clearly not the case. Helping children understand what is happening and thinking through what they might want to tell others can be helpful. It can also be useful to pass the burden of informing others by giving regular bulletins to an adult in the community to pass on, in order to spare the sibling some of this.

Most of the information received by siblings will be from family members or the sick child. Rarely are they included in meetings with the doctors or, even if present, have any of the explanations addressed to them. It can be a very positive experience for them to have their own time with the doctor or nurse, and to have an opportunity to ask questions directly. This can help them to feel an important part of what is happening.

It is also important that siblings are given a role or position within the family care of the sick child. At a time when the child is very sick or dying, siblings may feel displaced and estranged from the family. During lengthy hospital admissions siblings can be placed with a variety of relatives and friends and may suffer considerable disruption to family, social or school life. Some end up staying with a parent for weeks or months in hospital, while their parents seem to care tirelessly for their brother or sister, but with no time or patience for themselves. The frustration of this is reflected in the comments of a five-year-old who angrily asked his mother why she just sat and watched his brother's chest go up and down all day long!

Hospital schools can have a very important role both for the child receiving treatment and for brothers and sisters. School can give both a structure to the day, and stimulating and purposeful activity. It is also a distraction from the ward and provides emotionally responsive adults who can be attentive to what the child is doing and feeling.

Visiting someone who is so ill is very stressful and difficult. Siblings who only visit occasionally can easily feel in the way, bored, and resentful for the lack of attention they receive. However, it can be important and helpful if a member of the nursing team welcomes visiting siblings to the unit, makes special time available for them and perhaps gives them responsibility for some aspect of care.

For other families, where children are cared for at home, the household routines will undoubtedly revolve around the sick child. In addition, there is likely to be a stream of visitors, community nurses or doctors, allied medical professionals, relatives and friends. If siblings' needs are not properly addressed, they may feel in the way and excluded from the important events around them. Again, they can be helped to feel valued by being given important caring tasks and considerable praise for their helpfulness. The task for one child was to tell her sick brother the day's gossip from school and to read to him and keep him company in the evenings. Another child was particularly good at rubbing sore legs, another at telling jokes. The actual care undertaken is not the issue; what is important is that they feel comfortable with the task and feel valued and involved in helping. It may be so important after the child's death that siblings are able to feel they were able to help, as a concrete sign of love for their brother or sister.

Keeping routines as predictable and normal as possible

Good friends can be an invaluable protective factor for siblings, but unfortunately visits to hospital or staying away from home with relatives can disrupt these relationships. It is particularly helpful if siblings remain in their normal environment, or at least are in regular contact with their friends, with a clear plan for each week. The familiarity of one's own school and established relationships with teachers and peer group can be very supportive. If siblings are staying in hospital, it is important that the school is aware of this and can send messages and greetings to them as well as the sick child.

Sensitivity to the sibling after the death of the child

At a time when the whole family is grieving, children may feel most vulnerable, distressed and abandoned, finding that adults are so absorbed in their own grief that they are emotionally unavailable to them. Parents may also find it difficult to understand the way siblings are grieving or showing distress, since it may be quite different to the adult's experience of grief. For example, young children are not able to sustain prolonged expressions of intense grief. They may be very distressed for a little while and then appear to play happily. Sometimes their activities can provide a healthy distraction for their parents, but at other times adults may be easily irritated with noise or disturbance, or frustrated that the child does not seem to care about their brother or sister.

Some children show their distress in physical ways, and develop symptoms which may resemble the physical problems of the child who died. This perhaps reflects both the child's preoccupation with the physical condition and ultimate death, and fears that it might also happen to him or her. It may also reflect the fact that such physical symptoms are likely to draw close attention from distressed parents. What this implies is that siblings may need considerable reassurance about their own safety and health at a time when the world has suddenly become a frightening place where children can die. They may also seek reassurance that parents or other family members are not going to die and leave them.

Some children may also suffer 'survivor guilt', where they struggle to make sense of the death, and wonder why it was their brother or sister who died and not them. They may feel guilty about it, or may think that the terrible upset in the family might have been lessened if they had died instead. They may also feel guilty about being able to enjoy activities, to laugh or feel happy. Children need a clear message from adults that life is for living and having fun, and there is still a time for memories of the dead sibling and feelings of both sadness and joy about them.

Many parents question whether siblings should be allowed to see the dead body or to attend the funeral service. Although there are no absolute rules about this, they should not be excluded from these events, but the decision should be made taking account of what they would like. There should be an open discussion with them if possible. However, they should certainly not be forced to do anything against their will. If they take part (for example, see the body) they should be carefully prepared for the experience, and a supportive adult should be available to them during and following the event to give them an opportunity to talk. Funerals can facilitate expressions of sadness and support for the child and family and may be helpful for the child in terms of saying goodbye. If the siblings do not attend the funeral service, other ways of saying goodbye can be arranged, such as a small family memorial service.

For staff on a ward or unit it is important to consider the needs and distress of children outside a particular bereaved family. We have already briefly mentioned how other children in the ward may be affected by the death of a friend. It is good practice for families to be informed about a child's death and given an opportunity to attend a funeral or memorial service. Giving such information in a controlled and proactive way is preferable to them finding out by chance. It is also important that opportunities are made for children to talk to staff about the dead child, as it enables them to share their feelings, but it also gives children an important message that once dead, people still remember and care about you.

Summary

❑ The aims of helping are to provide the highest quality of living (and dying) which involves dignity and comfort.

❑ To facilitate communication with children about dying, it is important to hold a developmental perspective of their understanding about death, the situations/events which may trigger worries, and the ways children raise questions or worries, directly or indirectly. It is also important to be sensitive to the emotional coping strategies used by children to manage their situation.

❑ Children's knowledge of death and what happens after death will be determined by cognitive abilities, religious and cultural teachings, and their direct or indirect experiences.

❑ Death is not an all or nothing concept. It is comprised of a number of components, including: realization, separation, immobility, irreversibility, causality, dysfunctionality, universality, insensitivity, and appearance. By the age of eight or nine years, almost all children will have a comprehensive understanding incorporating all of these components.

❑ Research findings are only a guide, and it is important to listen sensitively to what children understand and what they actually want to know.

❑ Children may find it difficult to talk about dying directly, but do find indirect means of alerting adults to a worry or need to talk. Their play, drawings, dreams and indirect comments can be very revealing.

❑ A number of different situations may prompt children to worry or think about their own death: when they are frightened or in pain; when they perceive their parents to be scared or upset; when they are given their diagnosis; if they overhear or mishear comments; if they know another child has died; or when they are aware of a change in their condition or a change in the treatment plan.

❑ Children's emotional responses to life-threatening conditions will depend on their understanding of death and the emotional support they perceive to be around them, including whether it is possible to talk about their worries and fears with a supportive adult.

continued

continued --

❏ Talking to children about dying needs to be done with great sensitivity to what they really want to know. A supportive relationship allows them to talk openly about worries or fears and ask any questions they would like.

❏ Much, if not all, information given to children will be based on their questions and the context in which the discussion is held.

❏ The skills and process of information giving are relevant here (see *Chapter 8*), taking into account the highly emotive nature of the subject and the child's response to talking and thinking about dying.

❏ Siblings need to be involved in the care of the dying child, and to have their own emotional needs attended to both before and after their brother or sister's death.

11

Final Remarks

We hope that this book has given an indication of the importance of psychosocial issues in caring holistically for children with chronic medical conditions and disability. We also hope that the examples of children's experiences will have enabled a greater understanding of their needs and the help that can be offered at each and every stage of a child's illness. Although there are no absolute rules for helping, our aim has been to offer some practical guidance relating to the process, skills and qualities of helping, both to enable people to identify their own strengths or training needs, and to be able to apply these skills more appropriately and confidently. The assumption implicit in the text is that everyone can develop their communication skills to enhance the quality of their care for children and families.

When working with children, in addition to helping them set goals and evaluate the changes they have been able to make, it is important to reflect on and evaluate one's own role and contribution. It is also important to acknowledge personal or professional limits and to access more specialist services as required. Furthermore, it is very important to be aware of one's own needs, particularly as working with sick children can be so emotive and challenging. Issues regarding referral on to other services, training, support and supervision will be considered in this context.

Referral to Other Services

There may be a number of reasons which make referral to another professional organization or service appropriate. These include factors relating to the child, the helper or the context in which the child is seen.

Factors relating to children and their situation

Referral on to specialized child mental health professionals is appropriate when children's distress or problems are persistent, complex or severe. It may also be appropriate where children are not able to make use of the help currently offered, because they are depressed or resistant in forming a relationship, or the child's situation does not give any opportunity for change, as, for example, when there are significant relationship difficulties with one or both parents. More specialist therapeutic help includes cognitive behavioural interventions, psychodynamic approaches or more systemic help involving the family, school or medical team. For a helpful introduction to different therapeutic approaches, please refer to Lane and Miller (1992).

If the child's situation is not safe, for example, if there are concerns that the child may harm him or herself, or any form of abuse or neglect is suspected (emotional, physical or sexual), this will need to be addressed immediately before any other help can be utilized. It is important that concerns are, in the first instance, discussed with senior colleagues, and referral made, if appropriate to child mental health services, or in child protection matters, to social services, who will have a legal responsibility to investigate and protect the child's welfare. It is important that there is good documentation of concerns, and it is likely that following referral to social services, attendance at a Professionals Planning Meeting or even a Child Protection Conference will be required. It is important to be familiar with the Child Protection Policy in your own health establishment as these can vary from one area to another.

Although conversations with children and families are private and confidential, the child's safety and welfare is paramount. Wherever possible, any referral to social services should be discussed carefully with children so that they understand why the referral is being made, and what help can be offered, even if they do not initially want the referral to be made. Although discussion and agreement with the family about the referral may be possible or even desired, permission is not required, and in certain circumstances, it is not helpful for parents to be informed at the early stages of child protection proceedings, as there may be an opportunity for some parents to put pressure on and silence their children.

Factors relating to the helper

No one can be expected to be expert at everything, and there will inevitably be times for every one of us when we are not in the best position to help. It can be very difficult to accept that we have not been able to change a situation or make things better for a child that we care about, as this can be seen as failing. However, success is not necessarily determined solely by changes in the problem, and it is important to recognize that there is a role for defining and exploring problems, and facilitating or supporting the child's access to specialist help, rather than being the sole agent of change.

Careful consideration needs to be given to the commitments made to children and the sort of work undertaken, particularly if a helper is only available to work with children for a short period of time, and will not have the opportunity to follow through what is begun. Relationships with children can become intense very quickly, and children may experience a considerable loss if the person they have come to trust, and with whom they feel comfortable, is suddenly not available to them. As with any ending in the helping process, it is important to put aside enough time to prepare children and give them an opportunity to work through their feelings associated with this loss.

Context

Referral should be considered if the context in which children are seen does not allow the time or the regularity of contact which may be needed. For example, it may be more appropriate for help to be given locally if children live a considerable distance from the clinic or hospital, and regular visits are difficult. Help may also be more easily given by professionals who have greater access to the child, such as those working within the child's school.

The referral process

Referral on to another professional should always be discussed carefully with the child and family. It is important that they do not perceive it as a rejection, or feel that they are losing the current support completely. It is possible, for example, to continue to see them even after referral, if appropriate. The aim is to obtain the most appropriate form of help possible by facilitating this transition and by helping both children and their carers recognize what help they need.

Naturally, their agreement to the referral is essential for it to occur, but it is also important to negotiate what information will be given with the referral. For example, it can be very helpful to write the referral letter as much as possible with the child (and family) and for them to keep a copy of it. This not only demonstrates the principle of working in partnership, it can also be a very constructive way of enabling the child to clarify the problems or issues and what help they would like.

There may frequently be a delay of weeks or even months before a referral is taken up by another service. This is usually the case, unless the child's problem is seen as a priority (for example, the child is in danger or a danger to him or herself or others). If there is a delay, it may be important to keep in contact with the child and to offer support as frequently as necessary.

Consultation and collaboration

If a good relationship has been established with a child and family, instead of referring them elsewhere, such as to a child mental health specialist, an alternative strategy is to consult the specialist directly and to discuss the difficulties with them. This may save everyone time, be just as effective, and avoid the difficulties of transferring and re-engaging with another person. Another useful strategy, however, is to invite the specialist to join you and the child, to be a consultant to you both, helping to clarify issues or plan appropriate strategies for helping. A further possibility is that you might accompany the child and/or family in their appointment with the professional to whom they are referred. This can be seen as something akin to an advocacy role. It may also enable you to help them understand what occurred in the session, if complex information has been given, or they did not remember everything that was said. If you have established a good relationship with the child, just your presence in the room may give him or her sufficient support to enable better use to be made of the meeting. It may also be that you can facilitate the process by raising questions, concerns or areas for discussion that the child has already raised with you.

Support, supervision and training

In order to ensure that the quality of services remains at a high level, it is important to acknowledge the stresses and strains that are experienced by all staff working in this area. To enable them to cope effectively, they require appropriate support, ongoing supervision, and their further training needs should be identified and met.

The stresses most commonly identified by health professionals are inevitably related to the nature of the work in terms of the constant suffering that is seen and the lack of resources available (including time) to meet the perceived needs. Relationships with staff can be very protective and supportive; however, feeling unsupported, unvalued or being undermined by colleagues can be a significant stress. In a study of a children's hospice (Woolley *et al*, 1989) 25 per cent of the staff showed significant stress, with the main symptoms being anxiety, difficulties sleeping, somatic symptoms and difficulties in social relationships. The highest levels of stress were attributed to caring for children with uncontrollable symptoms, and witnessing children in physical or emotional pain and distress. In addition, 80 per cent of the staff reported that difficulties in staff communication and interrelationships were also an important source of stress.

Children in particular can evoke very powerful feelings in their carers. When they are frightened, upset or hurt, their distress signals lead to intense protective responses from adults. Children exhibit many behaviours (such as rejecting help from all others but co-operating and visibly calming with particular people) which clearly demonstrate their dependence on their carer, who is likely to respond by feeling important to and needed by the child, but also desperate to protect and make things better for him or her. Although the work can be intensely rewarding, there is most certainly an emotional cost to supporting children with chronic and life-threatening conditions. Failure to acknowledge and care for oneself while constantly trying to meet the needs of such a needy population can lead to physical and mental exhaustion. Complete exhaustion, or 'burnout', is well recognized as a consequence of chronic stress and neglect of one's own needs.

To some extent we can all protect ourselves by using our professional boundaries to help distance us and to prevent over-identifying with children and families. However distressing the situation, the pain and distress belongs to the family. We can understand, empathize, and even suffer *with* them for a while, but it is not our child or our problem, and we cannot suffer *for* them. However, there will undoubtedly be particular children or situations which draw us in emotionally, leaving us more vulnerable and open to distress. At these times, it is important to have supportive colleagues, or even one's own family and friends, with whom to talk through the feelings. In this way, we have an opportunity to reflect on the characteristics of the child or the nature of the relationship which led to more personal involvement. This may enable us to manage the stress more effectively. However, although support can, and even should, be derived from supportive colleagues and good communication networks, more formal structures should be in place to provide all staff with ongoing support. These might include psychosocial meetings, formal support meetings, debriefing meetings, or regular individual supervision.

Psychosocial meetings

Many wards, units or clinics hold regular psychosocial meetings for those involved in the care of the child and family. These multi-disciplinary meetings provide opportunities for staff to share their concerns about families and to pass on information that would otherwise have been overlooked in meetings with a more medical or physical focus. The purpose of such meetings is to enable the team to give the best holistic care possible. However, they also serve a secondary function in offering feedback and support to the professionals caring for the children on the unit. It is important that the staff do not experience the burden of feeling alone in caring or worrying about particular children, and these meetings give an opportunity for everyone involved to discuss their part and talk about areas of progress or difficulty. As the focus of the psychosocial meetings is on the child and family, rather than on the staff need for support, some workers find it easier to protect time for this and derive the support they might not feel comfortable receiving in more formal support meetings.

Support group meetings

The aim of these meetings is to provide a safe and supportive place in which feelings aroused by children and their families or work situations can be vented and shared. Recognizing that you are not struggling alone with these feelings can be an important support in itself. Other members of the group may listen or even offer suggestions and feedback about the situation discussed.

For such groups to be effective, it is important that group members feel comfortable with each other and able to speak openly. Members, therefore, need to have respect for each other's viewpoint and absolute confidentiality has to be agreed. Care also has to be taken over the composition of such groups. Although mixed professional groups can be formed, it is usually more helpful if they consist of staff from similar backgrounds and seniority, otherwise, non-medical and more junior staff can feel intimidated by senior consultants and may feel unable to contribute. It can be most helpful if these groups are facilitated by someone who is perceived as coming from outside the unit or ward, and who has experience in the area of group dynamics.

Great demands on professionals' time can make attendance at any regular support meeting very difficult. When time is so limited, many staff feel uncomfortable about taking time out of their work for themselves. As a result, many tend to rely on more informal routes for their support. However, in reality, attendance at such meetings is entirely justifiable in terms of it ensuring their continued ability to provide the most effective care possible for children and their families.

Debriefing or ad hoc meetings

Following a particularly difficult or distressing situation, it can be helpful for all those involved to meet and to talk through the events. The purpose of this may be to explore how well the case was managed and to identify key problems and to evaluate what was particularly helpful or unhelpful. However, they can also be a way of debriefing in the sense of enabling the staff involved to share feelings of frustration or even joy about the situation. Although such discussion may happen informally, meetings of this kind can ensure that all those concerned have an opportunity to be heard. If managed properly, they can be very supportive and even enhance the working of a group of people as a team.

Formal individual supervision

For those working in mental health services, formal supervision is regarded as essential. In fact, relevant professional associations such as The British Psychological Society (BPS) and the British Association for Counselling (BAC) regard it as unethical for people to practise without it. It involves regular meetings (weekly or fortnightly) between the helper and a more senior colleague. The content of the meetings should largely be led by the needs of the helper, but the aims are to go through the helper's caseload and to review what has happened with each case. The idea is to evaluate what is being achieved, but also to explore difficulties and facilitate decisions about where to go next.

Within many other professions, formal supervision is not a regular practice, and meetings with senior staff do not tend to cover the emotional and psychological aspects of working with children. In these situations, it may be valuable to identify a colleague who is in a position to meet your needs in terms of supervision and negotiate some time for this purpose. The qualities required in the supervisor include an advanced knowledge of counselling and interest in your work. You need to get on with them well, and they should be a good listener and have good counselling skills themselves. Overall you should feel that they are able to facilitate your helping skills.

Supervision enables time to reflect on practice and to evaluate how effective you have been in your attempts to help in a supportive way. It also helps you explore your own feelings, whether positive or negative, about yourself, your role and the people with whom you work. Without protecting time for reflection, we are more likely to become reactive and rigid in our practice, with little opportunity for developing skills.

Supervision groups

Supervision can also be effective if conducted in groups. This is in some ways more economical of supervisor time, but may not allow the opportunity for a detailed handling of the needs of each person in the group. Such groups are likely to have a more formal structure than support groups, with an agenda, for example, that enables each person to present and discuss particular cases. These groups are most helpful if led by an experienced member of staff, with expertise in counselling or mental health problems. This can make it possible, as the need arises, for sessions to be given over to specific training issues such as working on relationships, behavioural methods, and bereavement, if several members of the group are facing such problems in their work.

Further education and training

As implied in the last section, training and supervision can be viewed as a continuum and much may be achieved in both aspects within specific services. However, if one is to become highly skilled in working with children and families psychologically, a formal training in counselling, for example, is inevitable. Group sessions or workshops focusing on stress management or communication skills (including role play with observers giving feedback) can be invaluable in the workplace. Nevertheless, the requirements of a good counselling training which has to be spread over several months or even two to three years are beyond what most services can offer their employees.

As counselling increases in terms of acceptability and popularity, a bewildering number of different courses and training are becoming available. The British Association for Counselling (BAC) runs short courses and provides information on training throughout the UK. If you are intending to take any courses, it is important they are run by an accredited college or organization and lead to a qualification which is recognized by others. It is also important to consider the theoretical orientation of the courses, since they differ enormously from the cognitive-behavioural, to the psychoanalytical and the non-directive client centred models, for example (Davis and Fallowfield, 1991).

If you are considering a career using these skills, further details are available from The British Psychological Society, the British Association for Counselling, or the British Association of Psychotherapists (see *Appendix C* for details).

Children's Rights

This text has been concerned with identifying children's emotional needs and how these can best be met by those caring for them. Our aim has been to help the reader think about communicating with children and to help them to improve their knowledge and skills in this area. It can be argued that services have been largely focused upon physical needs and have tended to neglect other issues. However, there is a general movement within current society to address the broader needs and to specify the rights of children, perhaps stemming from the work of the United Nations Convention of the Rights of the Child (recognized in the UK in 1991). This convention established that children have the right:

- *to be protected from harm;*
- *to take an active part in society;*
- *to express their views and have them taken into consideration;*
- *to services which meet their needs.*

In the UK, perhaps the most comprehensive document looking at the rights of children in hospital is the following charter produced by Action for Sick Children (formerly, NAWCH), in 1985. We have presented this in full, because of its importance.

A Charter for Children in Hospital

1. Children shall be admitted to hospital only if the care they require cannot be equally well provided at home or on a day basis.
2. Children in hospital shall have the right to have their parents with them at all times provided this is in the best interests of the child. Accommodation should therefore be offered to all parents and they should be helped and encouraged to stay. In order to share in the care of their child, parents should be fully informed about ward routine and their active participation encouraged.
3. Children and/or their parents shall have the right to information appropriate to age and understanding.
4. Children and/or their parents shall have the right to informed participation in all decisions involving their health care. Every child shall be protected from unnecessary medical treatment and steps taken to mitigate physical or emotional distress.
5. Children shall be treated with tact and understanding and at all times their privacy shall be respected.
6. Children shall enjoy the care of appropriately trained staff, fully aware of the physical and emotional needs of each age group.
7. Children shall be able to wear their own clothes and have their own personal possessions.
8. Children shall be cared for with other children of the same age group.
9. Children shall be in an environment furnished and equipped to meet their requirements, and which conforms to recognized standards of safety and supervision.
10. Children shall have full opportunity for play, recreation, and education suited to their age and condition.

Finally in the UK, The Children Act 1989 has had immense implications for the rights of all children. The key concept in the Act is that the child's welfare is paramount and that before any legal decision is made about a child, the local authority has a duty to ascertain the wishes and feelings of the child, with consideration for his or her age and understanding.

In considering children with illness and disability, the Act outlines the criteria for children in need, and makes the local authority responsible for providing services to allow children to live as normal a life as possible and to safeguard and promote the welfare of these children. Certainly, listening to children in order to learn about their experiences and problems, and providing holistic care to promote their well-being as covered in this text is an essential part of this.

Although it would have to be clarified in law, the implication of these kinds of documents and policies are that children have rights to know what is happening to them and to make decisions about it. For example, they might be considered to have the right to discontinue treatment or refuse tests and certainly to know what tests are conducted for (for example, HIV testing) and to know their diagnosis and prognosis.

In conclusion, we are firmly committed to the principle that children are to be fully respected and their views taken into consideration in everything that happens to them, whether in health or in suffering. Even when pain cannot be removed, they should be treated with dignity as befits their competence. Their strength should never be underestimated. Although it may be hard to do, the most respectful course of action that can be adopted under all circumstances is to provide them with the opportunities to talk, and to listen carefully, very carefully, to what they say and to act upon it. We hope that this book has communicated the significance of this principle, even if we have not been successful in making the task any easier for you.

Appendix A: *A Relaxation Exercise*
(Loosely based on exercises suggested by Bernstein and Borkovec, 1973)

First, find a comfortable position (sitting or lying down). We are going to do some exercises to look at the difference between feeling tense and relaxed, and will use this to learn to relax our bodies.

Now, I want you to make a fist with your hands . . . squeeze tightly for a count of three (for a younger child, you might ask them to squeeze their parent's hand or your hand). *Now relax. Good. Notice the difference between tensing and relaxing your hands . . . How does it feel for you?* (At this point, you might suggest that the child's hand feels warm and tingly, or heavy and relaxed). *Now we are going to help the rest of your body to get that lovely relaxed feeling.*

The relaxation exercise can be adapted to suit the individual child with consideration to the child's cognitive ability, concentration skills, and the aims of the exercise.

1. Breathing – most important of all is to relax the breathing. Suggest the child takes a few deeper breaths in and lets them out really slowly, breathing in to a count of three, and exhaling to a slow count of three. Actually saying the word 'relax' when exhaling can be helpful for some children.

2. Muscle groups – work through all the muscle groups as indicated above, tensing and relaxing to a count of three. Older children may enjoy naming and identifying the muscles they are using whereas younger children may benefit from concrete suggestions such as 'See if you can make your shoulders touch your ears', or, 'Try and smile as widely as you can, stretching from one ear to the other'. Move through the arms, shoulders, face, abdomen, legs and feet in this way.

Appendix B: *Books for Children*

Specific Medical Conditions and Disabilities

Althea (1983). *I Use a Wheelchair*. London: Dinosaur Publications.

Althea (1987). *I Have Epilepsy*. London: Dinosaur Publications.

Althea (1989). *I Have Cancer*. London: Dinosaur Publications.

Althea (1983). *I Have Diabetes*. London: Dinosaur Publications.

Amenta, C.A. (1992). *Russell is Extra Special. A book about autism for children*. New York: Magination Press.

BACUP (1989). *Coping with Hair Loss*. London: BACUP.

Brazier, L., Trapp, A., and Yales, N. (publication date unknown). *Simon has Cancer*. Newcastle Upon Tyne: Victoria Publications. (Available from Victoria Publications, Royal Victoria Infirmary, Queen Victoria Road, Newcastle upon Tyne NE1 4LP, UK.)

Larsen, H. (1974). *Don't Forget Tom*. London: A.& C. Black Ltd. (About a child with learning difficulties.)

Marshall, A. (1989). *I Can Jump Puddles*. Harmondsworth: Penguin Books. (A story of a boy with a physical disability.)

Merrifield, M. (1990). *Come Sit By Me*. Ontario, Canada: Women's Press. (An educational book about AIDS and HIV infection for young children ages 4–8 and their carers).

Mills, J., and Crowley, R. (1988). *Sammy the Elephant and Mr Camel. A story to help children overcome bedwetting*. New York: Magination Press.

Mills, J. (1992). *Little Tree. A story for children with serious medical problems*. New York: Magination Press.

Moss, D. (1990). *The Rabbit with Epilepsy*. USA: Woodbine House.

Petersen, P. (1976). *Sally Can't See*. London: A. & C. Black Ltd.

Rogan, P., and Perret, A. (1987). *Epilepsy – The detective's story*. Liverpool: Roby Education Ltd.

Books Dealing with Social Situations/Bullying

Browne, A. (1984). *Willy the Wimp*. London: Little Mammoth.

Stones, R. (1993). *Don't Pick on Me*. London: Piccadilly Press.

Other Books

Althea (1986). *Going into Hospital*. London: Dinosaur Publications.

Balkwill, F. (1990). *Cells are Us*. London: Harper Collins Publishers.

Balkwill, F. (1990). *Cell Wars*. London: Harper Collins.

Beswetherick, H. (publication date unknown). *Wiggly's World!* Newcastle upon Tyne: Victoria Publications.

Handford, M. (1989). *Where's Wally?* London: Walker Books.

McKee, D. (1980). *Not Now, Bernard*. Italy: Grafiche AZ.

Books Specifically for Siblings

Muscular Dystrophy Group. *Hey, I'm Here Too. A guide for brothers and sisters of children with muscular dystrophy*. (Available from the Muscular Dystrophy Group, 35, Macauley Road, London. SW4 0QP. Tel: 0171 720 8055.)

Peterkin, A. (1992). *What about me? When brothers and sisters get sick*. (Ages 4–8). New York: Magination Press.

Bereavement/Loss

Burningham, J. (1984). *Granpa*. London: Jonathan Cape Ltd.

This is a large printed book with very little text. It is about a little girl and her granpa and the things the two of them enjoy doing together. Towards the end of the book he is seen to be unwell, and the last picture is of his empty chair. This is most suitable for an adult to look at with a young child and to facilitate the child describing what is happening in the pictures. Suitable for pre-school age and upwards.

Cowlishaw, S. (1993). *When My Little Sister Died*. Derby: Merlin.

Harper, A. (1994). *Remembering Michael*. London: SANDS (Stillbirth and Neonatal Death Society). A story about a family where a baby brother dies at birth.

Hollins, S. and Sireling, L. (1994). *When Mum Died*. London: St. Georges Mental Health Library.

Hollins, S. and Sirling, L. (1994). *When Dad Died*. London: St. Georges Mental Health Library.

Johnson, J. and Johnson, M. (1982). *Where's Jess?* Nebraska: Centring Corporation.

Lamont, S. (publication date unknown). *Ewen's Little Brother*. Newcastle upon Tyne: Children's Cancer Unit, Victoria Publications. A simple but effective story of the loss of a younger brother.

Maple, M. (1992). *On the Wings of a Butterfly. A story about life and death*. Seattle: Parenting Press Inc. This tells the story of a child who is dying with a brain tumour.

Mills, J. (1993). *Gentle Willow. A story for children about dying*. New York: Magination Press.

Nystrom, C. (1990). *Emma Says Goodbye. A child's guide to bereavement*. Oxford: Lion Publishing plc. This is a sensitively written book about a young girl coming to terms with the death of her aunt. There is a strong and supportive Christian text. This book would be suitable for children of middle to upper primary age.

Schultz, C. M. (1990). *Why Charlie Brown, Why?* (A story about what happens when a friend is very ill). West Sussex: Ravette Books Ltd.

Simms, A. M. (1986). *Am I Still a Sister?* Starline Printing Inc. (Available from Big A and Company, PO Box 20882, Albuquerque, New Mexico 87154, USA.) This asks questions and expresses feelings that may be experienced by bereaved siblings.

Stickney, D (1982). *Water Bugs and Dragonflies – Explaining death to children*. London: Mobray. This is a wonderful book, which although does not mention the word 'dead', can be used as a safe introduction to the topic.

Varley, S. (1985). *Badger's Parting Gifts*. London: Lion Publishing House. This is a lovely book about the death of an old badger and the working through of the sadness and grief of his friends. The book is beautifully illustrated and is appropriate for primary-school age children (and above).

White, E.B. (1963). *Charlotte's Web*. Harmondsworth: Puffin Books.

Wilhelm, H. (1985). *I'll Always Love You*. London: Hodder and Stoughton. This introduces death as a result of old age in the story of a little boy and his faithful old dog.

Other Useful Resources

Barnardo's (1992). *All About Me* board game. Barkingside, Essex: Barnardo's.

Cancer Research Campaign. *Welcome Back! How teachers can help children returning to school after treatment for cancer.* (Free publication.) Available from the Cancer Research Campaign, Dept. of Public Health, University of Manchester, Oxford Road, Manchester, M13 9PJ.

Heegaard, Marge. *Drawing Out Feelings* series. These workbooks provide parents and professionals with an organized approach to helping children aged 6–12 cope with feelings resulting from family loss and change. A facilitator's guide is also available to accompany the following titles:

When Someone Very Special Dies. Children can learn to cope with grief. (1988). Minneapolis USA. Woodland Press.

When Someone Has a Very Serious Illness. Children can learn to cope with loss and change. Minneapolis, USA: Woodland Press.

When Something Terrible Happens. Children can learn to cope with grief (1991). Minneapolis: USA: Woodland Press.

Phillips, K. (1996). *What Do We Tell the Children? Books to use with children affected by illness and bereavement.* Available from Paediatric AIDS Resource Centre, 20, Sylvan Place, Edinburgh. EH9 1UW. Tel: 0131 536 0806.

Slater, M. (1997). *Caring for All Our Children. A training pack in multi-cultural healthcare for providers.* Available from Action for Sick Children (Argyle House, 29–31 Euston Road, London NW1 2SD, UK).

Ward, B. and Houghton, J. (1988; 1989). *Good Grief-Talking and Learning about Loss and Death.* Volume 1-over 11 year olds, 1988 (ISBN 095128888 0 6). Volume 2-under 11s, 1989 (ISBN 0–9–51288–2–2). These have been designed specifically for use by teachers in schools to help teach about grief and loss among children.

Videos

Somewhere Over the Rainbow. Victoria Publications. (Royal Victoria Infirmary, Queen Victoria Road, Newcastle upon Tyne NE1 4LP, UK.) This video shows the techniques used by Malcolm Sargent Social Work in their direct work with children – patients and siblings. The video includes work with a child on treatment as well as with family members of a child who has died. Accompanying the video is an excellent handbook, *All about the Rainbow* by M. Hitcham (1993).

- Videos for children of three age categories about cancer and leukaemia and about bone marrow transplantation are available through the Malcolm Sargent Fund.

When a Child Grieves (1997). Designed for all child carers to help understand the experiences of bereaved children. Available from The Child Bereavement Trust (see p. 207 for the address).

Appendix C:
Useful Organizations/Agencies – UK

A.C.T. (Association for Children with Life-threatening or Terminal Conditions and their Families)
65, St. Michael's Hill
Bristol BS2 8D,UK
Tel: 0117 922 1556
Fax: 0117 930 4707

This is a national resource for parents and professionals, aiming to provide information about available services for terminally ill children.

ACTION FOR SICK CHILDREN (formerly 'NAWCH')
Argyle House
29–31 Euston Road
London NW1 2SD, UK
Tel: 0171 833 2041

An excellent resource for parents and professionals, providing information to help care for and support children in hospital. Reports and policy documents from this organization have been instrumental in the development of better provision for children in hospital.

AIDIS
1, Albany Park,
Cabot Lane,
Poole
BH17 7BX, UK
Tel: 01202 695 244

This organization provides computer communication equipment for people with severe disabilities.

BARNADO'S
Tanner's Lane
Barkingside
Ilford, Essex
IG6 1QG, UK
Tel: 0181 550 8822

Barnado's run a large and diverse number of projects to support young people, including children with disabilities and those affected by HIV/AIDS.

BEING YOURSELF
73, Liverpool Road,
Deal
Kent CT14 7NN, UK
Tel: 01304 381 333
Fax: 01304 381 255

This is a valuable resource for ordering reference and practical materials for working with children.

BRITISH ASSOCIATION FOR COUNSELLING (BAC)
37a, Sheep Street
Rugby
Warwickshire CV21 3BX, UK
Tel: 01788 550899

A national organization which offers information and advice concerning both counselling (and training courses) and counsellors.

THE BRITISH PSYCHOLOGICAL SOCIETY (BPS)
St. Andrews's House
48, Princess Road East,
Leicester LE1 7DR, UK
Tel: 0116 254 9568
Fax: 0116 247 0787

The professional and learned body for psychologists in the UK, promoting the advancement of the study of psychology and its applications, and ensuring high standards of professional education and conduct are maintained. Incorporated by Royal Charter, it is authorized to maintain a *Register of Chartered Psychologists*.

CHANGING FACES
1 and 2 Junction Mews
Paddington
London W2 1PN, UK
Tel: 0171 706 4232
FAX: 0171 706 4234

This organization provides help, advice and information for anyone with a facial disfigurement. A range of publications is available and particularly helpful for teenagers, including *Everyone's Staring at Me* and *Meeting New People, Making New Friends: A step-by-step guide.*

C.H.A.T.A (CHILDREN IN HOSPITAL AND ANIMAL THERAPY ASSOCIATION)
87, Longland Drive,
Totteridge
London N20 8HN, UK
Tel: 0181445 7883
Fax: 0181 445 7883

Provides animal therapy services to sick children in hospital.

THE CHILD BEREAVEMENT TRUST
Harleyford Estate
Henley Road
Marlow
Bucks SL7 2DX, UK
Tel: 01628 488101

The charity cares for bereaved families by offering training and support to the professional carers.

COMPASSIONATE FRIENDS
53, North Street
Bedminster
Bristol
BS3 1EN, UK
Tel: 0117 953 9639

Bereaved parents who have themselves suffered the loss of their child offer their support to grieving parents.

CONTACT-A-FAMILY
170, Tottenham Court Road
London WIP OHA, UK
Tel: 0171 383 35555

This organization produces an excellent and comprehensive index of support groups all over Britain (and some overseas) for families caring for a child with any type of disability or special needs and particularly rare conditions and syndromes. The organization works to link families who can provide support for each other and to provide updated information about support groups.

MAKE A WISH FOUNDATION
Suite B, Rossmore House
26–42 Park Street
Camberley
Surrey GU15 3PL, UK
Tel: 01276 24127

This organization provides once in a lifetime treats for families of children with life-threatening conditions. The child is granted his or her wish, and the whole family is involved in making this wish come true.

MEDITEC
York House
26, Bourne Road,
Colsterworth,
Lincs. NG33 5JE, UK
Tel: 01476 860281

A specialized bookselling service covering a variety of topics including counselling, and nursing care within oncology and other medical conditions.

NAESC (NATIONAL ASSOCIATON FOR THE EDUCATION OF SICK CHILDREN)
18, Victoria Park Square,
Bethnal Green,
London E2 9PF, UK
Tel: 0181 980 8523

Works for equal access and entitlement to a good education for all sick children.

PHAB (Physically Handicapped and Able Bodied)
Summit House
Wandle Road
Croydon CRO 1DF, UK
Tel: 0181 667 9443

A national organization with local branches which organizes joint activities for physically handicapped and able bodied people.

RTMDC (Research Trust for Metabolic Diseases in Children)
Golden Gates Lodge
Weston Road
Crewe
Cheshire CW1 1XN, UK
Tel: 01270 250 221

This is an umbrella organization providing support and information for families and professionals caring for children with rare metabolic conditions.

SARGENT CANCER CARE FOR CHILDREN
14, Abingdon Road
London W8 6AF, UK
Tel: 0171 565 5100

This organization offers counselling, practical and financial support for families caring for a child with cancer. It is also a good resource for information with a number of helpful publications for schools, families and professionals, including videos for children about cancer.

THE THEODORA CHILDREN'S TRUST
1, Riding House Street,
London W1A 3AS, UK
Tel: 0171 580 1379
Fax: 0171 323 2816

This charitable organization introduced clown doctors to the UK.

WHIZZ-KIDZ
215 Vauxhall Bridge Road
London SW1V 1EN, UK
Tel: 0171 233 6600

A leading provider of mobility aids to children with disabilities.

WRITE AWAY
29, Crawford Street,
London WIH 1PL, UK

A penfriend club for young people with special needs.

Appendix D:
Useful Organizations/Agencies – North America

COMPASSIONATE FRIENDS
P.O Box 3696
Oak Brook
IL 60522–3696, USA
Tel: 708 990 0010

National organization which supports parents following the death of their child.

THE ASSOCIATION FOR THE CARE OF CHILDREN'S HEALTH
7910, Woodmount Avenue
Suite 300
Bethesda
Maryland 20814, USA
Tel: 301 654 6549
Fax: 301 986 4553

This organization promotes collaboration among families and professionals of all disciplines. Its principal aim is to promote family-centred healthcare policies and practices through education and advocacy.

NATIONAL INFORMATION CENTRE FOR CHILDREN AND YOUTH WITH DISABILITIES
PO Box 1492
Washington D.C. 20013
USA
Tel: 1 800 695 0285
Fax: 202 884 8441

This is an information and referral centre that provides information on disabilities and disability-related issues.

NATIONAL PARENT TO PARENT SUPPORT AND INFORMATION SYSTEM, INC. (NPPSIS)
PO Box 907
Blue Ridge
GA 30513
USA
Tel: 706 632 8822
Fax: 706 652 8830

This organizations links parents of children with special healthcare needs and rare disorders.

PEN-PAL PROGRAMME
Children's Hopes and Dreams Foundation Inc.
280 US Highway 46
Dover
New Jersey 07801, USA

Offers an international pen pal scheme for children with chronic or life-threatening illnesses.

References

ACT: *A Guide to the Development of Children's Palliative Care Services* (1997). Report of a Joint Working Party of ACT (Association for Children with Life-threatening or Terminal Conditions and their Families) and the Royal College of Paediatrics and Child Health. Available from ACT.

Action for Sick Children (1985). *Charter for Children in Hospital.* London: Action for Sick Children (formerly NAWCH).

Alderson, P. (1993). *Children's Consent to Surgery.* Buckingham: Open University Press.

Bernstein, D. A., and Borkovec, T.D (1973). *Progressive Relaxation Therapy: A Manual for the Helping Professions.* Illinois: Research Press.

Beresford, B. (1994). Resources and strategies: How parents cope with the care of a disabled child. *Journal of Child Psychology and Psychiatry, 35,* 171–209.

Bloch, J.H., Block, J. and Morrison, A. (1981). Parental agreement-disagreement on child-rearing orientations and gender-related personality correlates in children. *Child Development, 52,* 965–974.

Bluebond Langner, E. (1978). *The Private Worlds of Dying Children.* Princeton: Princeton University Press.

Breslau, N. (1985). Psychiatric disorder in children with physical disabilities. *Journal of the American Academy of Child Psychiatry, 24,* 87–94.

Breslau, N., Weitzman, M. and Messenger, K. (1981). Psychological functioning of siblings of disabled children. *Paediatrics, 67,* 344–353.

Buckman, R. (1992). *How to Break Bad News.* London: Papermac.

Burbach, D., and Peterson, L. (1986). Children's concepts of physical illness: A review and critique of the cognitive-developmental literature. *Health Psychology, 5,* 307–325.

Burden, R., and Thomas, D. (1986). Working with parents of exceptional children: the need for more careful thought and more positive action. *Disability, Handicap and Society, 1,* 165–171.

Cadman, D., Boyle, M., Szatmari, P., Offord, D.R. (1987). Chronic illness, disability and mental and social well-being: Findings of the Ontario Child Health Study. *Pediatrics, 79,* 805–813.

Cadman. D., Boyle, M., and Offord, D.R. (1988). The Ontario Child Health Study: Social adjustment and mental health of siblings of children with chronic health problems. *Journal of Developmental and Behavioural Pediatrics, 9,* 117–121.

Cadranell, J. (1994). Talking about Death with Parents and Children. Chapter 3 in Hill, L. (Ed.), *Care for Dying Children and Their Families.* London: Chapman and Hall.

Davis, H. (1993). *Counselling Parents of Children with Chronic Illness or Disability.* Leicester: BPS Books (The British Psychological Society).

Davis, H. and Fallowfield, L. (1991). *Counselling and Communication in Health Care.* Chichester: John Wiley.

Davis, H. and Fallowfield, L. (1991). Counselling Theory. In H. Davis and L. Fallowfield (Eds), *Counselling and Communication in Health Care.* Chichester: John Wiley.

De Maso, D. R., Campis, L.K., Wypij, D., Betram, S., Lipshitz, M. and Freed, M. (1991). The impact of maternal perceptions and medical severity on the adjustment of children with congenital heart disease. *Journal of Pediatric Psychology, 16,* 137–150.

Department of Health (1989). *The Children Act.* London: HMSO.

Douglas, J. (1993). *Psychology and Nursing Children.* Leicester: BPS Books and Macmillan.

Drotar, D. and Bush, M. (1985). Mental health issues and services. In N. Hobbs and J. Perrin (Eds), *Issues in the Care of Children with Chronic Illness.* London: Jossey-Bass.

Egan, G. (1990). *The Skilled Helper, 4th edn.* California: Brooks/Cole.

Eiser, C. (1990). *Chronic Childhood Disease.* Cambridge: Cambridge University Press.

Eiser, C. (1984). Communicating with sick and hospitalised children. *Journal of Child Psychology and Psychiatry, 25,* 181–189.

Eiser, C. (1989). Children's Concepts of Illness: Towards An Alternative To The 'Stage' Approach. *Psychology and Health, 3,* 93–101.

Eiser, C. (1993). *Growing Up With a Chronic Disease.* London: Jessica Kingsley Publishers.

Eland, J.M.(1981). Minimising pain associated with pre-kindergarten muscular injections. *Issues in Comprehensive Paediatric Nursing, 5,* 327–335.

Gaffney, A. and Dunne, E.A. (1987). Children's understanding of the causality of pain. *Pain, 26,* 91–104.

Garrison, W. and McQuiston, S. (1989). *Chronic Illness During Childhood and Adolescence.* Newbury Park: Sage.

Harbeck, C. and Peterson, L. (1992). Elephants dancing in my head: A developmental approach to children's concept of specific pains. *Child Development, 63,* 138–149.

Hawton, K., Salkovskis, P.M., Kirk, J. and Clark, D.M. (1989). *Cognitive Behaviour Therapy for Psychiatric Problems: A practical guide.* Oxford: Oxford University Press.

Hitchman, M. (1995). *Somewhere Over the Rainbow* (Video and Handbook). Newcastle upon Tyne: Social Work Department, Royal Victoria Infirmary, Queen Victoria Road, Newcastle upon Tyne, NE1 4LP.

Hill, L. (Ed.) (1994). *Caring for Dying Children and their Families.* London: Chapman and Hall.

Horowitz, W.A. and Kazak, A.E. (1990). Family adaptation to childhood cancer: Sibling and family system variables. *Journal of Clinical Child Psychology, 19,* 221–228.

Ingersoll, G.M., Orr, D.P., Alison, J.H. and Golden, M.P. (1986). Cognitive maturity and self-management among adolescents with insulin-dependent diabetes mellitus. *Behavioural Pediatrics, 108,* 620–623.

Jenkins, J.M. and Smith, M.A. (1990). Factors protecting children living in disharmonious homes: Maternal reports. *Journal of the American Academy of Child and Adolescent Psychiatry, 29,* 60–69.

Johnson, S.B. (1980). Psychosocial factors in juvenile diabetes:A review. *Journal of Behavioural Medicine, 3,* 95–116.

Johnson, S. B. (1985). The family and the child with chronic illness. In D.C.

Turk and R.D. Kerns (Eds), *Health, Illness and Families: A life span perspective*. New York: John Wiley.

Johnson, S.B (1988). Psychological aspects of childhood diabetes. *Journal of Child Psychology and Psychiatry, 29,* 729–739.

Judd, D. (1989). *Give Sorrow Words: Working with a dying child*. London: Free Association Books.

Kane, B. (1979). Children's concept of death. *Journal of Genetic Psychology, 134,* 141–153.

Kazak, A.E., Reber, M. and Carter, A (1988). Structural and qualitative aspects of social networks in families with young chronically ill children. *Journal of Pediatric Psychology, 13,* 171–182.

Kelly, G. (1991). *The Psychology of Personal Constructs: Second edition*. London: Routledge.

Kendrick, C., Culling, J., Oakill, T., and Mott, M. (1986). Children's understanding of their illness and its treatment within a paediatric oncology unit. *Association of Child Psychology and Psychiatry Newsletter, 8,* 16–20.

Kister, M.C. and Patterson, C.J. (1980). Children's conceptions of the causes of illness: understanding of contagion and use of immanent justice. *Child Development, 51,* 839–846.

Koocher, G. P. (1984). Terminal care and survivorship in pediatric chronic illness. *Clinical Psychology Review, 4,* 571–583.

Kübler-Ross, E. (1969). *On Death and Dying*. New York: Macmillan.

Kübler-Ross, E. (1983). *On Children and Death*. New York: Macmillan.

Lane, D. and Miller, A. (1992). *Child and Adolescent Therapy: A Handbook*. Buckingham: OUP.

Lansdown, R. and Benjamin G. (1985). The development of the concept of death in children aged 5–9 years. *Child: Care, Health and Development, 11,* 13–20.

Lansdown, R. and Sokel, B. (1993). Commissioned Review: Approaches to Pain Management in Children. *Association of Child Psychology and Psychiatry Review and Newsletter, 15,* 105–111.

Lansdown, R. (1996). *Children in Hospital*. Oxford: Oxford Medical Publications.

Lask, B. and Fosson, A. (1989). *Childhood Illness: The psychosomatic approach*. Chichester: John Wiley.

Ley, P. (1988). *Communicating with Patients. Improving communication, satisfaction and compliance*. London: Chapman and Hall.

Lloyd, M. and Bor, R. (1996). *Communication Skills for Medicine*. London: Churchill Livingstone.

Mayled, J. (1986). *Death Customs*. Religious Topics series. East Sussex: Wayland.

Melamed, B. G., and Siegal, L.G. (1975). Reduction of anxiety in children facing hospitalisation and surgery by use of filmed modelling. *Journal of Consulting and Clinical Psychology, 43,* 511–21.

Melamed, B.G., Dearborn, M., and Hermecz, D.A. (1983). Necessary considerations for surgery preparation: age and previous experience. *Psychosomatic Medicine, 45,* 517–525.

Melamed, B.G. (1992). Family factors predicting children's reactions to anaesthesia induction. In A.M. La Greca, C.J. Siegal, J.L. Wallander and

C.E. Walker (Eds), *Stress and Coping in Child Health*. New York: Guilford Press.

Melzack, R. and Wall, P.D (1988). *The Challenge of Pain. 2nd edn*. London: Penguin.

Mercer, A. (1994). Psychological approaches to children with life-threatening conditions and their families. *Association of Child Psychology and Psychiatry Review and Newsletter, 16*, 56–63.

Moos, R. H., and Tsu, V. D. (1977). The Crisis of Physical Illness: an overview. In R.H. Moos (Ed.), *Coping with Physical Illness*. New York: Plenum Press.

Oaklander, V. (1978). *Windows to Our Children*. Utah, USA: Real People Press.

Olness, K., and Gardner, G. G. (1988). *Hypnosis and Hypnotherapy with Children*. Philadelphia: Grune and Stratton.

Parkes, C. M., Relf, M., and Couldrick, A. (1996). *Counselling in Terminal Care and Bereavement*. Leicester: BPS Books (The British Psychological Society).

Peterson, L.(1989). Coping by children undergoing stressful medical procedures: some conceptual, methodological and therapeutic issues. *Journal of Consulting and Clinical Psychology, 57*, 380–7.

Pless, I. B. (1984). Clinical assessment: Physical and psychological functioning. *Pediatric Clinics of North America, 31*, 33–46.

Rogers, C.R. (1959). A theory of therapy, personality and interpersonal relationships as developed in the client-centred framework. In S. Koch (Ed.) Psychology: A Study of a Science. New York: McGraw-Hill.

Rogers, C. R. (1965). *Client Centred Therapy: Its current practice, implications and theory*. Boston: Houghton-Mifflin.

Ross, D.M. and Ross, S.A. (1984). Childhood pain: the school-aged child's viewpoint. *Pain, 20*, 179–191.

Sabbeth, B. and Leventhal, J.(1984). Marital adjustment to chronic childhood illness: a critique of the literature. *Pediatrics, 73*, 762–767.

Saunders, D. (1996). *Counselling for Psychosomatic Problems. Counselling in practice series*. London: Sage.

Smith, S. (1985). *The Collected Poems of Stevie Smith*. Harmondsworth. Penguin Books.

Smith, S.C. and Pennels, M. (Eds) (1995). *Interventions with Bereaved Children*. London: Jessica Kingsley Publishers Ltd.

Soukes, B. (1995). *Armfuls Of Time. The psychological experience of the child with a life-threatening illness*. London: Routledge.

Spence, S.H. (1994). Practitioner review: cognitive therapy with children and adolescents: from theory to practice. *Journal of Child Psychology and Psychiatry, 35*, 1191–1228.

United Nations (1991). *Convention on the Rights of the Child*. London: HMSO.

Varni, J.W., Thompson, K.L., and Hanson, V. (1987). The Varni/Thompson paediatric pain questionnaire. 1: Chronic musculoskeletal pain in juvenile rheumatoid arthritis. *Pain, 28*, 27–38.

Wallander, J. L., Varni, J. W., Babani, L., Banis, H. T., and Wilcox, K.T. (1988). Children with chronic physical disorders: Maternal reports of their pyschological adjustment. *Journal of Pediatric Psychology, 13*, 197–212.

Wallander, J. L., Varni, J. W., Babini, L., DeHeen, C.B., Wilcox, K.T. and Banis,

H. T. (1989). The social environment and the adaption of mothers of physically handicapped children. *Journal of Pediatric Psychology, 14,* 371–388.

Weiland,S., Pless, I., and Roghmann, K. (1992). Chronic illness and mental health problems in paediatric practice: results from a survey of primary care providers. *Paediatrics 89,* 445–449.

Woolley, H., Stein, A., Forrest, G. C. and Baum, J.D. (1989). Staff stress and job satisfaction at a children's hospice. *Archives of Disease in Childhood, 64,* 114–118.

Woolley, H., Stein, A., Forest, G.C., and Baum, J.D. (1991). Cornerstone care for families of children with life-threatening illness. *Developmental Medicine and Child Neurology, 33,* 216–224.

Index
Compiled by Mary Kirkness

action plan for helping 76–8
adaptation to illness 5–8, 10–27
    as aim of helping 63–7
    by children 14–22
    by family 12–14
    and Personal Construct Theory 22–6
adherence to treatment *see* compliance
adjustment *see* adaptation
adolescents
    information needs of 129–30
    and problems of dependence 16–17,
        39–40, 50–1
    and transfer to adult services 54–5,
        151–2
    understanding of 29, 39, 167
adult services, transfer to 54–5, 151–2
aetiology of conditions 16–17
age and adaptation 16–17, 19
All About Me (board game) 113
anger
    in face of death 174
    at health professionals 54
    at parents 49–50
    of siblings 53
animal therapy 148
anxiety 25–6, 41–2
    about death 175
    pre-procedural 145–8
asthma, incidence 3
attending *see* listening
autonomy, need for 39, 57
awareness of impending death 168–72

bedside, meetings at 84–5
behavioural problems 7, 15, 49
    in face of death 173–6
Big T, The (poem) 11–12, 111
blind children 96
blocking *see* denial
body, understanding of 30–1
body language 87–9, 90
books
    by children 112–13, 128, 184
    as information source 127–8, 141
brainstorming, in planning action 76–7
British Association for Counselling
    (BAC) 196, 197
British Association of Psychotherapists
    197
British Psychological Society, The (BPS)
    196, 197
brothers and sisters *see* siblings
bullying 59–60, 77–8

causality, understanding
    of death 165–6
    of illness 31–7
central nervous system, involvement in
        condition 15–16
change, and anxiety 25–6
changes in condition
    ambivalence about 41–2
    and thoughts of death 171
characteristics, adaptation and
    of child 18–19
    of condition 15–18, 40–4
    of parents 6–8, 19–20
Charter for Children in Hospital 198
child, characteristics of, and adaptation
    18–19
child abuse 5, 191
Child Protection Policy 191
Children Act (1989) 68, 198–9
'Circle of Friends' 151
Clown Doctors 157
cognitive impairment 16, 58
cognitive–behavioural work 71
collaboration/consultation 193
communication
    with children *see also* information, giving
        basic skills 86–90
        difficulties in 22, 95–6
        need for effective 33, 62, 66
    in counselling 2–3
compliance with treatment 56–7
    encouraging 148–50
    problems in 7, 14, 39, 66, 74
concreteness of children's thinking 29,
    33–4
conditions, chronic 3–4 *see also* changes
        in condition
    causality, understanding 31–7
    characteristics of, and adaptation 15–18,
        22, 40–4
    constructions of 28–9
    and personal experience 37–8
confidentiality *see* privacy
congenital conditions 28
    and parental guilt 49–50
consent to surgery/treatment 134
constructions
    of death 163–6
    of family 49–52
    of illness/disability 28–9, 31–8
    of professionals 53–5
    of self 44–7
    of siblings 52–3

of treatment 33–4, 55–7, 122–4
consultation/collaboration 193
Contact-a-Family 17
contagion theory 36
control, increasing sense of 65–6
co-operation with treatment *see* compliance
coping skills 19
  developing 65–6
counselling *see also* engaging children; exploration; helping; information
  defined 2
  training in 197
cultural differences and communication 96

deaf children 96
death
  awareness of impending 168–72
  characteristics 164–6
  children's understanding of 163–6, 172
  emotional reactions to 173–6, 181
    management 176–8
  life after 167–8
  mutual pretence about 52
  siblings and 183–7
  talking about 162, 179–83
debriefing
  meetings (for staff) 195
  post-procedural 148
demonstrations, of procedures 141–2
denial/blocking, in face of death 173–4, 180–1
  management 177–8
dependence, problems of 16–17, 39–40, 50–1
depression, in face of death 174–5
desensitization, in pain management 158
developmental tasks, challenges to 38–40
diabetes, incidence 3
diagnosis
  and awareness of death 170
  communicating about 130–4
  and effect on construct system 25–6, 44–7, 119
diaries in exploring experience 114–15
  of pain 155–6
disability
  constructions of 46
  defined 4
diseases *see* conditions
distraction, in pain management 156–7
distress, pre-procedural 145–8
drawing
  as exploration strategy 105–9

in giving information 128
Drawing Out Feelings (workbooks) 113, 180

eczema, incidence 3
education *see also* school
  at home 59
emotions, in face of death 173–6
  management 176–8
empathy 78
  demonstrating 89–90, 104
engaging children 72–3, 99–101 *see also* meetings
  difficulties in 94–5
  skills involved 86–90
enthusiasm of helpers 80
epilepsy
  incidence 3
  stigma of 42
equipment, use in play 83, 110, 140–1
ethnicity, and communication 96
experience *see* constructions; exploration
expert model of helping 68
exploration
  of experience 66, 73–4, 99–117
    of medical/surgical procedures 139–40
    of pain 153–6
    skills/strategies
      non-verbal 105–11
      structured 111–16
      verbal 101–5
  of information needs/wishes 122–5
extended family, and adaptation 13
eye contact, in communication 87, 90

facial expression, in communication 88
facilitative responses 104
family *see also* parents; siblings
  and adaptation 4–5, 6, 7, 12–14, 20–1
  constructions of 49–52
  informing, about diagnosis 133–4
  relationships within 4–5, 20–1, 49–52
fear, about death 169–70, 175
  management 178
friendships, problems with 13, 59–60
funerals, and siblings 187

games
  in exploring experience 113–14
  in pain management 156
gate control theory of pain 152
gaze, in communication 87, 90
genetic diseases *see* hereditary conditions
genuineness, in helpers 79

germ theory of illness 36
Ghost (film) 163–4
goals, setting 74–6
graphs/scales, in exploring experience 115–16
  of pain 154–5
guided imagery 157–8
guilt 51
  parental, and hereditary illness 17, 49–50
  of siblings 35, 53
'guilt, survivor', of siblings 187

handicap, defined 4
handpuppets, using 110–11
hearing-impaired children 96
heart disease, congenital, incidence 3
helper attitudes 78–80
helping
  aims 63–7
  models 67–71
  process 71–8
helping relationship 67–71
  building 72–3
hereditary conditions 28
  and parental guilt 17, 49–50
home tuition 59
home visits 85
honesty, in giving information 119, 120–1
hospital
  admission, preparing for 142
  children in, charter 198
  children's problems with 37–8
  information giving in 121
  leaving, preparing for 150
  meetings in 84–5, 91–2
hospital schools 185
humility, in helpers 79–80
hypnosis 157

illnesses *see* conditions
independence, need for 39, 57
individual experience *see under* exploration
infants *see* pre-school children
information 58–9
  giving 66, 121–30
    about death and dying 180–3
    about diagnosis/treatment 130–4, 142–5
    and consent 134
    principles 120–1
  need for 28–9, 118–20
  right to 119
  through schoolwork 58–9
  updating 129–30

witholding by parents 119–20
information needs/wishes
  exploration of 122–5
  of siblings 184–5
interpreters 96, 121
introductions, in meetings 91–2

jokes, in pain management 156

language differences, and communication 96
language/vocabulary
  in giving information 121, 124, 125–6
  mirroring 89
learning difficulties 16, 58
life after death, concepts of 167–8
Life after My Operation (poem) 44
Lion King, The (film) 163
listening 64, 86–7 *see also* empathy
  demonstrating attention in 87–9
literalness of children's thinking 29, 33–4

magical thinking 29, 34–5, 36
Make a Wish (organization) 172
medical procedures *see* procedures, medical/surgical
meetings (of staff)
  debriefing 195
  psychosocial 194–5
  support group 195
meetings with children/families
  aims 82, 93
  organization and conduct 90–4
  privacy in 82, 84
  settings for 82–6
mental health problems of parents, in adaptation 6, 19–20
mental health services
  referral to 190–1
  and supervision 196
model of world, child's 23–4
  and adaptation 24–6
modelling, in pain management 158–9
models of helping 67–71
movements, bodily, in communication 88–9

non-compliance *see under* compliance
non-verbal behaviour
  in communication 32–3, 87–9, 90
non-verbal strategies in helping 105–11, 128, *see also* games; play; scales/graphs
Not Now, Bernard (book) 64

note-taking, in meetings 88–9

On Call (poem) 41
onset of conditions 16–17
Ontario Child Health study 15
operations *see* procedures, medical/surgical
outings, and meetings 84–5

pacing, in giving information 125
paediatric care, transfer from 54–5, 151–2
pain 152
  in dying, fear of 178
  exploring experience of 153–6
  intensity, scales of 154–5
  management 144, 156–60
  psychogenic 154
pain diaries 155–6
parents
  and adaptation 4–5, 6, 8, 12, 19–20
  and distress in face of death 169–70
  and helpers 4–5, 91
  and hereditary conditions 17, 49–50
  informing, about diagnosis 130–2, 133
  meetings with 90–1, 92–3
partnership model of helping 67–8
  applied to children 68–71
PCAs (patient-controlled analgesia pumps) 159
peer relationships 36, 59, 60
  in adolescence 39–40, 50–1
perceptions *see* constructions
Personal Construct Theory 23–4, 71 *see also* constructions
  and adaptation 24–6
personal experience *see under* exploration
physical disability, as risk factor 15
physical examination 84
Piaget, Jean 29–30
pictures, using
  in exploration 105–9
  in giving information 128
play
  in exploring experience 83, 90, 109–11
  see also games
  in giving information 128, 140–1
  materials 83, 109–11, 140–1
Playmobil hospital kits 83, 109–10
positive thinking in helpers 80
praise/reinforcement 53, 57, 65
  in pain management 158
pre-school children
  and developmental challenges 38
  understanding of 29, 32–5
privacy 39, 52

in helping relationship 68–9, 72, 79
  in meetings with children 82, 84
problem-management approach 71
problem-solving in counselling 2, 66
procedures, medical/surgical
  and anxiety 145–8
  debriefing after 148
  preparation for 137–45
professionals
  constructions of 53–5
  support by 22
protection
  mutual, of parents and children 52
  of parents by children 20, 51–2, 64
protective factors in adaptation 14
psychosocial meetings 194–5
punishment, illness as 35–6

questions, in exploration 101–3

rarity of conditions 3, 17
reactions, emotional *see* emotions
reactions, others' 16, 22, 36, 42–4
  changes in, and thoughts of death 171–2
  and construction of self 46–7
realization of death 164
referral 95, 190–2
reinforcement *see* praise
relationships
  within family 4–5, 20–1, 49–52
  with helpers 5–6, 54, 67–71
  forming *see* engaging children
  with peers 36, 50–1, 59, 60
  with siblings 35, 52–3
  social 13, 59–60
relaxation techniques 157, 158, 200
religious beliefs 36, 163
  in life after death 167–8
'rescue fantasy' 79
resistance factors in adaptation 14
respect 78–9
response, others' *see* reactions
responsibility
  helpers', for children 68–9
  for self-care 18, 39, 54, 151
rights, children's 119, 197–9
Rights of the Child, UN Convention 197
risk factors in adaptation 14
Rogers, Carl 71, 78
rooms for meetings, requirements 83–4

scales/graphs, in exploring experience 115–16
  of pain intensity 154–5
school 39, 57–9, 185

preparing for return to 57–8, 150–1
school visits 85
self-efficacy, increasing 65–6
self-esteem, increasing 64–5, 80
self-harm 69, 191
self-image 44–7
sentence completion, structured 111
sentence story, incomplete 112
severity of disease 15
shut down, in face of death 175–6
siblings
   and adaptation 12–13, 21
   caring for, in face of death 183–7
   constructions of 52–3
   relationships with 35, 52–3
   role in terminal care 184–6
skills learning 25, 57, 67
   in pain management 159–60
social acceptibility of conditions (stigma)
   13, 22, 42, 46
social relationships, problems with 13,
   59–60
Social Services, referral to 191
social support 21–2
stereotyping 43
stigma of conditions 13, 22, 42, 46
stories, in pain management 156–7
story books, in exploring experience
   112–13
stress see also adaptation
   of carers 193–4
   chronic illness as 18
   external 21
   parental 6, 19–20
      and children 51–2
structuring
   of experience 104–5
   of information 126–7
supervision of carers 196
support

   for carers 193–6
   for children/families 21–2
surgical procedures see procedures,
   medical/surgical

teenagers see adolescents
terminology see language
thinking, children's, development 29–30
toys 83, 109–11, 140–1
training in counselling 197
translation services 96, 121
treatment see also compliance
   change in, and thoughts of death 171
   constructions of 55–7
   demands of, and adaptation 17–18
   giving information about 130–4, 142–5
   understanding, development of 31–7
trust, in helper–child relationship 119

uncertainty of conditions 16, 40–2
unconditional positive regard 78–9
understanding, development of 29–30
   of body 30–1
   of death 164–6
   of illness and treatment 31–37
unpredictability of conditions 16, 40–2

verbal skills
   children's 32–3
   in helping 89, 101–5
videotapes, for information 128
visibility/invisibility 16, 42–4, 46
visually impaired children 96
vocabulary see language

wish-granting 172
withdrawal, in face of death 175–6

young children see pre-school children
young people see adolescents

DATE DUE
